Escape to Miami

Escape to Miami

An Oral History of the Cuban
Rafter Crisis

ELIZABETH CAMPISI

OXFORD
UNIVERSITY PRESS

OXFORD

UNIVERSITY PRESS

Oxford University Press is a department of the University of Oxford. It furthers
the University's objective of excellence in research, scholarship, and education
by publishing worldwide. Oxford is a registered trade mark of Oxford University
Press in the UK and certain other countries.

Published in the United States of America by Oxford University Press
198 Madison Avenue, New York, NY 10016, United States of America.

© Oxford University Press 2016

Library of Congress Cataloging-in-Publication Data
Names: Campisi, Elizabeth, 1961–
Title: Escape to Miami : an oral history of the Cuban rafter crisis /
    Elizabeth Campisi.
Description: New York, NY : Oxford University Press, 2016. | Series: Oxford
    oral history series | Includes bibliographical references and index.
Identifiers: LCCN 2015044421 | ISBN 978–0–19–994687–7 (hardback)
Subjects: LCSH: Cubans—Florida—Miami—Biography. | Boat
    people—Cuba—Biography. | Refugees—Florida—Miami—Biography. | Illegal
    aliens—Cuba—Guantánamo Bay Naval Base—Biography. | Oral history. |
    Psychic trauma—Case studies. | Adjustment (Psychology)—Case studies. |
    Cuba—History—1990—Biography. | Miami (Fla.)—Biography. | Guantánamo
    Bay Detention Camp—Biography. | BISAC: HISTORY / Latin America / General.|
    HISTORY / United States / State & Local / South (AL, AR, FL, GA, KY, LA,
    MS, NC, SC, TN, VA, WV). | HISTORY / United States / 21st Century.
Classification: LCC F319.M6 C295 2016 | DDC 972.91/67—dc23
LC record available at http://lccn.loc.gov/2015044421

9 8 7 6 5 4 3 2 1
Printed by Edwards Brothers, USA

Frontispiece: Tent with improvised porch furniture, Camp Bravo.

Contents

Preface

In January 1995 I took a job as a temporary worker in a field office of the Justice Department's Community Relations Service that had been set up on the naval base in Guantánamo Bay, Cuba, as part of the government response to an outflow of 34,000 Cubans who had left the island on rafts in August and September of 1994. After a year of being alternately fascinated by the Cuban rafters' creativity in coping with being detained in camps, and disgusted by many elements of the operation, I wanted to tell the story of the Cuban rafter crisis. I arrived on the base already disillusioned by President Clinton's false outrage at Fidel Castro for having unleashed tens of thousands of people on rafts. In the run-up to the rafter crisis, Congress had tightened a decades-old embargo intended to maximize misery among the Cuban population while leaving in place a long-standing open arms policy toward anyone fleeing Cuba. Since this policy tacitly encouraged people to leave the island while it limited the Cuban government's options when the island's economy collapsed in the early 1990s, what did he think would happen? Fidel Castro's cynicism neatly matched Clinton's. He had made it nearly impossible to leave the island. Mass exodus was the only alternative to jail time for leaving without authorization. Such a dysfunctional relationship only hurt ordinary Cubans while denying people in the United States opportunities to know the richness of Cuban culture.

After a few weeks on the base, I became aware that President Clinton and his predecessors had been interning people at the base to avoid giving them due process rights. I found this troubling, since the United States had interdicted them and taken them to a territory under its control. Had I been naïve in actually believing in the principles upon which this country was founded?

Sending politically inconvenient populations to a remote military base with limited media access also makes it difficult for the wider public to find out what goes on in its name. For example, since President Clinton had decided to change the policy of admitting all Cubans to the United States at the last minute, it was obvious to anyone on the ground that the camps were anything but a haven, despite the military's best efforts to make it one, and regardless, the rafters were not about to return to Cuba. Media accounts at the time did not provide much detail about the living conditions, nor did they note the strength of the rafters' determination to complete their journeys at all costs. It was frustrating to see some articles that seemed to be no more than rehashed military or administration talking points.

The fact that people were detained and deprived of due process wasn't the only thing that bothered me about the operation. It seemed that the higher one went in the Justice Department, the less compassion government officials had for the people entrusted to their care and the more incompetent the people they picked to run the field offices were; officials in Washington did not seem to have given much care or attention in choosing whom they sent. I often wondered how a bus driver could have been the best choice to run the Community Relation Service's field office. A symptom of this was that even ten years after the operation was over, both federal and local officials would express no remorse or even admit to lessons learned at a conference on the rafter crisis organized by the University of Miami, but merely gave each other a public patting on the back for emerging from the crisis with their careers intact.

All of this was only half of the reason I wanted to document the rafter crisis. For much of the operation I was literally in awe of the Cuban rafters' idealism, intelligence, determination, and creativity in the face of overwhelming experiences. Therefore, I really wanted to document not just their trials and tribulations but also the inspiring ways in which the rafters, whom I will call by their Spanish name, *balseros*, worked to overcome them. The balseros left me fascinated with Cuban history and culture, which eventually led me to study anthropology and oral history. In the end, working for a year in the hot, stressful camps for an agency that was not set up to support field staff properly took its toll. As I delved more deeply into trauma theory, I realized that I had had symptoms of secondary trauma; I felt numb and had difficulty re-engaging with family and friends. A psychologist specializing in refugee trauma later told me of his observation that offices run in the harsh and rude manner in which the Community Relations Service field office was operated did indeed foster secondary trauma among field workers (Dr. Jack Saul, personal communication, April 2013). I also found that I avoided writing some sections of this book in a manner that seemed similar to ways that some of the people I sought to interview in Miami had avoided talking to me about the camps. In the end, by writing about how the Cuban rafters dealt with their trauma, I also processed and released my own. I also had more respect for the people who allowed me to interview them, since they had run the risk of having the feelings associated with their own traumatic experience surface again during the interview. This oral history is my tribute to the perseverance and spirit of all the balseros in the face of overwhelming circumstances.

Acknowledgments

I owe a debt of gratitude to many people for help with this project. First, I would like to thank my editor at Oxford University Press, Nancy Toff, for recognizing the value of this work and for her superb ability to save me from myself in places where I failed to follow my true writer's instincts. I also thank her for her patience when I struggled with some sections of the book. I would also like to thank her assistant, Elda Granata, for helping get all of the details in order in such an efficient and kind-hearted manner.

I am grateful to the balseros who invited me into their homes to share their stories with me, whether or not I officially recorded them. Not only did I appreciate their wonderful hospitality and assistance, but I also admired them for their bravery in bringing up memories that could be very painful. I also would like to thank a group of people from the Cuban community in Miami who befriended me and helped me understand Cuban Miami: Angela Valella, Roberto Montes de Oca, Ileana Casanova, Manolo Casanova, Martha Corvea, Neri Torres, and Jorge Del Rio. I also thank Roberto Montes de Oca and Lourdes Quirch for helping me find people to interview.

I would also like to thank the group of people who were at the University of Miami at the time for welcoming me as a visiting scholar at the Center for Latin American Studies: the late Dr. Robert M. Levine, and Drs. Diane Just, Holly Ackerman, Lillian Manzor, Max Castro, and Martha Corvea.

Many people supported me when my mother began dying from pancreatic cancer while I was writing this oral history. Louise Burkhart went above and beyond the call of duty by copy editing my work when I became too stressed to think and Martha Corvea and Linda Pershing provided the right words of support so that I could keep going. I am particularly indebted to Dr. Jill Swensen, first for her assistance with processing my own secondary trauma issues from the camps and then for helping me get through life as the primary caregiver for my mother. Without Dr. Swensen, I might not have held up enough to complete this work.

I thank the following institutions at SUNY-Albany for financial support: the Dona Parker Fellowship, Initiatives for Women, the Benevolent Association, and the Graduate Student Organization.

Finally, I would like to dedicate this book to the memory of my mother, Jean Malay Campisi, for her loving support during the forty-eight years I was privileged to have her with me. I could not have completed this work, or many others, without her serving as a one-woman cheering section throughout my life.

Introduction

In 1991, Cuba was one of the many countries around the world that experienced severe aftershocks from the collapse of the Soviet Union. Since its economy had been heavily dependent on Soviet subsidies, the island nation plunged into an economic crisis so severe that some observers began to predict the Revolution's demise.[1] By 1993, the Cuban economy was in a free fall, with severe shortages of everything from food to gasoline, and the government was increasing its use of repression to keep a lid on the social tensions that began to bubble under the surface. By the summer of 1994, Cuba had become a tinderbox, making conditions ripe for a mass exodus; these departures had occurred on such a regular basis since 1959 that they can rightly be called a characteristic of the Cuban Revolution. Tensions came to a head in early August of 1994 with rioting in downtown Havana. Soon, a flotilla, mostly of flimsy rafts, of 34,000 people began to form, setting sail for Miami through the Straits of Florida. The rafters left the island knowing that since 1959 Cubans fleeing the island had been welcomed into the United States as heroic exiles from communism.[2] However, on August 19, President Clinton drastically changed the traditional US stance toward Cuban émigrés. In a press conference that day, he labeled them "illegal refugees" and announced that they would be interdicted at sea and taken to join the approximately 14,000 Haitians who were already being held at the US naval base in Guantánamo Bay, Cuba, while the administration explored other so-called safe haven options in the region.[3] Eight and a half months later, pragmatic considerations caused Clinton to admit most of the Cubans and a handful of the Haitians as special entrants to the United States,[4] but the last Cuban did not leave the base at Guantánamo for more than eight months after that. This meant that many people spent sixteen months on the base, where they created a distinctive camp culture around an identity and a story of a search for freedom that helped them cope with the trauma and stress inherent in life in the hot, dusty camps.

Housing a population in a remote location without free media access makes it difficult to document what happened to it there. Hence, a major goal of this book is to provide new information on the Cuban camps erected on the naval base in August of 1994 and officially closed on January 31, 1996. Having worked as a civilian employee in the camps, I was in a good position to do this.

I spent an entire year working in the Cuban camps in Guantánamo. From January 5, 1995, to January 31, 1996, I was a resettlement interviewer and then a mediator for the Justice Department's Community Relations Service (CRS). The agency was assigned to provide a variety of services for the operation, including mediation, resettlement interviewing, family reunification, and recreation. During the four months I spent as a resettlement interviewer, I did intake interviews with more than 600 families eligible for medical parole. I then worked inside three camps as a mediator between the Cubans and the military for nine more months. When I first began these interviews, the one thing that struck me the most about the *balseros* (rafters) was their emotional intensity; the stress practically emanated from their bodies. I also could not fathom what had driven them to launch themselves into the middle of the ocean on flimsy rafts, especially with children. Therefore, after many of my interviews, I asked them about their lives in Cuba, why they left, and what their raft journeys had been like. They often surprised me with their answers in response to my questions about why they took small children on the rafts with them, saying "we would rather die together in the middle of the ocean than live in a country where there is no hope." At times my stomach sank while I heard stories of people being eaten by sharks, of the black waves surrounding rafts like walls at night, of people nearly drowning, or of others who had been burned with cigarettes by guards in Cuban prisons. Many people also felt compelled to show me the disturbing outward signs of the medical conditions that had qualified them for medical parole, such as osteomyelitis or breast cancer. Although I was not yet an anthropologist, I was emotionally involved with the people I was there to help, which made me a vulnerable observer according to the term coined by Cuban American anthropologist Ruth Behar.[5]

I soon became tired of just interviewing people and felt I could be more helpful in the camps, so I requested a transfer. My job as a mediator in the camps was to prevent or ameliorate conflict. This entailed checking in with military commanders and soldiers at the command post to learn what was going on from their point of view, and then talking with the Cuban camp leaders, the *jefes*, to get their opinions. Every day, I walked around the camps, visited people in their tents, and noted what was occurring in the environment. I was thus witnessing the camp world at the same time I was participating in it.

I was even more fascinated by the camps than I had been by the stories I had heard as an interviewer. The balseros had re-created social institutions such as churches and schools, but the most interesting development was the amazing volume of artwork they produced. It impressed everyone, military and civilian alike. Their creativity was ubiquitous, from decorations in living areas and improvised furniture to paintings and carvings that pervaded the camp environment. Army cots became armchairs and rockers, caps from miniature Tabasco sauce bottles became chandeliers, and plastic spoon collections became "beaded" curtains. People who had never before created anything made paintings, drawings, sculptures, tattoos, and even monuments. Groups of people got together to create art galleries, organize poetry readings and variety shows, and participate in Santería rituals. Some people stayed in their tents, morose or depressed, but many more socialized, participated in sports, or went to English classes or vocational school. Their ingenuity and industriousness impressed the military so much that it allowed some people to paint permanent murals, redecorate the base's day care center, and hold low-paying jobs around the base.

Soon after the Clinton administration decided to admit the refugees to the United States, the military devised a lottery system to determine the order in which the balseros would leave the base. The two events completely transformed the social environment. What had been a palpable level of collective desperation and frustration turned into anxiety in anticipation of what each person's number in the lottery would be, and then nervous hope for their future lives in the United States. By that time, the razor wire surrounding each camp had been replaced with fencing, and the troops caring for them generally had become friendly instead of hostile. The artwork also seemed to change. By late 1995, I noticed that people tended to make things such as model ships, carvings of dolphins, and shell ornaments instead of carvings or paintings with political content or menacing images of the camps. Depictions of American and Cuban flags were also scattered throughout the artwork. I did continue to see Fidel Castro portrayed as the devil. That did not change.

The experiences of the Cubans in the camps at Guantánamo Bay have hardly been documented, and this lack became the impetus for this book, which uses trauma theory to explain why creative expression was so ubiquitous in the camps. I conducted life history interviews with ten men and two women, in which I asked questions about their lives in Cuba, their experiences on the ocean, in the camps, and their initial lives in the United States. To develop an understanding of the Cuban exile community and how the balseros fit into it at the end of their long journeys, I spent a year doing participant observation in and around the Little Havana section of Miami, and, to a lesser extent, in Hialeah, the predominantly Cuban city next to Miami. In particular, I spent many nights at the home of two of the interviewees and much time with a group of Cuban American and Cuban exile artists and academics, who explained the nuances of the community's social dynamics to me. I also observed one group that was working to create an art gallery, and spent time with other, more established, politically moderate Cuban Americans who were organizing another group to help open up social space for people who wanted to improve relations with the Cuban government. Additionally, I listened to Cuban exile radio stations and attended community events in Little Havana, such as Viernes Culturales, a monthly art and music show, and the annual Calle Ocho festival, both of which were held on 8th Street, the main thoroughfare of that section of town. Prior to doing research in Miami, I traveled to Havana, Cuba, for seven weeks and lived with three families while I examined common forms of folk art in the galleries and markets there. All of these things gave me a better idea of the social history into which the rafter crisis fits.

Because this oral history was compiled by an anthropologist and not a historian, a few points will be evident to an academic audience. The field of anthropology maintains that anonymity is necessary to protect its sources from community reprisal, since they are often marginal characters in their societies or have opinions that may be unpopular with their neighbors. In this case, I am protecting my sources' families on the island from reprisals by the Cuban government as well as their ability to travel to Cuba without being interrogated, which has already happened to a few of them. Oral historians prefer that people use their real names for the historical record, but many have eventually come to the same conclusion that I did about protecting the safety of families at home given the nature of the population movement being documented here. Additionally, as an anthropologist I am a bit more concerned with the relationship of Cuban culture and trauma to the way the culture of the camps unfolded. However, I hope that this book makes a contribution to the field of oral history, since so many of the subjects of oral histories these days have also been victims of trauma.

As Anthony Mollica, the founding director of the Harvard Program on Refugee Trauma, has noted, telling effective trauma stories has both individual and social benefits. In addition to providing people with an opportunity to bear witness to and create meaning from their suffering, oral history can sensitize the public to the plight of victims of trauma so that the society, and not just individuals, can create opportunities for healing victims of trauma. Society also gains from what victims of trauma teach us through their stories of survival. By telling the rafters' story, I hope not only to increase the public's understanding of the rafter crisis, particularly the spirit the balseros mustered to get through it, but also to reduce the possibility that decision makers will use extraterritorial detention for people escaping dire conditions in their own countries, either because this story has pricked policymakers' consciences or because a newly informed public will make the political costs too high for the decision makers to do so. Unfortunately, I am betting that the latter instance is more likely than the former.

1

No More Mariels

History and the Rafter Crisis

At the time President Clinton ordered the Coast Guard to interdict Cubans fleeing the island nation and take them to the US naval base at Guantánamo, a particular confluence of historical events had changed the way the government would respond to unexpected flows of Cuban émigrés. Deep historical ties between Cuba and the United States, the end of the Cold War, and domestic political concerns all combined to preclude the Cuban rafters' automatic admission to the United States. Prior legal precedents on due process issues[1] also affected Clinton's decision-making process, as did his interaction with the politically powerful Cuban American community.

The fact that the United States had the option of detaining a politically inconvenient population on a US Navy base situated in a remote part of a country with which it had no formal diplomatic relations reflected a historical dynamic between the two countries that developed as a result of US ambitions toward Cuba, expressed openly by government officials as far back as the presidency of John Adams. His administration deemed Cuba the "Pearl of the Antilles" and asserted that Cuba should be an extension of the United States. Subsequently President Thomas Jefferson wrote that Cuba was a "natural addition to [the United States'] system of states,"[2] and John Quincy Adams, as secretary of state, argued to James Monroe that it was natural law that Cuba would fall under United States control:

If an apple, severed by the tempest from its native tree, cannot but fall to the ground, Cuba, forcibly disjoined from its unnatural connection with Spain and incapable of self-support, can gravitate only to the North American Union, which, by the same law of nature, cannot cast her off from its bosom.[3]

The United States was able to act on its ambitions without risking war with Spain as a result of Cuba's Ten Years War (1868–78), the island's first great struggle for independence from Spanish colonialism. Long and bloody, the war ruined many planters and other businessmen, who sold their land at bargain prices to United States–based business interests.[4] Consequently, by the time of the final independence revolt in 1895, Cuba was exporting more than 90 percent of its sugar and the majority of its other products to the United States, which further undermined Spanish control over the island and gave the United States a stake in the outcome of the independence wars. This was the context in 1898 that led President McKinley to declare war on Spain after an explosion sank the *Maine*, a US Navy ship anchored in Havana Harbor, and killed the entire crew. The declaration ignited the Spanish-American War, which the US public backed due to the outrage the yellow journalists of the era had generated at Spain's brutality during Cuba's independence efforts. It took Spain only a few months to concede defeat and transfer control of not only Cuba but also Puerto Rico, the Philippines, and Guam to the United States under the Treaty of Paris. The war effectively turned Cuba's struggle for liberation from Spain into a war of imperial conquest for the United States.[5]

By the time Cuba formally became a republic in 1902 after five years of occupation, the United States had already taken steps to ensure that it would maintain the neocolonial relationship it had just established with the island. In 1901, Congress had passed the Platt Amendment to a military appropriations bill, which asserted the United States' continuing right to oversee Cuba's economy, international commitments, and domestic politics. Article VII provided for the establishment of a naval base on Cuba that would later fill with Cubans and Haitians. It reads:

> That to enable the United States to maintain the independence of Cuba, and to protect the people thereof, as well as for its own defense, the government of Cuba will sell or lease to the United States land necessary for a coaling or naval station at certain specified points, to be agreed upon with the President of the United States.[6]

The new Cuban Congress incorporated the language of the Platt Amendment into the new nation's first constitution as well. The country's first president, Tomás Estrada Palma (1902–06), then entered into the

Permanent Treaty of 1903, allowing the United States to lease land for a naval base in Guantánamo, which it built later that year. The United States had already experienced the value of the base's bays during the Spanish-American War, when it used the territory as the launching point for its 1898 invasion of the town of Guantánamo. The navy had noted that the island's location, stretching over both entrances to the Gulf of Mexico, gave it a great deal of strategic value since it could be used to dominate Atlantic coast routes to the proposed Panama Canal. When the Platt Amendment was formally repealed in 1934, the two countries entered into the Treaty of Relations, which ensured that the United States could rent the base in perpetuity.[7]

Cuba, therefore, had achieved independence from Spain at the cost of having its sovereignty mediated by the United States. For almost sixty years, the nation endured military interventions and venal dictators who acted on behalf of foreign interests more than Cuban ones. In fact, Cubans were so aware of US control over a large portion of life on the island that most thought nothing could be done without US approval. Fulgencio Batista was the last of the dictators before the triumph of Fidel Castro's 26th of July movement in 1959. Batista seized power through a military coup in 1952 and then ran unopposed for a four-year term as president. The Batista era was known for widespread government repression, malfeasance, graft, and cronyism, and a decade-long economic crisis, all of which became kindling for a revolutionary movement to sweep the nation.[8]

Cubans put their complete faith in Fidel Castro's 26th of July movement to restore faith, dignity, and prosperity to the nation. However, breaking free from a neocolonial relationship was dangerous, particularly during the Cold War. In March of 1960, only three months after the triumph of the Revolution, President Eisenhower put the Central Intelligence Agency (CIA) in charge of all Cuba operations.[9] Castro re-established diplomatic relations with the Soviet Union and proclaimed the Revolution communist two months later. He then began to nationalize petroleum-refining properties owned by companies based in the United States. In response, President Eisenhower cut the amount of Cuban sugar allowed for import.

The growing hostilities between the two countries were immediately tied to mass migration from Cuba. Although Cubans had traditionally gone back and forth between the island and the United States to shop and educate their children on a regular basis,[10] mass migration did not occur until after 1959.

The pattern that took shape during the early years of the Revolution endured until the Cuban rafter crisis in 1994.

The United States encouraged migration from Cuba during the Cold War, since refugees made the Revolution look bad. It began by having the CIA smuggle 700 visa waivers into Cuba for the children of people fighting in the counter-revolutionary underground.[11] In the early days of the Revolution, as the new government took increasingly repressive measures against the opposition, first targeting the upper class and then the middle class and business owners, thousands of people began to flee the island. By November 1960, 1,700 Cubans were reaching Miami each week. In response, President Eisenhower established the Cuban Refugee Center in Miami, which provided funds and social services for resettlement while he intensified efforts to evacuate children from Cuba, an operation that became known by the nickname it was given by the *Miami Herald*, Operation Pedro Pan.[12]

By October of 1962, 14,048 unaccompanied minors between the ages of six and seventeen had entered the United States under Operation Pedro Pan. Cuban parents agreed to let their children go to the United States unaccompanied, even though only about half of them had relatives in the country, because of changes that the Revolution was making to the Cuban education system and because the CIA was spreading rumors that the Cuban government was going to take away parents' rights to care for their children.[13] The operation sent children without relatives in the United States to live in foster homes, boarding schools, and other institutions across the country.[14]

Just before President Kennedy took office in January 1961, Eisenhower severed diplomatic relations with Cuba and issued additional visa waivers to fleeing Cubans, placing them on indefinite parole six months after their arrival. Eisenhower left office as the Revolution nationalized utilities, railroads, hotels, sugar mills, factories, and banks. In February 1961, newly elected president John F. Kennedy converted the Eisenhower administration's partial trade embargo into a total one[15] and created the Cuban Refugee Program, the largest, longest-running, and most expensive assistance program for Latin American refugees in the nation's history. At a cost of $1 billion, it assisted more than 700,000 Cubans with a large array of government services.[16] Kennedy expanded migration-promoting programs and policies in the belief that they would create a brain drain that would undermine the Cuban Revolution.[17] The result was that between January 1961 and the October 1962 Cuban Missile Crisis, 153,534 people emigrated from Cuba to the United States. The missile crisis temporarily ended all migration from Cuba since the United States instituted an air-isolation campaign against Cuba during that tense week.[18]

Successive presidents continued to promote migration from Cuba. President Johnson's 1965 Immigration Act liberalized immigration policy and specifically removed limits on Cuban immigration. In response, Castro announced that as of October 10, anyone whose American relatives requested their emigration would be allowed to leave the country, saying that he was taking action because the United States had cut off normal avenues for emigration and forced people to risk their lives on small boats. A boatlift of about 5,000 people left Cuba almost immediately, causing a refugee crisis in south Florida. When the American public began objecting to the new influx of Cubans, President Johnson entered into secret negotiations with Castro to normalize the exodus. When the boatlift became ongoing in the fall of 1965, the administration replaced it with an airlift dubbed the Freedom Flight Program. Castro terminated it in 1973, but while the program lasted, more than 250,000 Cubans immigrated to the United States, some through Spain.[19]

The Johnson administration promulgated the law that continues to have the most influence over Cuban immigration to the United States. The Cuban Adjustment Act of 1966 entitles Cubans to be processed for permanent resident status once they are in the country, even if they arrive by unauthorized means or overstay their visas.[20] This means that all Cubans who make it to United States soil are allowed to remain, request asylum, and after one year apply for permanent residency. No other immigrant group has been granted this privilege.[21]

Another wave of mass migration occurred in 1980 with the Mariel Boatlift, which set into motion a set of dynamics that would later affect President Bill Clinton's decision making during the rafter crisis in 1994. The Mariel Boatlift occurred partly as the result of the unforeseen consequences of several Carter administration policies put into place during a cautious diplomatic opening between the two countries that went sour. In 1977, the countries re-established limited diplomatic relations by creating "interest sections" in each other's capitals. The next year the Cuban government created a family unification program that allowed exiles to visit their relatives in Cuba, which resulted in about 100,000 of them traveling to the island. Castro also released 3,000 political prisoners and 400 others who had been arrested for minor offenses, allowing them out of Cuba at a rate of 400 a month. Both of these efforts backfired. Bureaucratic resistance to admitting the political prisoners to the United States reduced their entrance to a trickle, and, while waiting to leave Cuba, the dissidents strengthened local opposition to the Revolution. At the same time, when Cubans saw wealthy relatives and friends and heard about their new lives in the United States, they saw the Revolution's economic problems in high relief, which increased popular discontent.[22]

The Carter administration was also admitting Cubans to the United States in a way that favored people who arrived by boat over other means, which further increased tensions between the two countries. It was granting very few immigrant visas for flights out of Cuba but was admitting anyone who came by boat, even a hijacked one. Even worse, it was prosecuting people who hijacked airplanes but not boats. Some have speculated that the reason for the different treatment of people crossing to Miami by boat was that dramatic images of sunburned escapees from communism had a higher propaganda value, and were therefore more likely to appeal to the American public, than the less forlorn plane hijackers and visa recipients.[23]

When the Carter administration refused to discuss the hijackings in talks with Cuban officials, Castro issued the following warning:

> We hope they will adopt measures so they will not encourage the illegal departures from the country because we might also have to take our own measures. We did it once.... We were forced to take measures in this regard once. We have also warned them of this. We once had to open the Camarioca port.... [W]e feel it is proof of the lack of maturity of the U.S. government to again create similar situations.[24]

This set the stage for a series of events that unfolded in March of 1980, when a busload of Cubans rammed the gates to the Peruvian embassy and demanded asylum, which they were granted immediately. At first, Castro had the embassy surrounded and barricaded, but three days later he let an estimated 10,000 people cram into the compound. Carter declared that 3,500 of them would be granted refugee status if they met certain requirements; then he tried to organize an airlift of the rest of them to Costa Rica, where he hoped they would be resettled. President Carter had been trying to reap a propaganda victory, but instead Castro handed him a boatlift by inviting all Cuban exiles with relatives in Cuba to come get them by boat. As a result, approximately 125,000 Cubans, about 10 percent of whom had criminal records, flooded into Miami during the spring and summer of 1980. At its peak, more than 5,000 people overwhelmed the docks at Key West.[25]

President Carter sent almost half of the *Marielitos*, the 62,541 people who left Cuba as part of the Mariel Boatlift, to three camps outside of Florida, including one at Fort Chafee, Arkansas, where Bill Clinton was then governor, to await sponsorship. That summer they rioted in protest of their prolonged detention, which drew national attention and caused their fellow exiles to distance themselves from the detainees. Eventually Carter returned to Cuba about a thousand so-called excludables, people with criminal records; virtually all of the others were allowed to remain in the United States as "special entrants," not refugees. Although the move proved to be politically damaging to President Carter, in reality he did not have much choice, since Castro was not about to take them back. Carter did continue to use the same words as his predecessors to describe the Mariel Cubans—as heroic escapees from communism.[26]

Part of the reason President Carter had to classify the Cubans under a non-refugee category was because the Mariel Boatlift occurred soon after Congress had passed the Refugee Act of 1980, which reorganized refugee admission procedures. Congress had not considered the possibility that the United States might become a country of mass asylum. To get around this, President Carter had to create the new Cuban/Haitian Entrant, Special Status category.[27] Later on, Clinton would allow the rafters into the country under the same category.

The Mariel Boatlift damaged President Carter politically and marked the beginning of a period of heightened concern about immigrants and immigration. The problems at Fort Chafee, Arkansas, in particular were significant in terms of subsequent history. As it was the center for hard cases, there were problems not only with riots and escapes but also knives, drugs, and prostitution. The immigration concerns contributed to reelection defeats for Governor Clinton as well as President Carter and set the stage for future administrations to treat subsequent émigré flows differently, particularly for the subsequent Clinton presidency. In fact, staff members at the time related that President Clinton's decision making during the 1994 rafter crisis was guided by two principles: "no more Mariels" and "remember Fort Chafee."[28]

Not only did the mass flow of people remind President Clinton of the Mariel Boatlift; during the period leading up to the rafter crisis, the situations within and between the two countries contained significant parallels to Mariel. As in 1979–80, a rapprochement between the two countries had taken place that involved freer movement of exiles into Cuba, and Cuban officials again were complaining that the United States was reneging on its agreement to grant visas to a large number of people each year. The Cuban government had a point. In 1984, the Reagan administration had increased the number of visas to 20,000, and in 1990 Congress had further raised that number to 27,845; but in practice, the Immigration and Naturalization Service (INS) was actually granting only about 10 percent of that number. By August 1994, 19,700 Cubans were awaiting visas.[29] This provoked a key dynamic in the development of the rafter crisis. Under the Cuban Adjustment Act, any Cuban arriving in the United States, even by unapproved means, was eligible to remain. Combined with the small number of visas being made available, this tacitly encouraged people to leave the island any way they could. In 1980 they left by boat, and in 1994 by raft. Other parallels to Mariel included a bad economy, this time a near-complete collapse, and the Cuban government's resentment of US indifference toward people hijacking boats to Miami. By early August of 1994, Castro had threatened to stop blocking the departure of people leaving Cuba if the United States did not stop encouraging Cubans to flee by sea, another echo of Mariel.

By August 1994, the number of people the Coast Guard was picking up in the Florida Straits was growing while more people in Havana were preparing their rafts, which alarmed Florida officials. In response, President Clinton announced the existence of a classified contingency plan called Operation Distant Shore, which had been developed after the fall of the Soviet Union. Specific details were classified, but the plan was aimed at preventing another Mariel Boatlift. Forty different federal agencies would respond, the Florida Straits would be blockaded, and anyone trying to enter the United States through that route would be arrested. On August 12, Fidel Castro announced that he would consider a blockade an act of war, and quietly began letting people leave on rafts and small boats. By allowing tens of thousands of people to leave the island, he helped relieve social tensions in Cuba while reducing the number of mouths to feed. As a result of this announcement, the United States Coast Guard picked up 272 Cubans on rafts and other vessels on August 15, the largest number since the Mariel Boatlift. The next day it picked up 339 people, and the day after that 527.[30]

At this point, domestic electoral considerations became a huge factor in the US decision-making process and directly impacted the thousands of people who had already launched themselves into the Florida Straits. Governor Lawton Chiles, a Democrat, was in an extremely tight reelection campaign. Evidently, he had decided that given anti-immigrant sentiments across the country he did not want to be seen welcoming tens of thousands of Cuban refugees to Florida. Since Cubans in south Florida traditionally voted Republican, he did not have to give much weight to their opinion or worry about whether they would support him. Chiles began to pressure federal officials to halt the flow of rafters, arguing that the federal government was not recognizing the crisis as escalating. The situation became even more complicated on August 16 when Clinton rejected the State Department's proposed resettlement plan under Operation Distant Shore, which had called for the Cubans to be distributed among military bases across the country,[31] a plan that must have given him bad memories of Mariel.

On August 18, Governor Chiles played his hand and officially declared a state of emergency in Florida, which activated the state's Immigration Emergency Plan and mobilized the National Guard to hold the Cubans for processing. He then prohibited Cubans who had been transported from detention camps in Key West from getting off buses in Miami and had them arrested and quarantined instead. Chiles made these moves even though that very morning US Attorney General Janet Reno had declared that the number of rafters was manageable. After Chiles's announcement, Clinton's foreign policy advisors decided to end the old policy of welcoming all refugees fleeing Cuba, with the specific aim of avoiding another Mariel Boatlift and accompanying accusations that Cubans and Haitians were being treated differently (which soon would be true at Guantánamo anyway). Later that day, the attorney general told Florida officials that the detentions could continue and that President Clinton would release a new policy the following day. Governor Chiles's pressure together with Clinton's refusal to implement the resettlement plan were essentially responsible for the change in policy.[32]

By the 1990s, the Cuban American community was a force to be reckoned with in Washington, DC, and it would eventually influence the general trajectory of the rafter crisis. When Governor Chiles began pressuring the administration to detain the rafters, President Clinton felt that he could avoid major political repercussions for the Democrats in Florida if he could gain the assent of Cuban American community leaders. Thus, as he began to receive reports that the exile community was angered by the shift in Cuban immigration policy, Clinton asked Governor Chiles to arrange a meeting with several of Miami's Cuban American community leaders. Clinton wanted their support for both the new interdiction policy and the establishment of the camps in Guantánamo.[33]

The community leaders agreed to the plan to send the balseros to Guantánamo, with the condition that Clinton put new sanctions on the Cuban government. The late Jorge Mas Canosa, president of the Cuban American National Foundation (CANF) at the time, insisted that remittances, the money that Cuban exiles send home to their families on the island, be cut off completely; CANF was mercenary in its ambition to punish the Castro regime and was willing to compromise on the detention issue in exchange for a more hostile stance toward Cuba. Thus, on August 20, the Clinton administration issued rules prohibiting remittances and eliminating direct charter flights to Cuba. However, no community is ever monolithic, and far right-wing CANF leaders did not necessarily represent the totality of the community's sentiments. During the eight and a half months before the Clinton administration finally decided to admit the balseros to the US mainland, a large number of other Cuban Americans continually protested their detention on the base.[34]

The outcome of all of this behind-the-scenes maneuvering was that on August 19, 1994, President Clinton announced that all Cuban rafters would be taken to the naval base at Guantánamo Bay, Cuba, and not directly admitted to the United States. This was the first time that any administration had refused outright to admit Cubans fleeing Revolutionary Cuba.[35, 36] The president described the situation in the following manner:

> This action is a cold blooded attempt to maintain the Castro grip on Cuba and to divert attention from his failed communist policies. He is trying to export to the United States the political and economic crisis he has created in Cuba in defiance of the democratic tide flowing throughout this region. Let me be clear: the Cuban government will not succeed in any attempt to dictate American immigration policy. The United States will do everything within its power to ensure that Cuban lives are saved and that the current outflow of refugees is stopped. Today I have ordered that

illegal refugees from Cuba will not be allowed to enter the United States. Refugees rescued at sea will be taken to our naval base at Guantánamo while we explore the possibilities of other safe havens within the region.[37]

Clinton purposely reinterpreted the history of Cuban migration and redefined the rafters in a way that precluded their automatic admittance to the United States; instead of being considered exiles or special entrants, they were now "illegal refugees." Historically, American immigration policy had allowed Cubans unlimited entry. Moreover, Castro had not in fact dictated US migration policy; he had only used it for his own domestic political purposes.

After the announcement, President Clinton dispatched three more US Navy ships to join the three ships and nineteen Coast Guard cutters that were already patrolling the Florida Straits. However, increasing the number of ships patrolling the Florida Straits only encouraged more people to leave Cuba, since they knew help would be waiting for them. Consequently, on August 20, the Coast Guard picked up 1,189 people. After people had a few more days to consider the implications of the new policy, the numbers really began to surge. On August 23, the Coast Guard picked up 3,253 people, a post-Mariel record. Between August 20 and September 8, the day before the immigration accords were signed, the Coast Guard picked up 26,000 Cubans. Operation Able Vigil, which involved thirty-eight Coast Guard cutters interdicting Cubans on rafts in the Straits of Florida, and Operation Able Manner, which patrolled the coast of Haiti for people on boats, together picked up 63,000 people, during the summer and fall of 1994, its largest peacetime operation since the Vietnam War.[38] In all, approximately 34,000 people left Cuba on rafts or small boats during the next five weeks.

In early September, with tens of thousands of Cubans and Haitians on the base, the administration began migration talks with the Cuban government. On September 9, the administration announced that new migration accords had been reached. The accords reiterated a version of the statement that had been read to the balseros after they arrived at Guantánamo on the Coast Guard cutters: "migrants" rescued at sea would be taken to so-called safe haven facilities outside the United States and not admitted to the US mainland. The Cubans in these "safe havens" would have to return to Havana to apply for immigrant visas or refugee status. The administration also agreed to admit at least 20,000 people each year directly from Cuba, not including immediate relatives of United States citizens or the people being held on the base.[39]

Officials in Florida and Washington needed a long time to accept how steadfast the balseros were in their refusal to return to Cuba and stalled for an additional eight months before making the final decision to allow them to enter the United States. The balseros' stubborn commitment not to return to Cuba was supported by members of the Cuban exile communities in Miami and New Jersey who continued to demonstrate vociferously for their release,[40] and the people in the camps were aware of this. The degree to which members of the community were upset with the situation was evident in Mas Canosa's subsequent actions. After a few months, in an attempt to buy the balseros' way out of the camps, CANF began promoting the idea of getting sponsors for them so they would not be a burden to the state. News of this initiative created false hope and much confusion in the camps, since it was announced with fanfare on Miami radio stations and transmitted throughout the camps but never implemented.

The efforts of the Cuban American community to get the balseros admitted to the United States and improve the conditions in the camps eventually had a big impact on the general trajectory of the rafter crisis and some of the specific policies implemented on the base.[41] By 1994, not only was Cuban exile leadership a force to be reckoned with politically, but other members of the community increased their assistance to the rafters while they were crossing the Florida Straits—which they had actually been doing for years. One of the first Cuban exile groups to become involved in the 1994 rafter crisis was Brothers to the Rescue, a group of pilots who in 1991 had begun to patrol the Florida Straits after the death of a fifteen-year-old rafter from dehydration drew their sympathy. In 1994, they flew over the Florida Straits in small planes and often dropped water to rafters in distress before notifying the Coast Guard of their location.[42]

Another measure of the degree to which the Clinton administration was willing to accommodate the community was a Justice Department initiative in February 1995 to create a family visitation center on the base under the assumption that the operation could last for up to five years (the few remaining Haitian detainees were never offered family visits). Some of the Cuban exiles working for the US Justice Department's Community Relations Service would have been in charge of the center, but the idea was dropped within a couple of months. Additionally, working with the communications company AT&T, the government set up phone banks in the camps, which allowed the balseros to place collect calls to anyone in the United States. Since reporters from the *Miami Herald*, and its Spanish-language counterpart, *El Nuevo Herald*, regularly visited the base, some of the balseros had reporters' phone numbers so they could call the press if anything went terribly wrong in the camps. The Haitians held on the base at the time were never provided with this level of phone service and the access to the news media that it afforded.

Therefore, from the start, the balseros themselves interacted with many individuals from the Cuban exile community, by phone, in person, or by radio. Seeing the Brothers to the Rescue flights while they were in the Florida Straits was the first signal to them that the Cuban exile community supported their cause. The second signal was the presence of community representatives in the camps at the beginning of the operation. Initially, a group of exiles went to the camps to check on the conditions and report back to the exile community in Miami. Although the balseros whom I interviewed were cynical about its effectiveness given the terrible initial conditions in the camps, the presence of these representatives did indicate solidarity with their cause in the Miami community. Another Cuban American, a professor at Miami-Dade Community College, Juan Clark, was also allowed to collect data on the balseros in the camps.

Three other groups of Cuban Americans also visited the base: lawyers, doctors, and entertainers. The group of doctors was known as the Miami Medical Team. It arrived in the fall of 1994 to assist with medical care and with initiating medical parole cases. According to the balseros I interviewed while I worked on the CRS resettlement team, many of the doctors promised medical paroles that either never materialized or that needed several additional signatures of base doctors before they became official. Additionally, later in the operation, a Miami United Way effort called GRASP, the Guantánamo Refugee Assistance and Service Program, sent small groups of Cuban Americans to the camps about once a month to give short presentations on adjusting to life in the United States.

A number of Cuban exile and Cuban American performers and athletes also went to the base to show their solidarity with the balseros' cause. In the fall of 1994, the salsa singer Willie Chirino visited the camps in Guantánamo and Panama.[43] José Canseco, the baseball player, visited Guantánamo. In June of 1995, Arturo Sandoval, the jazz trumpeter, gave a concert there, followed in August by Gloria Estefan, her husband Emilio, and the actor Andy García, who played the conga drums during Estefan's concert. All of these visits reinforced the story that the balseros told each other and the camp workers about an impeded search for freedom and solidified their determination to stick it out in the camps. In turn, the Cuban exile community used the balseros as a potent symbol for its cause—of getting the rafters into the United States.

Without such a powerful community advocating for it on the mainland, the Haitians never had a chance for such preferential treatment, whether in improved living conditions in the camps or in migration policy itself.

In addition to the external pressure coming from the Cuban exile community, elements internal to the operation were making it untenable. First, to house, clothe, and feed such a large population was costing more than $1 million a day, with total costs eventually exceeding half a billion dollars.[44] More ominously, intelligence from inside the camps indicated that people intended to riot or engage in other violent acts against camp personnel if they were not released by the summer. Finally, under all of this mounting pressure, on May 2, 1995, Attorney General Janet Reno announced that the administration would admit most of the Cubans and a few Haitians, the majority of whom were unaccompanied minors.

Barely a week after the announcement that the Cuban rafters would be admitted into the United States on a case-by-case basis, President Clinton had to enforce the migration accords. In an unprecedented action, the Coast Guard rescued a group of thirteen people on two rafts and summarily repatriated them,[45] and then took the others back to the base to investigate their asylum cases. Some were put in Camp X-Ray, but none of them were considered part of the group eligible for mass asylum. All were housed in a camp set apart from the main population, an action that was supposed to be kept secret to both civilian base workers and balseros alike.

2

Post–Cold War Cuba

The Special Period, Disaffection, and Escape

The migration-promoting laws and policies that the United States adopted during the decades of conflict with Cuba may have helped in the propaganda war against Fidel Castro, but they also provided Castro with an escape valve for internal tensions that built up during periodic economic crises. Former US House Speaker Tip O'Neill's famous aphorism, "all politics are local" provides a useful lens through which to view the situation on the island after the fall of the Soviet Union. Local factors played a determining role in ratcheting up the tensions between Cuba and the United States. Castro's complaints that the United States was not adhering to migration agreements and not prosecuting people who were hijacking boats to Miami were related to social tensions on the island. In the summer of 1994, the Cuban economy was suffering due to the demise of the Soviet Union in 1989 since Cuba had long been over-reliant on Soviet-bloc countries for trade. The Soviet Union had supplied more than 90 percent of Cuba's oil, 100 percent of the wheat used to make bread, 65 percent of the powdered milk, 55 percent of its fertilizers, and 40 percent of its rice. Without those and other items, Cuba could not provide enough food or other essentials for its population. One indicator of this, the country's gross national product, declined by 50 percent from 1991 to 1993.[1]

Tensions with the United States had an impact on the options the Cuban government had at its disposal to deal with the economic crisis. The United States had succeeded in isolating Cuba economically by imposing a trade embargo and keeping it out of membership in international lending institutions. In 1992, Congress had further tightened the screws through the Cuban

Democracy Act; this legislation prevented subsidiaries of companies based in the United States from doing business in Cuba and prohibited ships that delivered goods to Cuba from docking in ports in the United States for six months. This effectively added 40 percent to Cuba's shipping costs.[2]

All of these factors meant that Castro's options for responding to the economic crisis were very limited. Out of necessity, he created an extreme austerity program called the "Special Period in Peacetime" that focused on reforms and shared sacrifice among Cubans while preserving the ideology of the Revolution. The Special Period, as it was commonly known, focused on food rationing and increased food production, energy conservation and market reforms, and maintenance of social services such as schools, day care centers, and hospitals. It profoundly affected everyone on the island. Food shortages developed and rationing was tightened so much that people simply could not get enough to eat. Food available through the *libreta*, the ration book, kept decreasing, especially in proteins and fats; the daily per capita available caloric supply fell from 3,103 calories in 1988–89 to 2,000 in April 1993. In 1992, Cubans had to live for a month on the following basic goods: five pounds of rice, twenty ounces of beans, six pounds of sugar, two servings of fish, four ounces of coffee, and sixteen eggs. Milk, which was formerly available to everyone, was reserved for children under seven.[3] My observations in Havana in 1998 led me to conclude that this amount of food lasted a family only about ten days.

Consequently, the average Cuban adult lost an estimated twenty pounds in the early 1990s. In June of 1993, 40,000 people lost their eyesight to optic neuropathy caused by vitamin deficiencies, which the government addressed by distributing vitamin tablets to everyone and involving 18,000 family doctors in early diagnostic activities. The scarcity of food meant that people had to make numerous trips to stores to obtain their allotments, waiting on line for hours a day. Families typically spent fifteen hours a week in lines for food, with the burden falling disproportionately on women. The amount of time people had to stand in line fostered discontent as people shared their grievances and gossip while they were waiting.[4]

The reduction in available imported goods combined with the Cuban government's reluctance to devalue the peso exacerbated shortages, and demand increased in response to low prices when output contracted. By the end of 1993, while the official exchange rate for the dollar (the possession of which was legalized that year) was one for one, on the black market it was

130 pesos to one, and soon shot up to 170 to one. While salaries could cover the price of rationed goods, they could not buy enough for survival since black market rates put the prices out of the reach of most people.[5]

Government reforms introduced further contradictions into the system, since the official effort to "equalize sacrifice" had the unintended consequence of encouraging lawlessness. Because salaries were insufficient to cover the cost of black market items, people had to find things to sell. This provided them an incentive to steal from work at unprecedented rates. Producers and distributers of everyday goods routinely siphoned them off, and shop managers began to set aside some stock to sell at premium prices. Everyone bought things illegally out of necessity. Since everyone was stealing from work, anyone could be subject to arrest at any time, and everyone knew it.

Although the scarcity of food was probably the most potentially traumatic element of the Special Period, the drastic measures affected every sector of society and placed the entire population under great stress. To conserve energy, the government reduced petroleum supplies to the state sector and private consumers by 50 percent and closed down the energy-intensive Che Guevara nickel plant[6] and the country's oil processing plants. Although it officially called for a 10 percent reduction in electricity consumption, by 1993 the government was cutting off electricity supplies for six to seven hours per day, in the infamous *apagones*, or blackouts. Tractors and plows were useless without fuel or spare parts, and the government replaced them with oxen. Some factories had to close down, and the government paid laid-off workers 60 to 70 percent of their salaries. Soon, public transportation nearly came to a halt, blackouts became constant, and the water supply was erratic.[7]

Prostitution, a phenomenon nearly unknown to revolutionary Cuba, also returned. This time it included people who normally never would have entered into the trade, such as college students, professors, and doctors, and included men as well as women. Prostitution mostly focused on the tourist industry, since people were desperate for such things as a pair of new shoes and wanted a reprieve from the misery and boredom of the times in the form of dates with foreigners.[8]

In 1991, the government cut back on bus runs in Havana, first by 31 percent and subsequently by even more. To make up for the lack of public transportation, it imported a million bicycles from China and sold them to students for 60 pesos and to workers for 120. By the end of 1992, residents of Havana were relying on bicycles for one third of all their trips, and half of all households had bicycles from the Special Period era. Ironically, this only exacerbated the theft problem, as demand again far exceeded supply. Moreover, bicycles relied on a source of fuel that was also scarce: food. Hunger further increased as people had to burn extra calories to ride their bicycles everywhere.[9]

Although the Revolution was organized around the idea of the worker, because wages could no longer provide for individual and family well-being, the economic crisis also had a negative impact on the ideology the Revolution used to further its existence.[10] Increasing numbers of people began to question its value, albeit more in private than in public. In the Cuban government's own poll in 1990, half of all respondents said they were unhappy with the material situation, a remarkable number given the potential for punishment for open complaint. Interestingly, higher-income respondents voiced the most unhappiness about their salaries relative to how hard they worked. There were also complaints about bureaucracy, too many "meetings," *sociolismo* (trading favors among *socios*, the Spanish word for "partners"), abuse of office, private use of government vehicles, corruption, and the like. Another poll revealed disillusionment with Fidel Castro himself.[11]

Fernando[12] had worked in the tourist sector in Cuba and had access to enough currency to meet his and his family's needs on the black market. However, as a former member of the military who had dedicated his life to his country, the situation that it was in really pained him. For years he had resisted leaving Cuba, beginning when his father, who had emigrated earlier in the Revolution, sent a boat to take him to the United States during the Mariel Boatlift. The contradictions that had built up over the years, along with his own experience of state repression, made him decide to leave the country. He explains how he felt:

I dedicated many years to Cuba. The moment arrived when I said to myself I will be 30, 35, or 36 years old and I will still not have resolved this problem in Cuba. I'm not going to resolve it. I'm not going to be able to resolve this situation. The Cuban people's minds have been very brainwashed for a long time, I'm not going to be able to resolve it. As much as it hurts, as patriotic as I may feel, I know what my limits are. I'm not the kind of person who is going to sit in jail defending a cause for people who don't want to hear about it; I don't have a martyr's spirit. State Security grabbed me and put me [and my wife] in prison, they detained me, and we decided to leave.

Sylvia described her children's growing rejection of the system as initially a rebelliousness that was typical of their age.

Their initial rejection of the internal contradictions was a product of their age. But I was already separated from their father and I could, you know.... Ah, another thing that helped my children [reject the Revolution] a lot, but that also hurt them was that their father and grandmother belonged to ... they were informants. They belonged to all of that, so that bothered them a lot. When they went to their house to ask for Fulanito or Menganito, you know they were well-known people from the block. So it bothered my children a lot. They told their grandmother, "Why does it have to be you? Why does it have to be you giving information about somebody?" "Why can't you mind your own business? One day they are going to grab you and drag you around the street," they told her.

With the implementation of the economic austerity of the Special Period came increased repression. Any government that truly believes in the power of its ideological underpinnings does not need to resort to the persecution of its people. However, in addition to a legitimate need to address criminal activity such as theft, Cuban law also made the failure to report such activity a crime. Another criminal offense was attempting to leave the country without permission—and this betrayed Fidel Castro's cynicism in complaining that the United States was not allowing enough people to immigrate. Perhaps the most oppressive legal concept was dangerousness, or *peligrosidad*, which Human Rights watch described in the following manner:

Indications of dangerousness include not only habitual drunkenness, alcoholism and drug-addiction, but also "anti-social behavior." The law defines it as "the habitual disturbance of the rules of social co-existence through violent or provocative acts, violation of the rights of others, living like a 'social parasite' from the labor of others, or practicing socially reprehensible vices."[13]

Being declared "dangerous" also meant that one was under surveillance and could possibly be arrested. The government rounded up hundreds of young people as dangerous during 1993. Once in Guantánamo, many of the balseros also reported having been previously jailed or threatened with imprisonment for attempts to leave the country or for knowing people who did.

To appease the international community, at this time the government released some political prisoners at the end of their terms, relaxed travel restrictions, promoted fewer acts of mass vandalism, and ordered fewer mass dismissals of dissidents from their jobs.[14]

Because of the increasing number of thefts of almost everything, the government did have an urgent and legitimate need to crack down on illicit activity. For example, during the first half of 1990, 2.5 million pesos were unaccounted for. In 1991, the government had to halt railway parcel delivery services because too many food packages were being stolen. The situation was so bad that farmers were requesting armed protection because of rampant theft of their crops. In 1992, the country witnessed the largest bank robbery in its history, more than two dozen people were arrested for drug trafficking, and 500 people, from all walks of life, were arrested in a draconian anti-corruption campaign. Since the illegal activity was generally not being committed by habitual criminals, the arrests did not generally deter anyone from taking part in illicit activities. By August 1994, the economic base of the entire Cuban experiment seemed to be collapsing. The economy had been declining for five years in a row, power was being cut off, sugar production was falling, unemployment was increasing, many enterprises were operating at 15 percent of capacity, and food was scarce.[15]

Throughout 1994, a series of incidents within Cuba involving individuals openly defying the government in dramatic ways revealed mounting tensions on the island. On January 4, 1994, the crew members of a Cuban tourist plane heading to Jamaica diverted it to Grand Cayman Island, where they all defected; on February 8, a man windsurfed 110 miles from the Cuban coast to Marathon Key in Florida; and on February 12, hundreds of people clashed with Cuban police at the United States Interests Section in Havana, attempting to obtain visas after hearing rumors that the Clinton administration was granting them. These types of incidents only increased during the next few months. On May 8, a Cuban pilot diverted a government plane to Miami; on May 28, 114 more Cubans seeking asylum jammed the residential complex of the Belgian ambassador and occupied the grounds, the largest such incident since 1980. On June 4, sixty-one people fled on a state dredging boat and successfully made it to Florida. One week later, twenty-one people smashed a truck through the gates of the German embassy in Havana to demand asylum. On June 17, seventy-two Cubans escaped to Florida aboard a stolen tugboat.[16]

Tensions began to come to a head on July 13, when the Cuban Coast Guard sank a stolen tugboat called the Thirteenth of March, which was loaded with sixty-three men, women, and children, thirty-two of whom drowned. Though this incident was not reported on the news, it enraged the population, which learned about it by word of mouth. Between July 26 and August 4, two ferries were hijacked, one of them twice. On July 26, nine people hijacked the ferry connecting Havana and Regla and made it to international waters. The US Coast Guard took thirteen of them to Florida, and the rest, who had not wanted to leave, returned to Cuba. On August 3, another ferry was hijacked and ran out of fuel in international waters; the US Coast Guard then transported 117 of the passengers to Key West, repatriating those on board who had not wanted to leave Cuba. The third time a ferry was hijacked, on August 4, a police officer was killed in the process. The ferry ran out of fuel while still in Cuban waters and was seized by the Cuban authorities. The next day, when the ferry was being returned to Havana, a large crowd of people gathered to watch it arrive and gawk at others leaving on rafts. A riot broke out after a crowd attacked and killed a policeman who had attempted to stop a group of people from leaving on a raft. The disturbance quickly spread to downtown Havana, and speculation about another Mariel Boatlift spread throughout the city. Fidel Castro quickly appeared to assess the situation.[17]

Augustín, a balsero who was in his thirties when he spent fourteen months in Guantánamo, describes the scene:

> Fidel arrived fast. Fidel comes surrounded by a group of people. I saw a mess of them come. When they got there, I get up on one of the lions on the Prado, and I see a bottle they threw from the building at Fidel, and it broke about a meter and a half ... at Fidel! Incredible. They almost hit Fidel with a bottle. So, the bodyguards go up, I don't know, to those buildings, and at best they made a lot of problems for the [people in the] buildings [laughs] ... and then they made everybody get out of that building

[laughs]. But yes, somebody threw a bottle at Fidel from that building. Many people don't believe that they threw a bottle at Fidel like that. They threw various bottles, and one landed half a meter from Fidel.

That happened the fifth of August of 1994. From then on, the government understands that the pressure cooker is about to explode. So it uses a very old tactic, that it had used in '73, that it had used in '80, and that they decided to use in that moment, because if not it was going to get out of hand. Fidel then says that those who want to leave can go by their own means, they can go.

Yes, I was there. That same night, the fifth of August, when I get to my house at about ten o'clock at night, I had to walk from almost the tunnel [of Havana harbor] to my house [in Havana del Este]. Fidel is speaking. He says that he is not going to hold back the borders, that they [the crowds] had killed a policeman, that he isn't going to protect those who want to leave, and that whoever wants to leave should go. That had been coming since the day before, with the people on the rafts. We already had some rafts prepared. We had begun them days before, a week before. When they said that, we took them out to the roof fast and I say to them [the workers], "What I want today is that you finish all of this."

The situation was very bad.... The pressure cooker was about to burst. We had already told ourselves, "They have to free this up, because this is bad." They had already killed, they had stolen two ferries from Regla, the people were out on the street, grabbing whatever they felt like, and the government was not going to permit things to get out of hand. I said that the same thing had to happen as happened in '80. They took out a guard from the [Peruvian] embassy in Havana, and in less than a day ... 10,000 people jumped in there, they enter the embassy, in less than a day. That what was made Mariel happen, the bad deeds at the Peruvian embassy.

Later that day, Fidel Castro held an internationally televised news conference in which he blamed the Clinton administration for encouraging migration and said that he would not keep blocking people from leaving if the United States was going to keep encouraging them.[18]

On August 8, a Cuban Navy lieutenant was killed during another hijacking, this time of a Navy utility boat. The hijackers then picked up passengers at the port of Mariel. The next day the US Coast Guard found the boat sinking in international waters and took its twenty-six passengers to Key West.

The growing number of incidents led Fidel Castro to go on Cuban television on August 11 and place responsibility for the crisis on US immigration policy. The following day, he ordered his Coast Guard to stop impeding people from leaving the country. Two days after the announcement, hundreds of people stormed onto a tanker registered in Malta but were forced off the boat the following day.[19] Thousands of people began leaving on rafts or preparing to do so.

A balsera, Sylvia, a woman in her forties who ended up in camps in both Panama and Guantánamo with her daughter (despite the fact that they had landed at Key West and had a meal there), described the situation:

> The disturbances began on the Malecón [sea wall] with a boat that tried to leave. Everything began there. That day, everything was very calm and pretty soon a fight happened there. We were shut up in our house and our neighbors began to come over and say, "*Oye*, a tremendous fight just happened on the Malecón."
>
> And it touched the world, you know? And it happened and the thing was supposedly getting tough [laughs hard], but everything was getting really good! It was a chain reaction that had already begun. The people began to make preparations, because everybody thought of a mass exodus like that of Mariel. You know? Everybody thought, "And now it's going to start, it's going to happen like Mariel, you are going to get out like in Mariel," when family members began to bring boats for their family members who were here and they would take them back there in the boats [laughs]. . . .
>
> Well, you know, the government wanted it to happen. It was provoked by the government, the people didn't provoke it, so they could come out clean, so that all the counter-Revolutionaries would leave, and they would clean house. Because things were bad in Cuba then. Writing was appearing on walls, appearing on the streets, "Down with Fidel," and things like that. It was a charged atmosphere. And Fidel said, "Let me get these people out of here." . . . He knew there were a lot of intellectuals, they weren't falling for the usual tall tale. And he got afraid of that, and that's how things were.

Given the acute economic crisis and increased repression, it is not surprising that many people would want to leave Cuba. Some of the people who jumped on rafts and small boats to cross the Florida Straits had been disaffected for years and were waiting for the opportunity to leave while others made the decision to jump on a raft at the last minute, with little thought about the dangers once at sea. Some people had been experiencing threats from agents of the state in varying degrees of severity, others were political prisoners who had been released from prison and ordered to leave the country, while others simply were desperate to leave because of constant hunger, regardless of how they felt about the Revolution itself.

The situations in which the interviewees found themselves immediately prior to leaving Cuba aptly illustrate the kinds of things that were driving people out of the country in the early 1990s. Maria and Fernando had not endured particularly difficult material hardship because they had access to dollars in their positions as managers in the tourist industry and their association with the military. However, immediately prior to the rioting in Havana, each one had been arrested and subjected to traumatic military interrogations at two different facilities by commanders wanting to know whether they had helped anyone leave the country, and then whether they were planning to leave the country themselves. Separately, each was put in a small cell into which freezing cold and then extremely hot air was blown. They were threatened with death during the subsequent interrogations. Agents threatened Fernando with disappearance, but he was able to think quickly and told them that he had let everyone at home know where he was, so they would not be able to do this secretly. The couple had come to the attention of the authorities because some of their friends had already left the country by raft and because Fernando had quit his job out of complete disgust with the contradictions he saw at work every day. For example, one day he had been particularly frustrated when only one tourist boat was available for hire in the entire city of Matanzas because the only person who was authorized to order repairs on the other ones had not shown up to work for weeks. Mostly, it seems, the authorities wanted to know if they were helping people leave the country.

Their friend Mario was not under direct threat, nor was he hungry, but he had partaken in black market activities as a government official and knew he could be arrested at any time. He also felt bitter about the contradictions he saw within the Revolution. He describes being disillusioned by the constant economic problems as well as the contradictions he saw between what government officials said publicly and how they behaved with their families.

For years and years there was no relief. It really hit home with the workers—in their pocketbooks, in their way of life. Cuban people are very hardworking. I would have been a millionaire if they had paid me for the hours I worked overtime on my job.

The Cuban people didn't get any kind of breather. The standard of living was really, really low. Cuba didn't know how to use the billions of rubles the Soviet Union sent, in payments and in many things. . . .

I begin to note that there was a contradiction between Marxist philosophy and what was happening in Cuba. In Cuba there is a caste system. I had a lot of friends [while I was studying] at the university who were sons and daughters of ministers and vice ministers, whose fathers were in State Security or colonels in the military, et cetera, et cetera. I start to notice that they only married among themselves. They had to marry someone like them. In other words, a son of a General had to marry the daughter of the Transportation Minister, et cetera, et cetera. When some of the young people tried to marry someone who wasn't part of that cupola, they would encounter immediate rejection from their fathers. Fathers who would say to the press that everyone was the same, that we were all the same, that what the society valued were workers, the proletariat, the children of the workers, and farmers who represented Cuban society. In other words, what the people said as part of the official discourse was one thing, but what [they] thought and did among themselves and their own homes was another.

Another person I interviewed, Juan, had been pursued by agents of the state from one end of the island to the other after he got the wrong person to sign a paper giving him permission to study overseas. Raul, his partner, was disenchanted by the injustices he saw around him, in addition to the problems with getting enough food to eat, and he wanted to leave with Juan.

Miguel was one of seven medical students from his class who were refusing to go into the army. When they had signed up for medical school they had understood that they would do social service in the countryside, but not that they could be subjected to forced military service. Miguel told me that after he refused to be an army doctor he had not been threatened with incarceration, but he knew that he was putting his career in jeopardy, so he decided to take advantage of the opportunity to leave. Another of my interviewees, Augustín, had worked with computers, but he did not have access to many black market goods and felt bitter that he could no longer support his family. The incident that seemed to have put him over the edge was not being able to buy a doll for his young daughter.

Marcos had just been released from prison; he had been in and out of prison for years and severely abused there for creating paintings that criticized the Revolution. Guillermo was a completely non-political art student whose apathy had gotten him on the government list as "dangerous," even though his family was "integrated" with the Revolution. However, he claimed to have left Cuba because of music: he wanted to know more about the grunge rock he listened to in Havana.

Sylvia and her daughter, while not in the middle of any kind of direct confrontations with the state, also knew that they were on the list of dangerous, anti-social people, but they had been so disgusted with the Revolution for such a long time that getting out at the first opportunity was more of a concern than the consequences of whatever their State Security files said about them.

Pancho was not aware of being on any list, but he was disenchanted and had had a terrible time doing military service without enough to eat. His half-brother had just been released from many years in jail as a dissident, so they left the country together. Roberto, a *jinetero* (technically the term means "jockey" in Spanish, but in Cuba it is used to refer to people who work as prostitutes or escorts in the tourist sector) from Havana, had avoided scrutiny but had had great difficulty getting enough food; he left out of economic necessity. He was also hoping to be reunited with his parents, who had fled to Panama a few years earlier. Roberto had been prohibited from going with them because he had been at the age for compulsory military service at the time.

In a society where everyone has had some kind of involvement with a mass organization and a high level of daily social interaction with their neighbors, where people know that what they say in public has the potential to bring them problems with the state, where information is controlled, and where there can be a lot of social pressure to conform to the Revolution's mandates, disenchantment necessarily involves emotional pain and feelings of loss. A rejection of revolutionary ideology subjects one to feelings of isolation and then to the need of seeking out people with similar belief systems, even though that itself may be dangerous and nerve-wracking because, as one of my interviewees told me, "You don't know who's who." There is a high level of distrust among Cubans because throughout the course of the Revolution people have been known to report each other to the state to curry favor with officials.

In the process of addressing the various crises that it has gone through since 1959, the Cuban government has introduced an increasing number of internal contradictions into the island's political economy. This has meant that each time there is a crisis, more people become disaffected by new contradictions that often compound the old ones. For example, egalitarianism is a value that has been internalized by the majority of people in Cuban society. During the Special Period, in its search for new sources of foreign currency the Cuban government opened new hotels and beaches in joint ventures with private European and Canadian companies. However, as it did so, it also prohibited Cubans from entering these hotels or using the beaches. Moreover, in Havana, it took 50 percent of the taxi fleet out of public service and made it available to the tourist sector, further exacerbating transportation problems. These actions contradicted revolutionary ideology, and many people complained about them while they were in the camps. One man bitterly commented that not being allowed into the hotels made him feel like he was not welcome in his own country.

My own observations in Havana in 1998 point to another reason that life can be so frustrating: extreme bureaucratic rigidity combined with a system of informers that restricts the ability of the people to adapt to economic downturns. The very nature of the centralized economic system where wages are extremely low also encouraged people to steal items from work and then barter them, but that has been a problem endemic to the Revolution.

This was illustrated by the family of a balsero with whom I stayed in Alamar, a Soviet-style block of apartments in the Havana del Este section with stark concrete faces built by and for workers during the 1970s. The apartments are not spacious, but they are sufficient for a small family and are airy and pleasant inside, in contrast to their dreary exteriors. I visited with my taxi driver's sister, her second husband, and her daughter, and I found them to be in a terrible emotional state, completely frustrated with life. She was angry and depressed because she had been forced to leave her job as a biology teacher, which she loved, but which, like all jobs at the time, did not pay enough to make ends meet. To provide food for the family during the economic crisis, she began cutting people's hair after work and on the weekends. Someone reported her for this and a government official had arrived at her door to tell her that she could do one job or the other, but not both. Two jobs were forbidden. If she chose to do any job other than teaching, her teaching certification would be revoked. She felt forced to take a job mopping floors at a local beach club patronized by Cuban exiles treating their local family and friends to a day at the beach while visiting the island. Although the tips were meager, because they were in dollars, she could at least put food on the table for her daughter (the girl's biological father was a rafter who had settled in the United States and initially did not make enough money to send them on a regular basis). She despised this job, which left her sore and sad at the end of each day. Being forbidden from adapting to economic crisis after spending a lifetime attending meetings and participating in mass organizations supporting the Revolution naturally led to alienation, disaffection, and dissidence.

An interesting aspect of the disaffection is that it is a process. As the balseros explained it to me, it usually involves a slowly evolving realization that culminates in an "Aha" moment of sudden awareness that the person's values and identity do not match the reality of the Revolution. After that, it is only a matter of time before the newly disaffected person has a run-in with an agent of the state or the neighborhood Committee in Defense of the Revolution, undergoes some negative social experience, or is put on a list of "anti-socials." These moments of realization are instigated by events like watching people being beaten during "acts of repudiation," or by more mundane problems that suggest there is little hope for the future, such as the inability to buy shoes for an important social event. In the lead-up to the rafter crisis, there was enough shared misery and government repression to ensure that more people were having these moments of realization, and were having them more quickly than usual. Together with Fidel Castro's propensity to use mass migration as an escape valve for social tensions, this was a recipe for exodus.

Sylvia was one of the professionals whose process of disenchantment had begun years before the rafter crisis. She told me how she had begun to feel dissatisfied just before the Mariel Boatlift, and how actions the government took during it created the moment that cemented her disaffection for good. There are many fascinating elements in the story she tells. First, she displays an outstanding level of self-awareness, which is not surprising given that she is a psychologist. Second, she discusses the emotional connection that Cubans have with the Revolution and the kinds of feelings that can be produced when one disconnects from it. She also provides insights into why most of the balseros would remember a particular incident that destroyed their belief in the Revolution, why Cubans worry about expressing their disagreements with the government, and how this creates a great deal of emotional stress. Finally, she is an expert storyteller who draws us into the suspense of her story before she resolves it.

> I stopped believing in the Revolution maybe a little before 1980, but what made me become conscious and notice what was happening inside of me, because all of that is a process that comes along slowly, and that change you don't do brusquely . . . that change is produced within you over time . . . until one day it jumps out. And what made it jump out for me were the things that occurred during the exodus of 1980. Yes, you know, right then I noticed that the Revolution didn't have anything to do with me, you know. Quickly I became a rebel without a cause, or a rebel with a cause, you know. It was there where I began to change drastically. Drastically. Until that moment . . . I can't tell you with such exactitude when it was that I changed.

Here she tells us that disaffection is the culmination of a longer process. By describing the moment as the recognition that the Revolution "didn't have anything to do with me," she is suggesting that her values and identity were in conflict with the daily realities of life under the Revolution. She discusses the meetings of the mass organizations, such as Juventud Rebelde (Rebel Youth), which everyone is supposed to attend. One of the purposes of these meetings was to study revolutionary values, and here she reveals more about her process of disenchantment and disaffection. She also talks about a "double role," which others, such as Juan and Raul, refer to as the *"doble moral,"* a reference to the public face of support that people must show for the Revolution, regardless of how they actually feel about it. We can see how the contractions between the pro-Revolution identities that people must project in public and their private feelings about it can create a great deal of emotional turmoil.

> I could say that before the year 1980, for example, I went to the meetings. When I went to the meetings, first of all I have to tell you, I went but I didn't feel like going, understand. And when I was in the meetings

I wasn't at all interested in what they talked about there. And if there was something that interested me, it was so I could go against what they were saying. So, I began to play this double role, you know. Consciously, I was doing it consciously. You had to survive and try not to make yourself sick, because it's a neurotic situation, a neurotic situation. . . . So, nothing, I was surrounded. I worked with other young people, and you know when one is young one takes things more lightly. Until things start to bother you, you enjoy them, no? So, it became a party. In one way we all laughed and we made our jokes, you know.

But what happened in 1980, when I tell you it was like that [snaps fingers] because I really made a 180-degree turn, because it made me really indignant. Besides, I saw myself affected, I saw myself affected because I lost my youth identification card in 1980.

I worked right in front of the Ministry of Justice. The first balcony of the Ministry of Justice was used as a tribunal for the Acts of Repudiation. The window of my office was in front, it was next to that balcony I told you about. In all the offices, and all around that thing, every day people arrived and put down their things, and you had to go to the Act of Repudiation. And the whole day went by and nobody worked. That lasted for a little more than a month over there, almost two months, the people didn't work. You had to go to the Act of Repudiation. So, I worked on the second floor. In a little office half, halfway in the back, half hidden like that, and during that time I went to work at seven in the morning so I could leave at four in the afternoon.

These "Acts of Repudiation" occurred during the Mariel Boatlift in 1980, another connection to the rafter crisis. They involved accusing people and then beating them up for being supposed "counter-Revolutionaries" because they wanted to leave the country. The passage suggests that she felt strongly about the situation happening while she was at work, perhaps because so many people wasted so much time for two months. It also conveys a sense of indignation that everyone stopped working to beat people.

I got in to work, I went into that little office, and since everyone was going out onto the street, nobody, nobody noticed. And I passed days and days and days and days like that until, I don't know how it happened, the Secretary of Youth, they told him, or he noticed; he saw that I wasn't participating

in the Acts of Repudiation and he went to tell me that I had to participate ... in the Acts of Repudiation. I told him no, that I wasn't going to
beat anybody, you know. That to be a Militant Youth, that wasn't within
the statutes of the organization. To the contrary, what it talked about was
humanity. But that independently of that, I wasn't going to beat anybody.

So they had a meeting there to analyze, you know, my militancy. But
I didn't give them time to analyze it, you know. What I did was hand
over my identification card. And I told them that I didn't want to be a
Militant Youth anymore. Afterward, a policy change came down from the
Party, with a new orientation. After they got tired of beating people, a
change came that made the beatings stop, that nobody could beat anybody anymore, that nobody could set fires, that it was inhumane, that
that was against Party policy. And, so the Party wanted to give me back my
identification card.

I said "That's it," and that I had handed it over, and that I believed that
all of them, those who had their card in their hand, now was the moment
to hand it over. So, those people who did the beating should hand over
their ID cards. Because they had gone against the statutes, you know, of
the organization, they surely should hand over their ID cards.

This passage illustrates an element of Cuban revolutionary culture: meetings to "analyze" one's "militancy." In other words, the group would decide
whether she was a proper Revolutionary or not. To defend herself, Sylvia
skillfully uses the language of the Revolution to overcome her entrapment
within it, pointing out the contradiction between the values it espoused and
the actual actions it took. This was exemplified by the organization's statutes
advocating humane treatment of all people at the same time the government
was promoting public beatings. Although the policy to beat people eventually changed, Sylvia symbolically gave her Revolutionary identity back to
the State anyway by returning her ID card. By doing this, she succeeded in
overcoming the emotional conflicts involved in the double moral problem
while avoiding state sanction for failing to beat people. Moreover, by telling
the people that *they too* should turn over their cards, she implies that they are
all hypocrites and therefore not true Revolutionaries either. This passage also
suggests that the Cuban government is not as rigid as it is often portrayed.
Instead of being thrown in jail for not following the government's edict,

Sylvia was allowed to defend herself, and her story was accepted, however reluctantly.

> That was an incident that evolved me a lot, because look. Above all, I'm going to tell you something. When I handed over that card, it had a very positive effect on me, it had a *very* positive effect on me. In the first place, because in that moment, very few people had the nerve to do that.
>
> And it was like an act of valor, no? I proved my own strength. I became conscious of what I was capable of doing. It served as positive feedback, no? From then on many people began to admire me, many people began to secretly become close to me, no? And they hugged me, and they congratulated me, for the valor that I had had to do that, you know.

The fact that people in her office admired Sylvia for her courage is an illustration of how difficult it is for most people to withstand the social and political pressure to perform mandated actions; it also shows that people did not agree with what they were being ordered to do but went along with it anyway. People do this in a variety of situations in Cuba. Sylvia had taken the risk of being socially and politically isolated by her protest but ended up becoming less isolated instead.

> So, after you take that step in a situation like that you begin to live with more liberty. It's like taking a weight off your shoulders, you know. I had done that, and nothing happened to me, because they didn't send me to jail or take my job away, or anything. I continued to do the same thing I was doing. So, because of that, you know, that made me see that I could do a lot of things. And I didn't need to live, eh, that double life that I was leading, you know? So, I also liberated myself, I liberated myself from belonging to that organization, and you know, I wasn't even a Pioneer anymore.

The passage also illustrates how burdensome the various requirements of "being a Revolutionary" are, so much so that people espouse values in public that are at odds with their internal belief systems. As we see in this case, however, while not acquiescing is risky, freeing oneself from the shackles of hypocrisy produces a great feeling of liberation.

In the next part of her story, Sylvia connects what she did in 1980 with her subsequent divorce, both overtly and by describing what it feels like to be a Revolutionary. She then spends some time discussing how she gave her husband more time to get used to the idea of the divorce, suggesting that she felt guilty about it on some level. By knocking on the table, she underscores the finality of her divorce.

> And six years later [knocks on table] exactly, I got a divorce from him. And that was another . . . second important step for me, because when that was finished I was liberated completely. His family was very integrated with the Revolution.

She then more overtly connects divorcing her husband with divorcing herself from the Revolution.

> And the act of divorcing him . . . to break from him was also to break from the Revolution [laughs]. You know, even though it doesn't seem so, maybe you don't understand that, but it's like that. Being a Revolutionary is the state of being wed to the Revolution. It's like a marriage. Yes. In practice it's like a marriage, yes, yes, yes, yes. Yes, eh . . . from an emotional point of view, from a psychic point of view, it's as if you were married to the Revolution. So, my separating from him was also like separating myself [knocks on table] from the Revolution. It was like another cleansing, that I broke another link you know. Because . . . his family, I just told you that his family was very integrated. And I couldn't fight directly with that, I couldn't fight with that, because I had two children with him. And to put myself in opposition to him, or against the Revolution, meant losing my children. Do you understand? I had to be *really* intelligent, you know.

Sylvia drives home her point by making an emotional link between divorcing her husband and breaking from the Revolution. Both the Revolution and a marriage take a lot of time, energy, and commitment, and it is painful to dissolve the connection. She also illustrates how dangerous it can be to make the break when she says "to put myself in opposition to him, or against the Revolution, meant losing my children." Both a husband and the Revolution can retaliate. Aside from questions of emotional compatibility, there are problems with mutual suspicion when things like this happen because the consequences can be grave. In this case, being known as someone who does not support the Revolution would have put her in a very weak position in relation to gaining custody of her children, and her husband could have retaliated against her by publicly accusing her of being a counter-Revolutionary. Her use of the word "intelligent" here seems to indicate that she had used the double moral as a strategy both inside the marriage as well as in public.

It is also interesting that Sylvia describes the divorce as "another" cleansing, as if to really rid one's self of the Revolution, one has to wash off its various layers. First, it seems, links have to be broken. In this case, Sylvia's own parents had moved back to Cuba from New Jersey to join the Revolution, but eventually she had much more contact with her husband's relatives, since they lived across the street from her, and, ironically, unlike her husband, most of them were not Revolutionaries. It is therefore understandable that she would feel as if she were in a social vacuum when members of her husband's extended family left during the Mariel Boatlift. They provided a place where she could express herself in a way that was consistent with her sense of self, which would have provided a great deal of relief from the stress of the double moral. Her story goes to the heart of why it is so emotionally difficult for people to be disaffected in Cuba.

Sylvia then reveals that while her husband's extended family may have not been particularly fond of the Revolution, his parents were members of the Committee for the Defense of the Revolution and informants for State Security. After discussing how being free of her husband, and presumably the burden of not being able to express herself sincerely, allowed her to take a more honest path that included speaking openly with her children, she discussed the fact that her daughter was the first of her children to become disgusted with the Revolution, and that it started with her not wanting to go to the summer schools in the countryside to help harvest crops.

Sylvia discusses how her son became disaffected during military service in Angola, a painful episode in Cuban history that is not discussed much on the island. She reinforces the idea that disenchantment comes on suddenly by using the word *pom* (a term that loosely translates as "bam") and reveals her own revulsion at the fact that her son was sent to Angola at a very young age through her repetition of the word "Angola."

Before my son studied medicine they sent him to Angola, to the war in Angola. My son was in the war in Angola for two years, at only seventeen. Two years. That was his obligatory military service, in the war in Angola. And that put him at that stage, *pom*. When my son got back from Angola, he told me, "I don't want to know about the Revolution anymore, I don't want to know about Fidel anymore, all that is a tremendous lie and a piece of shit. And I want to leave this country."

That was how the story of us leaving the country began. Because my daughter was already rebelling, rebelling, rebelling. Because she was already, she couldn't even stand to hear the word "Revolution." And my son, he was even more, whatever, when he came back from the war, when he came back he came back like a fireball. "Everything that I've seen about the Revolution is a lie, it's all a lie, they're all corrupt," and this and that and that. He didn't want to know about the Revolution anymore. So, there we were, the three of us were ready to leave Cuba already, because I didn't want to leave them behind. He came back from Angola in the year 1991. . . .

So there arrived a moment when the Special Period said, "Here I am," and that finished off the situation. So, we made, well, we made an attempt. We prepared the boat that we had.

She then went on to describe how they prepared their boat to leave, but that someone must have turned them in because the state confiscated it. However, the government returned the boat when the rafter crisis struck the next year. Sylvia already knew that she and her daughter had a file open on them. Apparently, the State was actively monitoring people it knew were disaffected, and it pushed or enabled some of them to leave. Sylvia describes how charged the atmosphere was in Cuba, and she bears witness to the passive types of protests that were occurring immediately before the crisis.

People began to get ready, yes. They began their preparations, because everyone thought of a massive exodus like Mariel, understand? Everybody thought about that. And "now it's going to begin, it's going to happen to you like when Mariel happened." When family members began to bring boats, the people began with their families that were here . . . they sent boats [laughs]. . . . The government wanted it to happen. It was something provoked by the government. The people didn't provoke it, the government did. [It wanted them] to leave, of course, so they would go, all the counter-Revolutionaries. And . . . because things were bad in Cuba. Things were appearing on the painted walls along the street, "Down with Fidel" appeared, and things like that. It already felt, the atmosphere already felt charged, you know. It felt charged. And Fidel said, "Let me get these people out of here, this thing here is going to burden me."

So he knew that there were a lot of intellectuals, he knew it. There were a *lot* of intellectuals, you know. They weren't people he could tell stories about. Oh, that tall tale (*cuento Chino*) that he had become accustomed to telling everyone, the people who believe in him. He knew that there were many thinking brains there. People that he couldn't, you know, tell a story about. And he was afraid of that. He was afraid. And . . . that was how things happened.

All people who leave their home countries to resettle elsewhere experience painful losses. Although most of the balseros were either disaffected or being actively persecuted, leaving Cuba was still painful, as people left behind homes, jobs, parents, spouses, children, and friends to embark on dangerous journeys through the Florida Straits, which immediately exposed them to trauma. Sylvia's journey with her daughter across the Florida Straits was uneventful since they had a proper boat and a motor. However, it did involve a betrayal by the US government, which blatantly violated the law by loading her group aboard a Coast Guard ship and taking it to Guantánamo many hours after it had landed in Key West, where all of them had eaten a meal. This kind of deception and disregard for the rule of law was present in other elements of the operation as well, particularly in the Immigration and Naturalization Service's operation on the base.

Augustín had not been in any particular trouble with the state, but he had become disenchanted and generally miserable from the constant struggle to get enough food for his family. As he told me, "I couldn't even buy a doll for my daughter." He describes the high levels of social tension in Cuba in the period preceding the rafter crisis, how he got ready to leave, and what kinds of things people did to get materials for their rafts. The number of times Augustín repeats the word "streets" suggests how public the unrest had become.

In the summer of '94 there were people who had gone into the Spanish embassy, there were people going into the Belgian embassy. It was full of people. I wanted to get into the Belgian embassy, but then we began to make the raft, so I say, "Well, let's go by raft." We were going to go in secret, but then it exploded; Fidel says, "All right, whoever wants to go can go." From all of the streets in Alamar, they were in the streets, in Alamar they went through the streets. I saw people making rafts in the street.

They left the public transport buses without tires. There were no buses in Havana because they had no inner tubes. The people grabbed the inner tubes from the buses to make the rafts, which were also made of Styrofoam. The people stole Styrofoam, they bought it, they invented things. The problem was to make a raft, from whatever there was. From iron tanks, they sealed them, they put the Styrofoam in a float of inner tubes, of anything. The problem was to leave.

It seemed like a regatta in Cojimar, in what used to be the weeds.... Everyone was there, and so ... we were already friends: "Let's go, let's go, I'm going, I'm going." "No, let's go, let's go," and so forth.

At first we wanted to leave from Alamar because there were already a lot of people [leaving] from Alamar. But we wanted to leave from a calmer place, which was Las Brisas del Mar. Over by Guanabo was a place that's called Feliciano.

On August 18th, the dawn of the 19th of August of 1994, about five in the morning [takes a breath, getting emotional], I saw that hour as belonging to the morning ... the hour that we launched the raft. The beach was deserted at five in the morning. What happened was that a pursuer arrived. He said [clapping] "Hurry up ... hurry up. Let's go fast and get out of here," the policeman said.

The morning of the 19th of August, that was a mix of happiness and sadness. Happiness because I was leaving Cuba, I wanted to leave Cuba. But, well, sadness because I left a lot of people behind, a woman ... children, parents. My father said goodbye to us there [at the beach]. He was there until we left. After that I never saw him again. I said to papi, "Take care, take care of mom," and my father died last year, as you know. I never saw him again. My papa helped me make the raft, and he wanted his children to leave. If he couldn't go himself, he wanted his children to go. So, he said goodbye to us. I remember that I was in the water, all the way in the water. I took off a watch that I had, and I gave it to him. I say, "Papi, here, I have a watch." From there, I turn around, I launch myself into the water . . . I get into the raft. That was the last memory of my papa.

The Florida Straits are a stretch of ocean between Cuba and Florida; as on any area of open water, anything can happen there. It is thought that thousands of people died trying to cross the Straits during the rafter crisis, and an untold number of people have died there before and after the crisis as well. People who make the passage in a raft tend to remember it very vividly. Augustín describes an emblematic rafting trip that highlights experiences common to the rafters: grief and loss, confrontations with death, physical discomfort, hallucinations, extreme fright, facing the fact that there is no going back, and, at every moment, a high degree of uncertainty.

So, we were in the water for only three days. We had gone like twenty, twenty-five, thirty miles . . . the hills of Havana were still in sight, the tower of the Santa Cruz rum factory was still in sight. So, there are some who want to go back, they were afraid, they got scared, the first night.

First of all, nights on the sea are terrible, terrible because you can't see anything, everything is dark. The sea gets as dark as chocolate, like espresso chocolate. All that you see are those little fish, they reflect the light of the moon. They are shiny, but the sea is dark. That part of the Florida Straits is very deep, the water is very dark. . . .

So, they got scared that first night, and they wanted to turn around. We told them, "No, there is no turning back here. Whoever wants to go back will have to jump in the water" [smiling]. I remember that the woman said, "*Pingas*,[20] there is no going back for anybody," she says, "from *pinga* there is no going back for anybody." And, he, it seems, hearing his woman say that yes [laughing], there was no . . .

We were myself, the two brothers . . . and the other people, we were all adults. Two friends, one older, the other like us, my older brother, who is the oldest [in the family], two children, one younger girl, like twenty-something years old, two children. The oldest one was about thirteen, and the little one about eight or nine. There were ten of us altogether. I saw the children when they got on the raft. One hit herself in the face, she would have killed herself if the Coast Guard didn't rescue us, because they got under some cloths. I thought that they were going to die, because they began vomiting . . . vomiting . . . vomiting . . . vomiting . . . vomiting.

I thought that they were going to die. They didn't eat for the whole trip, they were vomiting, vomiting, vomiting. And I didn't see them again until the Coast Guard rescued us.

Independently, those who have tried to leave Cuba say that one cannot go back to Cuba ... when you go without a motor. Because after you get into the current, it takes you out, it won't let you back in. You leave easily ... but you can't go back, if you don't have a motor, you can't go back ... by rowing, you can't ... that's impossible. So, if you are the one whom the currents grab ... yes. So, that was it, we rowed, we rowed, we rowed, we rowed, we rowed, we rowed ... until we couldn't see Cuba anymore, we lost Cuba. I didn't sleep for three days. I got upset with the oars, I was tired of them, and I said to one guy, "Take this one here, you." There were only four oars.

I ... I was afraid, of what everyone is afraid of [death], and I drummed on the inner tubes, on the deck, I drummed ... to make sure they hadn't gotten lost over there. They had planned what they were going to do ... if the raft turned over, or if the inner tube burst or lost air. There is sure death, without escape. They told each other, "Well, here we have to die as fast as possible to suffer less," that was what they thought.

So, the next day, having to row, the rowing, and only that, the burning, and rowing, rowing, rowing, rowing. I saw a huge shark, a huge, black and white colored. We saw a lot of movement in the water, it seems that there were sardines ... and many seagulls, and the hump of a shark like this [gestures], at about ten meters. Then it was as if they had put a motor on the boat, on the raft. We left rowing ... fast. Yes ... there were no more sharks outside of that area. We saw a flying fish jumping over the water. The second night we saw a lot of rafts that were calling us, so that we would get close to each other, and pass the night with them. Because on the high sea all of the rafts that met tied themselves together ... to pass the night together, everybody, no? But we couldn't get there, the current didn't let us. The ocean got very rough and there were waves of one or two meters. And that boat, up and down, up and down, up and down, up ... the waves were ... about two meters ... and we couldn't get over to where they were. And that night passed, we didn't see more rafts.

The third night arrived, and that was the worst of all. Because we were exhausted and sleepy. We finished the food, we didn't have any more food. Almost everyone was the most. . . exhausted physically. I began to feel bothered … on the buttocks, because they were … raw flesh already, because of the little stick I was sitting on for the trip. … So, my body began to peel, because I urinated on myself in the same seat. And the water came in, the salt, and the urine, and my legs began to peel … and that dampness, *ahh.*

Ah, that night we saw … so there had been many small planes from Brothers to the Rescue, but none passed over us. We made signs, but they … were already busy with other people. Brothers to the Rescue didn't … night arrived … and that was when that last night … because it seems that we arrived at a traffic point in the Straits of Florida, a point of much traffic begins by Florida … I saw many ships; we came to a night where there were many boats, but many boats. Many … boats were visible. So, we got caught in a whirlpool. I remember that there was a whirlpool, and we began to spin around. We couldn't get out of that whirlpool, and we would have died in that place. I took off the T-shirt I was wearing. … We poured alcohol on it and we lit it, and we signaled to the ships … and the ships shot red lights at us, *ch, ch, ch.* … We saw red lights as if we were in a danger zone. An Italian ship, that was called—I'll never forget it—Giuseppe, almost flipped us. Because it got on top of us, and we said "It's coming to rescue us"—but rescue us nothing! We began to row over to them, out of ignorance, and we continued rowing and we almost [hitting fist into hand] crashed into the boat. We almost flipped over there, because the boat had turned off all of its lights. The boat when it passed by us was totally dark, like a deserted ship … a ghost. An Italian ship. It almost flipped us. So, well, we found out that the United States had put out the order not to rescue anybody.

Afterwards in Guantánamo, the Marines themselves told us that yes … that the United States had given the order to the world, you know the United States does that in the world, you know that [jokingly, laughing], that no ship should take in any rafter in the Straits of Florida, that that was their problem, and they had named the operation "Sea Signal." So, that none of them were going to take in any … that that was the United States' problem, and everybody, all the countries said, well, that's your problem, take them in, that … and no Italian ship would take us in.

So, we said, "Well, gentlemen, what we need to do here is stop rowing, pull in the oars." The children began to cry, the women began to cry … and the man who was afraid started to say that the north wasn't in the north, that the north was in the south, and that he knew, that he had to send us over there, and there almost was a fight, because his nerves were so bad. And I had to throw him three or four *"pingas"* so that he would calm down [interviewer laughs]. Yes, because if not, we would have fallen overboard. Three or four of us came together, and he arrived as another one, and the other two together, who I met on the raft. I say that if he didn't calm down we would have thrown him overboard . . . because, apart from all of our problems, if we would have had people in a panic, panicked because they couldn't stand it, that would have been . . . the women crying. Well, I shut down the situation there, which was the most difficult. . . . I thought we were going to die. I thought that our own people were going to sink us.

It's because you see in the Straits of Florida, rivers of current, *ch, ch, ch,* another river over here . . . the river was really clear, because there are waves . . . *ch, ch, ch* over there, and waves and . . . there are a lot. In one place many currents converge. At the convergence of the currents, the opposing currents in the water make it revolve. It's a whirlpool that they make. So, we got caught in it. We were afraid that it was going to drag us in and take us toward the Gulf of Mexico, around there, yes. The Gulf of Mexico is a cemetery, because whoever gets caught in a whirlpool in the Gulf of Mexico doesn't come out . . . if he doesn't have a motor . . . or they [don't] rescue you. They say that it is impossible to get out of there. And that whirlpool that it could drag us in toward the Gulf of Mexico. But, well, we got out of the whirlpool . . . it eventually threw us out, the centripetal force threw us out. So, we got out of the whirlpool, we thought about the sea and that we have to continue rowing . . . there is nothing else to do.

When I woke up, without eating, we now had no food, water yes, but food no. I woke up there, everybody now exhausted. That sun, three days. It rose. We didn't even have a watch, just an old compass. I woke up. It was seven or eight in the morning, we see a white point coming toward us . . . fast. It's a ship that's coming, from the north, a white point. When, well, we continued rowing, the point gets bigger and bigger, until we see that it was a ship. When the ship . . . it had seen us supposedly . . . when we see the ship, which pulls up next to us, is an American Coast Guard cutter. I say, "Wow, an American Coast Guard ship." Nothing less than a movie. I say, "Wow," it was imposing, that

Coast Guard ship. The red stripes, and the big letters from one side to the other say "Coast Guard," and the American flag … in an official American thing nothing more than. … So, I say, "That is the American Coast Guard." The Coast Guard sees us, and pulls up next to us … and it speeds up its motor and leaves. The women began crying again, the men screaming [laughs]. Everybody upset, and that they weren't going to rescue us, the women say [high voice], "They aren't going to rescue us," now crying. I say, "Shit." For me, for me inside I say, "Shit, to hell, we're going to die like this" [laughs]. So, after it runs about two or three hundred meters, it turns around *shweeu*. It seems that it was looking for a way to get us on board.

This story illustrates exactly how dangerous and stressful the trip was. The occupants of the raft were continuously afraid, and sometimes someone would get out of control and have to be calmed by the rest of the group as everyone's life depended on all of them keeping their wits about them. The social solidarity that occurred in the middle of the ocean was then transferred to the camps. Additionally, the theme of loss is present again, in lines such as "we lost Cuba" and "there was no going back." Finally, the tension was relieved when the Coast Guard rescued them, but not until after one false alarm.

In addition to confrontations with death that occur during traumatic experiences, one of the major plotlines in all of the rafters' stories is a search for liberty. One woman told me that when they got far enough away from the beach to see the larger Cuban coastline, everyone started yelling, "Libertad! Libertad!" This scenario would later be repeated when journalists came to the base and groups of men would gather at the barbed wire surrounding the camps and yell the same thing, but this time it meant being liberated from Guantánamo as well.

By the time the Coast Guard ships rounded them up at sea, most of the balseros were physically exhausted and sometimes very ill; a few of them had to be evacuated by helicopter directly to Miami. Their subsequent journeys to the base on the Coast Guard ships were also stressful, and sometimes traumatic. Some of these trips lasted for days, as the ships filled with hundreds, and sometimes thousands, of people. The ships' crews often performed heroic rescues. Guillermo describes one of them. The situation is so surreal that his only reference point is the movie character Indiana Jones.

In our boat, well, we were thirty-one people, our boat was the first boat. I say it was ours, there wasn't anybody [else aboard] when we got on the ship, I tell you. But afterwards there were 300 of us, or something like that. That day, I tell you, and it was there, our first interaction with the Americans. Nothing, you know, and later, I don't know, but it was in a way dazzling, right, seeing all of those things. Like how respectful they were. When they got us out of the boat, they asked who the boat's captain was, and we said, "No, he's the captain," and they asked him if they had his permission to burn the boat and sink it. Things like that. *Vaya*, if we had been somewhere else they wouldn't have even asked, understand? The captain said, "Yes, do it already!" We saw all of that. After they set it on fire, the little boat began to turn over, until the ship sank. Well, it was very emotional. And also, I don't know, other things … there was one. When they began to pick up people, after the rain storm, it was like bad weather. They took out a little tiny launch, and they put it in the water, but it went almost hugging the Cuban coast, right there, entering the coast. And to them, nothing, it was like nothing.

It was around Matanzas. And that was illegal, because normally they can't enter the coast of Cuba, but they got within like seven miles, really close around there. They picked up everybody. And there was a girl, a girl came with a guy, a guy in the raft, and the rafts had low pressure. And the girl, she couldn't get up into the boat and fell into the water, she fell into the water. And they had already gotten the guy up there, and she was alone in the water, and there were sharks. There were little tiny sharks alongside of the boat. And one of the Coast Guard dove in, into the sea.

Damn, man, it was like *wooo*, everybody, *ahhh*. And the guy jumped in and the guy still had his glasses and his cap and everything on and he dove in, and nothing, and she fell out of his arms, and he looked like Indiana Jones, that movie Indiana Jones, that movie, and his hat didn't even fall off, like that. And we were *ahhhhh*, and in the end, the girl almost drowned the guy, what happened was that the people also are prepared, understand? And things got rough for him in there, he put the lifesaver on her and all, and then they finally got her up. But, besides that, eh, everything at sea was normal.

There were like a thousand people on the ship in the end, I don't know, like a thousand. Oh man. That was a disaster. Look, we went up in the front section, that's the upper level, the part in front of the boat. And that part, there was bad weather and the boat went like this … and the ocean like this *chufffff*, and all that water got us wet. And we were wet on the whole trip. Wet, wet, from the water.

In the next section of the story, Guillermo and his two friends have a more direct confrontation with death when after everyone had disembarked from the ship at the base they stay behind to learn what happened to one man who had been sick. Watching a young man react to the announcement of his uncle's death on the Coast Guard cutter reminds him of his own loss: a beloved girlfriend whom he has left behind in Havana. He starts the first segment of the story by going directly to the death.

And the people there … an old man died, on the ship … there. We were the last ones to get off, but we stayed there, on the upper deck of the ship there, we wanted to get wet, we wanted to be the last ones. And then since there was a guy … who they had … his uncle. We met him on the ship. His uncle, they had … put him in another place because … he had had a very big ulcer … from the trip, he had an ulcer that he had had since Cuba, and so on all of that trip … well, without milk, without anything, or the things he needed for the ulcer, you know we had been I don't know how many days at sea [takes a breath]. And he had had an attack of his ulcer, and was dying. And so, they didn't let the guy see him; they put him in another place on the ship. And we got off the ship, we were the last ones, on the last bus, the bus couldn't leave, because … it was waiting for the guy to give all of his papers, because his uncle had died. So, when we arrived, we were … at least, he came with … because …

I was very in love when I left, right? And I left there but … it was already three days that I hadn't been there, without her there, and I was … I arrived here like, I don't know, halfway in shock, right? Because … I was, well … because I really missed her so much, you know; three days had gone by and so you know that there wasn't any going back. … already, I was already, I was already changing my life completely, understand?

Yes. I was already in shock there really. Throughout the whole trip, then, everything was really uncertain. Well, if I get there … if I don't get there the worst thing is that I have to go back, to Cuba again, things like that. But not toward Guantánamo anymore, one knew that there wasn't any going back.

Guillermo slowed down considerably while he was telling the part of the story where the man died, as if the feelings associated with that memory are surfacing again. Further, on arrival he then had to come to terms with his own loss.

In addition to the physical stress of being on a ship with hundreds or thousands of people and inadequate sanitary facilities, sometimes the balseros were fearful of each other as well. Marcos's narrative also highlights the fact that many of them had had some kind of traumatic experience before they left Cuba. He describes his reaction to seeing a military officer who had tortured him in prison among those who had been picked up at sea.

I came in the Wilber, mother ship, the one called Wilber. It was on the Wilber that I saw one of the sixteen men who broke this hand in seven places, and my feet, ribs, and other places. There was one of them on that boat called Wilber. I didn't recognize him, my brother recognized him. Because he even came back to let me have it again after he had left [his shift at the prison]. He was a Colonel from State Security. In other words … he was a high-ranking military official. And he was among us, in the same group. When my brother recognized him … to tell you the truth, I've never felt the desire to kill, but … the person that did this to me … understand? The person who did this to me . . .

And I ask God, I ask God every day that I continue being who I am, not killing anybody, not hurting anybody. It made me feel like doing that. And I went to speak expressly with the ship's captain, because the Marines were the ones taking care of us on the ship. And I get to the chief of the mother ship, the mother ship had 2,000 people on board.

And I went and I said, "Look, before … um … cordially … Lieutenant, my head … it's that … there's a person on the ship who is a high-ranking Cuban military officer … and he participated in a beating that I was given while I was in Cuba. And he tortured me. I, yes, before he has me having to … and I kill him … can you do something so that I can . . ."

And he said, "Of course, show this person to me." And I didn't see him anymore after that.

There were two reasons that members of the Cuban military and State Security officers were on rafts. Most of them were posing as balseros to cause disturbances or gather intelligence in the camps, but some were defecting themselves. If Marcos had not been traumatized by anything up to that point, seeing the man who had participated in torturing him would have triggered Marcos's original trauma.

When the Coast Guard cutters pulled up to the docks at the base, a soldier or sometimes the nineteen-year-old daughter of a permanent employee of the Community Relations Service (CRS) read them an announcement telling them they would have to go back to Havana to apply for asylum. Once the government had placed them in camps, it constantly repeated that message in one way or another. One of my interviewees, Pancho, a barber who was in his twenties when he set to sea in a raft with his brother during the Clinton administration's about face, described his reaction to hearing the announcement aboard the Coast Guard cutter:

> A military woman stood there in front of everybody on the boat and then she read us a piece of paper. . . . They gave us a paper by the leaders of the United States, and the things that the president said to us, that by order of the president, we wouldn't travel to the United States and we are going to a secure place, which was the naval Base at Guantánamo. So, imagine, when I saw that, I thought that I was going to die there, I said "Ay, mi madre, please, back to Cuba again, it's not easy." Everybody began to feel bad, because the people didn't want to go back to Cuba again. You know about Cuba; that they would send you back isn't easy. Of course, everybody began to get desperate and worried because of that. Because they were afraid that they would send us back, understand?

The announcement made people feel frantic, but it did not make them consider returning to Cuba; although a few did swim around some base fencing to the Cuban side, and a few hundred returned through official channels, the vast majority were not about to go back under any condition.

Besides causing them great unease, the statement offended them on a number of levels, and it immediately crystallized the balsero identity. First, the US government was defining them in a way that differed drastically from the way prior groups of Cubans leaving the island had been treated. Since Fidel Castro was still in power, they could not understand the reason for this. Moreover, given that the word "migrant" had economic connotations, for the rest of their stay at the base, their identity was also tied to a narrative about a search for freedom. Hence, no matter what pressure the United

States put on them, the balseros remained steadfast in their determination to achieve their goal of getting to the United States. Not only did many of them think they would be risking persecution, and possibly death, but they had built a new identity around finding freedom that would not be so easily discarded.

Mario describes the situation:

There were confrontations with the military, serious confrontations with the military, but that was nothing compared to the [lack of] information. We didn't know. There's nothing worse than being in a place where you don't want to be, for no reason, or no reason and ... you don't know what's going to happen with you. It's like being in jail. We were in jail. A very nice jail. A temporary jail. We were very well treated, but we were in jail. For no reason. Because when you think objectively, "I was leaving my country looking for freedom and we are here. What is this? Is [this] the freedom I was looking for?"

Another balsero, Raul, elaborates on how they felt.

Telling us by microphone that we had to go back to Havana, that we would never enter the United States, that we were economic emigrants. So, that political pressure [hitting fist in hand] over months was a disaster because it discourages you, it disenchants you, because supposedly one left Cuba for all that injustice that you know was there ... so one left to get to this country, the country of liberty, the country of democracy.

So, the government of this country grabs us, and puts in Guantánamo, and begins that psychological treatment on us ... not wanting to give us attention, not wanting to give us clothes, but only food, not giving us any type of information, as Juan said so well. We spent months where we didn't know what was happening in the world. There wasn't a newspaper. In my camp, how many were they, I believe we were 2,000 people. There was a person who had a little tiny battery powered-radio, really little, like this [gestures], and imagine, 2,000 people to hear [laughs] THAT little radio to know what was happening in the world with us, or even to know the time. We imagined that the world was effervescent with the thing, because we knew there were 30,000 of us. And through some soldiers, through channels, we found out that there were negotiations, but we didn't know.

Camp on the McCalla airstrip, January 1995.

While the Clinton administration was debating internally about what to do with the tens of thousands of people it was dropping off on the base, the balseros themselves were being forced to mobilize all of the coping skills they could summon. Besides the difficult physical conditions they were about to encounter, the specter of indefinite detention loomed like a huge, dark cloud over the camps. This combination of trauma and stress could have been a recipe for disaster for many individuals had they not found the strength in numbers and supported each other in a common cause.

Juan describes the situation that he perceived:

Now, at the beginning, behind everything, everything the military was doing, of course there was a great political problem. The government, in this case Clinton's, didn't know what it was going to do with us and it could treat us all badly...because they didn't know ... what they were going to do with us. We had lost contact with the past ... we didn't know what was going to happen in the future, and I believe that that was the same case with the military.... They didn't know what was going to happen with us.

At the beginning they tried to maintain order in the camps, they tried the best they could to maintain order ... or, rather, they tried to have us maintain order ourselves. They didn't come into the camps, they weren't interested in anything that happened in the camps. If someone was sick ... if someone had a kidney pain, for example, if something happened to someone, they did not intervene.

3

Gitmo

From Navy Base to Immigration Detention Center

"Gitmo" is the name that members of the US Navy, Marines, and Coast Guard affectionately call the US Navy base in Guantánamo Bay, Cuba. By the time the Cuban rafter crisis began in 1994, the United States had been in control of the forty-five miles of bays and inlets that comprise the base for nearly a century, long enough for it to have evolved through a number of different uses. For most of the twentieth century, the United States used Gitmo only for military purposes, mostly as a deep-water training facility rather than an immigration detention center. Originally, the base served as a strategically-located refueling station, but it became a launching pad for military interventions during a period of intense United States neocolonial activity in the Caribbean basin in the early twentieth century. During World War II, the Navy spent $37 million to upgrade the base's facilities after a military readiness commission determined that the United States was vulnerable to German attack in the Caribbean. The upgrade resulted in a fully resourced base that included new airstrips on both sides of the bay, munitions, thousands of temporary and permanent housing units, a school, chapel, and additional recreational facilities. This effort required 10,000 Cubans, Jamaicans, and other West Indians assisting 4,000 servicemen and civilian contractors. Workers from all over the eastern end of Cuba went to the base in search of work on this effort.[1]

The commission's assessment of the German threat was correct, and that made Guantánamo an important defensive asset during the war. German submarines attacked commercial ships between Europe and North America as well as between the Panama Canal and the port of New York. In 1942, they sank 247 Allied ships carrying merchandise throughout the region. In 1943, the base became a linchpin in a convoy system from the Panama Canal to New York, which dramatically reduced the loss of ships to twenty-two by the next year.[2]

After that, the base was tranquil until the late 1950s, when Fidel Castro's 26th of July movement began fighting for control of Cuba. Given the chronic tensions that have characterized the relationship between the United States and Cuba since that time, it would seem logical that Guantánamo would be a flash point for tensions, but that has not been the case. After a few incidents in the early 1960s, Cuban protests over the base have been mostly rhetorical, with Fidel Castro's refusal to cash the annual rent check the United States sent to Havana being the major act of protest.

One incident was serious, though. In 1964, after the Coast Guard seized four Cuban fishing vessels that had wandered off course, Fidel Castro cut off the base's water supply. Until that time, under a contract signed in 1938 Cuba had provided 2 million gallons of water a day from the Yanter River, for which the Navy paid $14,000 a month. The Navy quickly installed desalinization equipment, tightened the base's defenses, and dismissed hundreds of Cuban workers. The water supply would become an issue in the mid-1990s during the rafter crisis. By then, the base had lost most of its strategic importance and was functioning as an important deep-water training facility.[3]

During the course of a century, "Gitmo" became an outpost of middle-class suburban America for members of the military assigned there. A number of generations of US Navy, Coast Guard, and Marine families have good memories of raising their children on the base, which has a small-town feel with an emphasis on safety, abounds with water-related recreational opportunities, and even has a shopping mall centered on the Navy Exchange, or NEX. When the rafter crisis struck in mid-1994, the mall contained a souvenir store, an ice cream and sandwich shop, and banks of war-themed video games. The only McDonalds on the island opened next to the mall in 1986. The base's isolated location near the eastern tip of the island, and its situation as a military base located in a sovereign nation with which the United States had no formal diplomatic relations, made Gitmo an island within an island. This is implied in the saying among military personnel that "what happens in Gitmo stays in Gitmo."

Haitians were the first group of refugees to be held at the base. In 1977, the Coast Guard interdicted a large boat called the *St. Joseph* carrying 101

Haitians and took it to the base for repairs. After the Haitians balked at being repatriated, they ended up remaining on the base for a month while the United States decided what to do with them. Eventually, Immigration and Naturalization Service (INS) officials went to the base and gave them perfunctory interviews, accepting the asylum claims of only four people. Apparently, the State Department feared that admitting more would open a Pandora's box of attempted refugee entries. In fact, denying Haitian asylum claims was already a trend. In the four years before the *St. Joseph* landed on the base, only 10 percent of 2,000 Haitian asylum petitions had been granted. Since more Haitians had been landing in south Florida and creating a backlog of court cases, the government launched a program to expedite deportations, declaring them to be economic rather than political refugees. It was around this time that the INS first considered using Gitmo's ambiguous legal and political status to get around giving Haitians due process, since on the base they would not even have access to lawyers.[4]

In 1980, Miami's Haitian Refugee Center filed a lawsuit, *Haitian Refugee Center v. Civiletti*, on behalf of 5,000 Haitians being denied political asylum in what officials were calling "The Haitian Problem." The suit accused the INS of discriminating against the Haitians on the basis of national origin in violation of the Immigration and Nationality Act of 1965. Part of the government's defense relied on interviews of 30 of the 97 people from the *St. Joseph* who were repatriated and had not been harmed by the Haitian government, despite the fact that the Duvalier regime tended to consider Haitian asylum seekers as enemies.

The government's response to the suit highlighted its reasoning process and revealed a set of tactics that would be resurrected in the mid-1990s: it was willing to set aside established international protocols, deliberately distort political conditions in other countries, exaggerate the threat that the asylum seekers posed to the United States, and use intimidation to compel the outcomes that officials desired.[5]

In the end, the Southern District Court ruled in favor of the plaintiffs and declared the policy toward the Haitians to be racist. District Court judge James Lawrence King found that the Haitians' due process rights were violated and was withering in his criticism of the way the government had treated and portrayed the Haitians. He noted how drastically the government differed in its acceptance of Cuban asylum seekers, commenting that "All of the plaintiffs are black. In contrast, for example, only a relatively small percent of the Cuban refugees who have fled to this country are black ... all of the Cubans ... were granted asylum routinely ... none of the over 4000 Haitians processed during the INS 'program' at issue in this lawsuit were granted asylum. No greater disparity can be imagined." The Mariel Boatlift began just as the case was being argued. The boatlift was accompanied by a simultaneous exodus of thousands of Haitians, which became more of an ongoing occurrence than Mariel.[6]

The outcome of the Civiletti case did not change anything about the way President Reagan handled the next exodus of Haitians. As Haitians continued to try to escape the brutal Duvalier regime, President Reagan made a unique deal with the government of Haiti to interdict those fleeing by sea and summarily repatriate them in exchange for keeping flows of US aid going to Haiti. The United States had no other agreement of this type with any country in the world. In announcing the policy, Reagan officially proclaimed the Haitians a threat to the welfare and safety of the United States, repeating the same behavior that had so incensed Judge King.[7]

Under Reagan's arrangement with Duvalier, a new Alien Migrant Interdiction Operation (AMIO) would transfer passengers on seized vessels to Coast Guard ships, where they would be quickly interviewed by INS officials to see if their fears of political or cultural persecution were "well founded." The interviews were perfunctory and the immense majority was forcibly returned to Haiti. This procedure ensured that the administration was technically not in breach of the principle of non-return of refugees contained in the international treaties the United States had signed after the Holocaust, although it was quite blatantly in violation of their spirit. The asylum statistics of that period provide evidence of the government's true intentions. During the first decade of the AMIO, only twenty-eight out of 23,000 people interdicted made it to the United States, and only eight of them were granted political asylum while the country was simultaneously accepting hundreds of thousands of refugees from all over the world.[8]

Though Haitians had been held at Gitmo only briefly in the 1970s and 1980s, officials did not embrace the idea of using camps on the base to get around due process issues until George H. W. Bush was president. In November 1991, the Coast Guard again had begun to interdict Haitians, this time in the wake of a violent coup d'état that deposed democratically elected Jean Bertrand Aristide. When the number of people being interdicted began to overwhelm the INS's ability to screen them aboard its ships, President

Bush declared a national emergency and ordered that a processing center be opened at the base in Guantánamo Bay, publicly asserting that the Haitians had left their country due to economic hardship. In May of that year, President Bush suddenly issued an executive order to halt asylum screening and forcibly return them all, pledging to monitor conditions in Haiti.[9]

The situation became infamous for the denial of due process. Many of the Haitians were held in camps on the base for up to three years in terrible conditions, with inadequate water supplies and sanitary facilities. Most were put in six camps on the McCalla Airstrip. Camp Bulkeley was reserved for special cases, for the "screened-in" people awaiting transfer to the United States, and eventually for people with HIV/AIDS. HIV-positive Haitians, besides being held in substandard living conditions, were given substandard medical attention and subsequently saw their health deteriorate. A facility known as Camp 7 was reserved for people with behavior problems, foreshadowing the creation of Camp X-Ray during the rafter crisis.[10]

The government relied on hysterical, racist images of contaminated bodies to justify its actions and the State Department pressured INS interviewers to screen out as many people as possible, which caused a drastic decline in the numbers admitted to the United States by early 1992. Additionally, in February of that year the INS lost the paperwork for nearly 2,000 screened-in refugees, after its chaotic screening procedures had made the asylum process miserable in the first place. Mishandled files resulted in at least one death after a women who had been screened in to the United States was instead repatriated and murdered in her bed soon after her return to Haiti.[11]

Hunger strikes and lawsuits helped free the Haitians from the base, although two circuit courts ended up divided over whether the Bill of Rights applied to people held on the base. This set the stage for President George W. Bush to send so-called terrorist suspects to the base, since in 1995 The Eleventh Circuit Court of Appeals had ruled that Cubans and Haitians held on the base had no First or Fifth Amendment rights, and that international human rights treaties only applied when refugees are "at or within the borders of the United States."[12]

That suit was the result of another double exodus of Cubans and Haitians in the spring and summer of 1994. In May, approximately 21,000 Haitians again fled their country on small boats to escape the continuing high levels of violence the coup government was perpetrating. Although Clinton had sharply criticized George H. W. Bush, president at that time, for interdicting the Haitians and sending them back to their country, as president he repeated and even extended those actions himself, through continuing a Coast Guard blockade of Haiti that ensured that few Haitians even made it far enough to request asylum.[13]

Operation Sea Signal began in May of 1994, first to interdict Haitians and then Cubans. The Coast Guard began running ships to interdict Haitians and then used the Navy's hospital ship, the USS *Comfort*, docked in Kingston Harbor, Jamaica, to house them while the INS processed their asylum claims.[14] When the numbers of Haitians again became overwhelming, President Clinton ordered a tent city be set up at the US Navy base in Guantánamo, where, as his predecessors had done, his administration relentlessly pressured them to return to their country. After 5,000 marines restored Aristide's presidency in mid-October, it sent most of them back to Haiti.

In early August, while the military was dealing with housing, feeding, and clothing thousands of Haitians living in hastily erected tent cities on the base, rioting broke out in downtown Havana and sparked a mass exodus of Cubans on flimsy rafts. This was on top of an increasing number of people who had been leaving the island on rafts before that. Over the course of five weeks, the number of people deciding to take the risky trip grew to 34,000. By deciding to send them to join the Haitians on the base instead of allowing them into the United States, the Clinton administration became the first one since the Triumph of the Revolution in 1959 to refuse outright to admit Cubans fleeing Cuba to the United States. The president's decision to create a massive "safe haven" of 50,000 people in Guantánamo strengthened the trend for presidents to use the base's anomalous legal status[15] to house people who would pose inconvenient political problems if provided access to the United States judicial system.

Operation Sea Signal was part of a Joint Task Force, JTF 160, in which all five branches of the military worked together to provide food, shelter, security, and general logistical support, and rotated members of the US Army, Navy, Air Force, and Marines through the camps every ninety days. Civil Affairs officers as well as reservists were present among the military personnel assigned to the base. In August of 1994, the Air Force dispatched the 59th Air Transportable Hospital (ATH) from the Williford Hall Air Force Medical Center at Lackland Air Force Base in Texas to treat members of the Cuban population who had serious medical conditions. More complex cases were taken to the Navy Hospital on the base and others were medically evacuated to Miami.[16]

The operation really engulfed the base and temporarily altered the use of many of its buildings. A huge tent city went up on the McCalla Airstrip and smaller ones were set up in the Camp Bulkeley area of the base, and on the rifle range and golf course. Two newborn baby clinics had to be set up for new mothers, one taking over a building on the McCalla airstrip and the other set up in the golf course's clubhouse. Mothers who gave birth were allowed to remain in the cool and clean clinics for two weeks, after which time they were sent back into their camps, where it was difficult to care for them due to the heat, coral dust, lack of privacy, and rationing of water. Since the base is a legal abyss, to add insult to injury, neither the United States nor Cuba would recognize children born on the base as citizens. Another building, which had been a jail, was put to use to house and treat members of the population who became mentally unstable during the operation. Yet another building would soon be set aside for the production of a camp newsletter.

McCalla camps from the air, January 1995.

The JTF 160 Migrant Operations Center was housed in a large pink building that the military affectionately dubbed the Pink Palace. It sat on a hill overlooking the thousands of little tents that had been broken up into six camps, called McCalla 1 through 6, on the McCalla airstrip. A building that had contained a restaurant called the Blue Caribe was put to use for producing a database of camp occupants as well as identification cards and bracelets for everyone on the base. The system the military used was called the Deployable Mass Population Identification and Tracking System (DMPITS). As people were dropped off on the base, they received a DMPITS bracelet; this resembled a black plastic, faceless watch that was riveted together around their wrist. Inside the "watch" face was a computer chip with identification information that could be read with a special scanner at the command post in each camp. Military and civilian personnel were given ID cards to hang around their necks on dog tag chains. Near the end of the operation, the military replaced the DMPITS bracelets with those photo ID cards and just a slice of the original piece of the bracelet, the blank watch face, which contained a computer chip with further identifying information.

While the operation was at its height, Camp Phillips housed members of the military in field morgues. While the real purpose of these buildings did not inspire glee, they had air conditioning, which was key to the inhabitants for getting enough sleep at night. The rest of the military personnel were initially assigned to tents without many more comforts than those in which the balseros lived, although some were housed aboard an old, stripped-down cruise ship with a number of the civilian employees who were working in the camps.

The military named the camps using the NATO phonetic alphabet, in which fixed words correspond to letters of the alphabet, such as Alpha, Bravo, Charlie, Delta, Echo, and so on. While the operation was at its height, it also gave some of the camps names that corresponded with their location on the base, such as the Rifle Range. Because women were only about a third of the population, people were quickly segregated into single male and family camps. Unlike the men, so few women arrived alone that they could only be given tents within the family camps. The family camps had a different feel from the all-male camps, and the people modified their living spaces differently. To create privacy for themselves and their children, the residents of the family camps would gather blankets and tack them up to create internal partitions that gave them some personal space, and then decorate them with found objects such as plastic spoons or miniature Tabasco bottles. When the population was moved to hardback tents, people extended their personal space by improvising porches out of wood, cots, and snow-fence material, and sometimes they covered their porches with netting. They obtained these things from the soldiers or, most often, the garbage dump, since the base's location in an arid part of the Caribbean allows many items to survive well. People would return from the dump with things ranging from rugs to air conditioners, lamps, and fans.

Most of the male camps had a more Spartan feel than the family camps, and their inhabitants did little to create private space aside from decorating the areas around their cots, sometimes with pornographic magazine images supplied by the military. An exception to this was the tents that housed the gay men, which they partitioned and decorated. There was usually a significantly lower amount of social tension in the all-male camps.

Some people had taken their dogs or other pets on the rafts with them. The dogs were sent to the base's kennel, which some people jokingly referred to as the "dog camp." Owners could visit their pets periodically.

Improved tents with improvised porches, Camp Bravo in Bulkeley, 1995.

There was also a jail, Camp X-Ray, to house people who acted out in the camps or who had been denied admission to the United States. The environment in Camp X-Ray was highly controlled, and civilians were not allowed to visit the camps until near the end of the operation. The legal abyss in which Guantánamo was situated echoed plainly in Camp X-Ray, since the prisoners had no access to due process and the INS forbade anyone to help them connect with lawyers. People were kept in the long, narrow, chain-link stalls that resembled large dog kennels, only worse, since they were topped with razor wire. The camp was clean, but heavily infested with mosquitoes, and it lacked tents, electricity, and freely available sanitary services. Guards accompanied the prisoners, men and women alike, to the toilet and the shower, which was merely a hose. Unlike the other balseros held on the base, no matter how hot it was outside, they could bathe only once a day at most, and had to do so under guard. Family visits were limited to once a week after the first two weeks of detention, during which time there were no visits allowed at all unless repatriation was imminent. Sometimes families were informed that their relatives had been repatriated only after the fact, depriving them of the chance to say goodbye. Camp X-Ray was reactivated after the September 11, 2001, terrorist attacks in the United States and became an infamous site where prisoners were tortured or otherwise abused.

One case involved a married couple being held in X-Ray because they had entered the base through the minefield sometime after May 2. Both had been wounded by an exploding mine and hospitalized. After they recovered from their injuries, the military placed them in separate holding areas inside of Camp X-Ray instead of incorporating them into the rest of the camp population. The man was put in with other people the INS had newly categorized as "Cuban Asylum Seekers," those interdicted at sea after May 2, and his wife was sent to a separate section with two very tough women who had been accused of prostitution in the camps. This was traumatic for the woman. Their status by the end of the operation was unknown.

Eventually, the military created an entire camp for people who fell under the category of Cuban Asylum Seekers, and they stayed there while the government investigated their asylum claims. This camp was shrouded in secrecy because neither the military nor the Justice Department would officially acknowledge that it existed, but everyone, including the balseros, knew about it anyway. Apparently the administration thought that if it admitted the existence of new rafters on the base another wave of them would leave Cuba. By the official end of the operation on January 31, 1996, about 200 people were housed in that camp, and since they were not heading to the United States any time soon, the Justice Department's Community Relations Service (CRS) was attempting to hire someone to work with them.

Corresponding to the adult X-Ray facility were two camps where Haitian and Cuban unaccompanied minors were sent if they acted out too much. Officially these camps were called by their numbers, Nine and Ten, but the CRS Haitian staff called them "Baby X-Ray." Each "camp" consisted of a couple of hardback tents with just a few cots inside them. The camps were so isolated and felt so lonely, and the few children in them so incredibly sad, that holding them there must have only made their emotional issues worse. In fact, during the summer of 1995, a Haitian child attempted suicide there. Fortunately, he was unsuccessful.

Until December 1994, when Clinton summarily returned all but a handful of Haitian adults and almost 300 unaccompanied minors after the marines invaded Haiti and restored Aristide to power, a small camp was set up next to a large gray hangar on the section of the McCalla airstrip near the Pink Palace to house the holdouts. Another 300 Haitian unaccompanied minors were housed there, under a huge banyan tree.

Additional governmental and nongovernmental organizations were necessary to process people and provide social services. The INS already had a presence in the camps screening the Haitians, and it sent more agents down to process the Cubans. When it ran out of agents willing to go down to sit in a hot hangar all day to process people, it sent Border Patrol officers to fill in. The State Department contracted with the World Relief Corporation to provide social services and education programs, and to distribute donations and mail. The International Organization for Migration was brought in to facilitate efforts to have third countries accept some of the Cubans. The State Department also had a representative at the base, as did the United Nations High Commissioner for Refugees.

The Community Relations Service and the private voluntary organization the World Relief Corporation were the two major civilian organizations in the camps. CRS normally provided federal mediators for various communities in crisis, but since it had experience working in Operation GTMO, the previous Haitian crisis, it was assigned to manage the larger operation again after the Federal Emergency Management Agency (FEMA) declined to take on the task.[17] In Guantánamo, the CRS provided preliminary resettlement services for the INS, ran a family reunification program, had a team of workers assessing tensions in each camp, and organized some of the recreational activities for the balseros along with the military and World Relief. Initially, CRS was also trying to develop an education program, but it quickly passed that task off to World Relief. That organization then created a large and very successful program called the Bulkeley School, named for the section of the base on which it was located. A smaller group worked in the Haitian camps, coordinating recreational activities and, after some pressure from World Relief, providing limited educational services to the unaccompanied Haitian minors. World Relief also coordinated the distribution of material donations and mail.

Despite all the effort that went into caring for the Cubans and Haitians who were being housed on the base in August of 1994, conditions in the camps were initially terrible. Both the balseros and the members of the military assigned to take care of them felt miserable. Press reports quoted some soldiers as feeling bad from merely looking at the conditions in which people were living, especially those with babies. Others expressed hostility toward them since Operation Sea Signal had forced military families to be evacuated from the base, and the soldiers themselves were required to live and work in the same poor conditions in which the people in the camps lived. The general in charge of the base, at the time Brigadier General Michael Williams, acknowledged the problems. "It's a mess," he said. "You can't help feeling sorry for these people."[18]

At first, there was not really enough clothing, medicine, or doctors, and although there was enough food, it was poorly distributed. Potable water was not in good supply, and people had to get it from large metal tanks called "water buffaloes." The tanks sat under the hot sun, ensuring that the water was warm and tasted bad. Part of the reason military families were sent off the base was to conserve water for the refugee population as the only source of water for the base was the desalinization plant.

With barbed wire, guard posts, high-intensity lights, guards who sometimes patrolled with dogs, severe limitations on movement, poor sanitation, scarce potable water, regimented food distribution, and no word on whether the balseros would be admitted to the United States, the camps were not a haven of any sort. In reality, they were a low- to moderate-security extraterritorial immigration detention center.

Guillermo, who had otherwise told me that he thought that Guantánamo was a party, describes his first few nights on the base, during which people were highly disoriented and frightened. This was no party.

For the first nights, when you got up, you got dizzy, like this, and you went back down dizzy, like this, *zziiii*. Because you get off the boat and everything makes you dizzy, it seems like you're still in the water, *chhhh*, walking. And that first night that we slept there, *psew*, man, everyone had a nightmare, everyone, everyone, everyone. I remember that I was sleeping, and the same nightmare came to me, because I heard people screaming, people right there next to me were really screaming. And it even made me scared because I hear noise, noise, noise . . . noise, noise, noise, and when I turn around like this, I wake up and turn back around; some lights came in, and it was the tractors that were making a camp right there next to us at night. They worked by night more than by day, because the sun is very strong during the day. And so they put those tractors in there at night, clearing that. *Oyyy*, that gave me a scare, that right here they're going to run us over with the tractors and they're going to bury us here. *Hmhum*. . . . And besides that, well it did that to everyone, so everyone was screaming, and they had their other things, the traumas from the trip and all of that, right. But that was the most dogged night. And when we arrived and they put us there, sitting on the ground, and the guards with machine guns like this, I was, *eeeee*, and everyone was super scared. The people said, "*Ay Dios.*"

One of the interesting elements of this description is that it communicates how disoriented all the émigrés were when they arrived on the base, still with their sea legs and nightmares. It also illustrates how easily individual trauma becomes collective, as people telegraph their feelings through affect. In other words, fright is contagious.

Sylvia's account of the early camp environment shows how stressful the supply and sanitation issues were for the women. This was just the beginning of the particular stress that women experienced in the camps.

When we arrived, it was tremendously disorganized. We hadn't bathed or brushed our teeth in exactly eleven days. Nothing, nothing. Eleven days without having any water to wash out our mouths, without clothing either, nothing, nothing, nothing, nothing. After eleven days they gave us some clothes. And they gave us a little pail of water for water . . . every day, it was white, like this [gesturing]. A little pail like this size. For everything. That little pail of water for all day. At first we only had drinking water, from some small tanks that they brought in there. We couldn't use it for anything else.

And my daughter was well, what can I say? Imagine, when my daughter left Cuba she was menstruating. My daughter smelled like, what do you call it? A dead mouse, a dead mouse. . . . I don't know how she didn't get an infection. The amount of shame she experienced, because in those conditions in front of thousands and thousands of men. . . .

And the food was little boxes, those little military boxes. The first brown ones were the worst ones of all. Nobody could eat them. Everything was hard, everything was raw, and spicy, spicy, spicy. If you ate it one day, you got hemorrhoids the next. People started to get hemorrhoids because it was so spicy. There wasn't anybody who could eat it.

In mid-September, when the Cubans in the camps found out that they were not going to be counted among the 20,000 new visas that the United States had agreed to provide under the September 9 accords reached by the US and Cuban governments to end the rafter crisis, they immediately breached the camps' boundaries, and very angry, they roamed around the base for two days before the military forced them back into their camps.[19]

Augustín had been writing a diary on scraps of paper, where he described the events:

September 11, 12, 13, 1995
The base seems taken over by the balseros, the soldiers make sure we don't get to the city, everyone is in the bush, hunting jutias[20] and iguanas! They steal what they can [to eat] and how embarrassing! We went from protestors to thieving pirates. It's embarrassing! The only place where we can't go is the city; a completely armed cordon of Marines jabs at anyone who gets near it.

September 14, 1995
In the morning through tall speakers they tell us that we have until 5 in the afternoon to return to the camps. Until 5, I was in [Camp] Kilo and in Camp India; you can see around 100 marines in anti-riot gear

[shields, helmets, and sticks]; that the balseros who enter Lima begin to throw rocks and break even the shields, and they begin to take balseros to prison, besides the film crews that film the "riot," from Kilo they also throw rocks. You hear troops saying the famous phrase, "Go back to your cabana and we won't consider you an enemy." The hunt continues in Kilo for everyone who is outside of the camp. They say that they will put the leaders in prison.

September 15, 1995

This morning we woke up surrounded by anti-riot police that are deployed throughout the camp and begin a search for arms. We have to hide a knife that we had brought from Cuba in the ground, I pass it hurriedly and they find some stakes from the tent under my bed, but everything gets cleared up. After that day the repression and bad treatment by the Military Police begins.

By October 1994, the Clinton administration was still instructing the populations in Guantánamo and Panama that they would have to go Havana to apply for asylum; however, it was admitting people who had become sick or who already had severe medical conditions to the United States under a medical parole protocol, which created a number of perverse incentives for the highly stressed camp population. The INS began by granting medical parole to people over age seventy, some unaccompanied minors (under thirteen), and people with serious medical conditions and their caregivers. On December 2, Attorney General Reno added another category, accompanied minors, but that protocol was not fully implemented for a few months. Initially, the children were considered only on a case-by-case basis if it was somehow determined that they would be adversely affected by their long-term presence in the camps—as if all of them were not enduring serious adverse impacts in such a harshly stressful environment. All together, these were known as the four protocols.[21] Under the provisions of the Cuban Adjustment Act, any Cuban reaching US soil can apply for refugee status. During the rafter crisis, this meant that even though the INS had written the medical parole policy as only a three-month reprieve from the camps in Guantánamo and Panama, in practice virtually everyone on the medical parole case would apply for and be granted refugee status once they arrived in the United States.

Thus, between October 1994 and early May 1995, the only way for the balseros to get to the United States was to obtain a medical parole, and a narrative was required for each step in that process. The first step was for the person to see a doctor at the 59th Air Transportable Hospital (ATH). This usually happened after a medical team at the camp decided that the case warranted a doctor's appointment. After a few examinations and after enough (usually from three to six) doctors had signed recommendations for medical parole, the base's surgeon, Dr. Rose, would review the case and sign a final recommendation, which put the case into the parole system.

The Community Relations Service ran a resettlement program in which it conducted the initial medical parole intake interviews for the INS. Because CRS inexplicably would not ask the INS exactly what kind of information it needed, the resettlement interviewers would just guess, and the officers would use whatever information they found useful. During the CRS interview, the sick person would describe his or her illness and relationship to each caregiver, who had to be a family member in most cases, involved in the parole case. After the information was entered into a database, it would be passed on to the INS, which sometimes would then lose it. If all went well, and the family went to the INS interview, the agent would check the veracity of the story by asking a series of questions. Because the INS decided which members of a sick person's family would be allowed to go to the United States, and it often rejected people included on the medical parole case, this was a big hurdle; it felt like a life or death situation to most people. It was also a problem because the agency tended to assume that all the interviewees were lying about their relationships with the people on their parole cases. It turned out that many people did in fact include people on their cases who were not caregivers, but just friends whom they wanted to help avoid an uncertain future in the camps, or people they considered were too sick to stay in the camps but who had not been granted a medical parole. This was really their only outlet for any kind of resistance to detention.

Since there were no documents or other types of written evidence available to prove family relationships, the INS agents devised a series of questions meant to determine how well each person knew the parolee. My friends who worked in the camps early in the operation told me that the internees rapidly learned from the way these interviews were conducted. They questioned people returning from INS interviews to discover who got parole and why; then they decided whom to put on their cases and memorized each other's life stories in preparation for their interviews. Sometimes they even mapped out each other's houses as practice. This way their stories would match when they were asked who they were, where they came from, and why they had left home.

The INS officers asked a myriad of questions, such as "How many rooms does the house have? What color is the kitchen? What is the name of your daughter's second grade teacher? Is the TV black and white or color? How many trees are in the front yard? How much money does your husband make? How long have you been married? What side of the bed does your husband sleep on?" Some went overboard with embarrassing questions including, "What sexual positions do you use? How many times a week do you have sex?" These types of questions deeply offended the women in particular. One woman, for example, saw the offensive questions as a trial by fire in which the balseros had to prove they were worthy of admittance to the United States and thereby freedom. Unfortunately, some of the agents particularly relished degrading pregnant women, telling them, "I know that isn't your husband's baby. I know you got pregnant just to get out of here, and this guy you say is your husband isn't going anywhere. And this woman you say is your mother doesn't look like you. She's not going anywhere either." Such statements were guaranteed to leave the woman in tears.

While it had obviously been given orders to reject Haitian asylum claims with perfunctory interviews, the INS was living up to its reputation for being undisciplined, disorganized, and inefficient in relation to the balseros' parole cases as well.[22] The agency was simply incapable of keeping track of everyone's paperwork. This posed two major problems: one for the individuals themselves, and the other one for the military officials in charge of each camp. First, many sick people sat languishing in the camps, some of them becoming even sicker. Second, as growing numbers of people sympathized with their plight, social tensions in the camp would increase. The camp workers and military personnel had to cope with these situations, but INS officials seemed immune to them. Eventually, solving these problems even through CRS intermediation became virtually impossible since the Justice Department was essentially mediating itself and there was no real pressure or leadership to improve anything. This meant that for the entire time the medical parole system was in place in Guantánamo, CRS camp workers' efforts to alleviate camp tensions were hindered every time they walked through the camps as dozens of people crowded around them, asking for help in finding their lost paperwork. The tensions that this caused also became a problem for the military in the camps, an issue that a Marine Corps colonel vociferously raised to indifferent INS officers toward the end of the operation.

To make matters worse, the INS suddenly sent back to Washington its only officer in charge who had been effective in correcting problems with lost paperwork and the behavior of some of his officers. Compounding this, for most of the operation, the INS had a difficult time convincing its regular officers to volunteer to work in the Gitmo morass. Eventually it was forced to order poor performers and Border Patrol agents to go to the base. These management issues became an abusive element of the camp world that challenged the balseros' adaptive capacities. The officers' hostilities were at their height during the time people were leaving on medical parole, since many of the balseros tried to pass off friends or sick acquaintances as family members. This frustrated the officers, who retaliated against them. One of the Border Patrol officers who identified himself as "El Jakal" to the balseros told me that he abused the Cubans out of resentment because he, as a Mexican American, had had to turn his own compatriots back at the Mexican-US border while the Cuban refugees were being let into the country.

Some of the INS officers ordered strip searches and harassed people who had tattoos; others seemed to get perverse satisfaction from making pregnant women cry, ignoring the effect that this abuse had on social tensions inside the camps. Some of the problems were clearly cross-cultural. Many balseros complained that they had been offended by the hand gestures the INS agents used. In particular, many of the officers called the balseros over to their interview tables by curling their index finger in the gesture that Americans interpret as "come here." Although even in the United States this is considered rude and condescending, for Cubans it is a vulgar reference to female genitalia.

The parole policy itself created a number of perverse incentives that seemed to surprise both the military and the Justice Department but which were entirely predictable. The worst one was a consequence of Clinton administration uncertainty, which caused a high level of desperation among the balseros. Each time a new illness or injury was considered cause for medical parole, a wave of self-destruction, usually among men in their twenties, ensued, challenging the base's medical facilities.[23] Ironically, the individuals involved in these actions were actually trying to save their own lives by damaging their bodies, since going back to Cuba was the same as a death sentence as far as they were concerned. Unable to feign or develop a real illness, or, as a few alleged, to get money to enlist the support of a Cuban doctor working with the Miami medical teams to exaggerate or create an illness on paper, a number of young men injured themselves. Some inhaled powdered laundry detergent to create the appearance of asthma. A few melted the thick, brown plastic food ration pouches and burned them into their skin. One man injected diesel fuel into his hip and had to be evacuated to the United States. Another man stuck gasoline-covered needles into his legs, hoping to cause an infection. When doctors began giving parole for hemorrhoids, some stuffed rolled towels or rope up their rectums to create them. One of the worst cases involved a man who injected dirty water into his scrotum. He at first refused treatment and displayed it to anyone who would look, proudly convinced that this was his ticket to the United States. Many medical officers in the military were not willing to recognize the balseros' actions for what they were: desperate attempts to save themselves from death if they were returned to Cuba. The officers accused them of malingering or, worse, attempting suicide, which could qualify someone for involuntary repatriation for mental illness. These kinds of observations then filtered into the media's accounts of what was going on in the camps.

Because of problems with the parole policy, the behavior of some of the INS interviewers, and lost parole paperwork, the CRS operation was initially extremely difficult. One of its more straightforward programs was its family reunification program. By coordinating with the military to help people find family members after they arrived in the camps, this program helped alleviate tensions and provided touching moments when people who worried that their loved ones were dead were reunited with them. Juan describes a common situation in which he and his brother had left Cuba on different rafts.

I was looking for my brother among all the people the Coast Guard ship was picking up, I was looking for him. Because I knew he had left the same night as I had, but in another raft.

My family knew that I was going to leave in something, but they didn't know when, how, or where. So, at the last minute, right before I left I had to go home and get a long-sleeved shirt and a hat, and I kissed my grandmother and my aunt goodbye and told them that I was leaving on a raft. And I left and they didn't know anything more about me until … Guantánamo [coughing].

They went through some difficult times. They had news about my brother. The idea was that my brother was going to leave … the same way I did … and we got the same transport down to the coast. … He left an hour before we did because we hadn't been able to get anybody else to take the raft down to the coast. And so my brother had to leave first and then us. And the idea was to meet up at sea. Since we were leaving from the same point, the idea was to meet at sea and tie the rafts together and continue the rest of the trip together. So, we never found each other, we never saw them again, and I thought something could have happened to my brother. I got to Guantánamo and everything and nobody had seen him or anything. The problem had been that my brother had left on the raft … the guys who went with him had gotten scared and they wanted to go back so my brother went back, and with the pieces of their raft he made another one, and five days later he left with other friends and they got to the base.

On the second trip they took a homing pigeon that would go back to the island if they arrived alive. So the agreement had been that the pigeon would die with them. If they were saved or arrived to a secure place, they would let the pigeon go. So, they let the pigeon go. They had taken three days and it took the pigeon six hours to arrive. They let the pigeon go at seven in the evening; no the pigeon only took three hours, it arrived in Havana at a little after one in the morning. It got to the house of some of our neighbors who bred pigeons professionally. So, his wife was making coffee and says to her husband, "Chino, you didn't give the guys the little brown pigeon, did you?" And he says, "Yes, China, China, that's what I gave them." Our family tells us this story months later in a letter. And so the wife tells him, "Well, look, I believe that's it resting over there on the other roof," and he says, "No man, no. They haven't had enough time to get there yet, that's another one, you're confused." The man was thinking that his wife didn't know which pigeon it was or anything. So she goes, "But Chino, get up, come over here so you can see that it's the one." And the man, "No, no, I'm sure it's not it." He didn't trust his wife, so she calls her son and says, "Come over here, grab that pigeon, I believe that's the one." In effect, when they grab him, it was the pigeon. It had gotten there so tired, so dead tired, that it arrived and rested on the roof without bothering to get into its nest.

When they picked up the pigeon it fell over on its side as if it were dead. So right away they go to my house and they tell them that the pigeon had arrived, because that was a signal that my brother was alive. But they didn't have information about me. It took another month before they found out about us.

My family knew that he was alive but they didn't know about me. I didn't know about my brother or my family either.

I came to know that my brother was alive but I thought he was in Cuba. Because … one day I was walking around in the camp and I meet with some people who said, "Are you from Santa Fe?" I say, "Yes, I'm from Santa Fe." And they tell me, "*Oye*, you know that I saw your brother over there, he had to go back with his raft … and *bfffff*, for me that was … you know, a tremendous relief, because I thought … that day … so that you see how coincidental it was. … I had been talking with some of the military that were going to look for my brother's name in the computer … and all of that, and so … he had heard that they hadn't found him, and in the afternoon they had come by and they had told me that "No," but I was on the computer I don't know where and I have to look for him there … and so, he came, he gave me the name of two other members of the military … and they went and came back at night, and told me "*Oye*, look … I looked all over and your brother's not here." So, for me that news was … like telling me that my brother was dead … and I remember that everyone in the tent was like … as if to say, "Wow" … and everyone came to me and said, "Wow, Juan, maybe nothing happened to him, maybe he hasn't arrived yet," whatever … and I told them, "Don't worry, I want to stay a little while, and think, and go" … and I went out, I left the tent, so I didn't have to have people all over me, you know. And when I was walking around there, I meet this individual that tells me that he's from Santa Fe … and he tells me that he had seen my brother … in Havana … and he had to go back. That's what it was like. … It was a tremendous coincidence.

Fernando and Maria had to cope with the anxiety of trying to find each other on the base after having decided to leave on separate boats. Fernando reported that Maria cried a lot in the camps. Maria commented on the things that were stressful for her, and what she did to cope.

I found Fernando through church representatives and through Mark in CRS who worked in Family Reunification. For me the scariest thing was using the bathroom [latrines] at night. I said, "Oh God, get me out of here."

Pretty soon I put myself to work in the mailroom. We divided up the letters and delivered them. I worked all day. I never sat on my cot thinking. It was the same with Fernando, he was camp jefe. The problem was just to wait in Guantánamo.

Being thrown together with many different kinds of people not only bothered the women. Pancho also told about this issue:

I was in three different camps. Of course, changing camps made us feel even more unstable. Imagine, they send you to different camps and you meet people you don't know, like a lot of people, because there were so many people there. And people who . . . you know. There were all types of people there, with all kinds of personalities. Not everyone was the same. You had to be mixed together with all those people, understand?

Sylvia was one of the 8,600 balseros who looked at the conditions in Guantánamo and decided that things had to be better in Panama, where the military had been able to prepare for their arrival. Unfortunately, they were put on a plane before being able to bathe.

It was only after sixteen days that we could bathe [once we got to the Panama camps]. We went to Panama by plane without bathing. The flight attendants, the airline personnel, went around, the whole trip they went by spraying air freshener. *Fwt, fwt, fwt* [making spraying motions] and they stayed away from us, *fwt . . . fwt, fwt,* because they couldn't stand the stench. We couldn't stand our own stench either. What can I say? When we got on the plane . . . the stench that was on that plane was . . . and the poor people who were there, the flight attendants and the others, they couldn't . . . they had to go around like this [covering nose and mouth with hand], covering up their nose like this and spraying deodorant, spraying deodorant until we arrived. I imagine that they had to fumigate the plane after we got off because . . . the stench was unbearable . . .

unbearable, unbearable. . . . The first shower that we had, my daughter and I . . . was when we arrived in Panama.

Panama was, that was . . . *vaya*. It was like night and day [from Guantánamo]. We had a shower, we had wash basins . . . for, you know . . . eh, and latrines, they were from here, those plastic latrines. Eh . . . everything was in better condition, understand.

Apart from that, we had communication with all parts of the world. In Cuba I had never spoken with my family from Spain, and from that camp I talked almost every day with my family in Spain. I have uncles, cousins and all of that on my mother's side. We talked with everyone. We had communication, we had telephone cabins and we could call all over the world. Besides all over the world, people went to visit us there. Because on the naval base in Guantánamo, nobody could go there. You know, with all the other restrictions that it had, being inside of Cuban territory.

But in Panama it wasn't like that. In Panama . . . people from all over the world went to see us and visit us. We had, you know, a lot, a lot of communication. In Guantánamo we were isolated, we knew nothing, nothing about anybody, nothing. [In Panama] I knew about my family, I could speak to my family anytime I felt like it. My family knew how we were. In Guantánamo, no . . . you know. We could write them letters, write. We felt, you know, we felt good, in that sense, no? Because over there we weren't isolated or anything. Besides we met a lot of people who helped us. A lot of people went to help us. A lot of Panamanians went to help us.

The food changed. They took away . . . because the restaurants. In Panama there are a lot of Cuban restaurant owners. There are a lot of people with money, Cubans down there in Panama who are restaurant owners. And they offered to cook for us. And we ate Cuban food for breakfast, lunch, and dinner. It was the most delicious food. Really delicious. We ate ripe plantains . . . they made them for us. It was exquisite and all of those things that we liked. Everything was completely different. Everyone felt much better.

Even with the more humanizing environment in the Panama camps, which had to have helped people feel more stable after their rafting journeys and the trauma of the initial conditions at Guantánamo, the specter of indefinite detention and the psychological war the military was waging on the population to go back to Havana took their toll. Severe riots broke out in December 1994 in the camps in both Panama and the Cayman Islands. The riots soured the governments of both countries on the balseros, and the population was reintegrated into Guantánamo in February of 1995.[24] Sylvia explained the genesis of the riots.

I had the luck of not being in the camp when the riots began. I was outside of the camp.... When I got back to the camp ... everything was already dust and ashes. I wasn't in the camp. I went out very early in the morning with my daughter and I got back in the evening. The Panamanian lady who would take us around came that day to take me out of the camp.

But I'm going to tell you what happened in the days before that. The camp was already, it had been days in which they were bombarding us ... with news ... eh ... that was affecting us psychologically. I alerted the military to the situation because they were playing around with people. It was constant, you know. So, for example ... they were constantly telling us ... that ... [President] Clinton wasn't going to authorize our entry ... that, I don't know, some organization was opposing our entry, and that it seemed like we weren't going to be able to enter the United States ... that, go figure, that they were going to see where it would go. So, a lot of times they said ... that they were going to construct like a community there. So we could stay there. That if Panama, they were going to see if ... countries, that they were making gestures so that, we would go to other countries.

Things like that. So, the camp jefe ... from the Cuban side, the camp jefe, began to align himself with the military that ... we demanded, you know ... that they stop that. That that psychological war that they were waging against us couldn't go on. That we demanded, that if there were a response, but we had already been there for a long time, it had been months, months were going by.... and well, they came to an agreement, the military and the Cubans, that they were going to transmit our concerns through the appropriate government channels ... that please give us some more time to make that gesture and get a response, you know. So then, it happened, when I left the camp, I know that it had been fifteen days to get a response to that and all of that over there ... to that situation.

And so, those fifteen days went by and that day that I left the camp [knocks on table]. When I left, everyone was already coming out of the front part of the camp, gathering around the front, waiting to see what was going to happen, what they were going to say, you know. So [claps],

I went out and when I got back I what I found was . . . ashes. Everything was ashes.

Really what happened there exactly, I [snaps fingers] . . . I have some compañeros who . . . some who were there, but it's that most of the people who were with me. . . . I was always . . . outside of the camp, by luck, you know. But they say that over there, they abused . . . they abused our patience. That many, many Cubans who were there tried to control the situation, because you know that in those huge groups of people there are always people who are more aggressive than others. So, there was one part that what they wanted was to take up things diplomatically, by way of conversation. But there was a group that what it wanted was [hitting back of hand into palm], you know, was to resolve the situation in any way. And so that . . . it began there, the fight began, no?

From here to there, the military saying, the Cubans responded to them and I don't know how many . . . and according to what they told me, they say that beginning, with the military grouping together, and moving in such a way that the Cubans noticed that they were going to take military action. Remember that Cubans have military training. Cubans, militarily Cubans know how to bear arms. Any Cuban woman or man can. I trained in the Territorial Militia also. Imagine, when I was studying for my bachelor's degree [knocking on table] in physics, chemistry, and mathematics, in the school where I studied . . . we were obligated to pass through military training. We did our rounds armed. You know, the Cuban people are trained militarily. So, they started to see, you know, the movements. They began to notice that SOMETHING was going to happen . . . you know, where . . . what happened there, where that thing happened. The Cubans began to defend themselves with rocks because that's what there was. They had arms, we were unarmed, but there were rocks there, and the Cubans . . . started to throw rocks.

At night, we got together like this, at the gates at the back of the camp. My tent was at the back of the camp. And I saw that every night. We were enclosed like that, with the fencing, that was there, how do you say it, the wire? We were surrounded by mountains, completely, the jungle. Barbed wire, and that. And we saw wild animals in the forest, the forest. We were surrounded by mountains like that. And in that place like that, we couldn't see anything, anything anything anything anything anything . . . in front of that mountain.

I also began a psychological war there.... A rumor began that we were going to stay there, that we weren't going to the United States, whatever. They began to get into groups and form work brigades ... to go on ... expanding and constructing the city. Because the idea that they gave us was that the city, of the base, that was the city, that they were going to keep us working and living in that city. They were going to construct housing over there for us. And so, they began to do that. And that was where the desperation really began. Because at the beginning it was, they only told us, but when the people began to see that they were starting to remodel the city, and they began projects, eh, to do this in the city, and to make whatever, and fix it up over here ... and do I don't know what, the people said [knocks on table], so "it seems to be true that they are going to leave us here ... " And so, it began to filter out from the military too, no? They started to tell us ... eh, that that was what they were planning, you know. To make a big city over there so we could stay working there.

After the riots, the military took reprisals against the population, particularly the women, since it thought that the energy behind the rioting came from nagging by women. Sylvia describes two stunning incidents that she witnessed in the immediate aftermath of the riots. She begins with a story about a group of soldiers in camouflage and face paint swooping into a camp and beating up groups of people. She then tells what happened to a group of women and then returns to the original incident to provide more details on it, linking the incidents both temporally and emotionally.

In Camp number two, there hadn't been a revolt. The revolt was in Camp One. But the military, as a product of what happened in Camp One, charged against the people in Camp Two. And by the dawn of the day after the riots, all of the soldiers mobilized, they disguised themselves, they painted themselves ... they were painted in a green paint, they painted all of their faces so we Cubans wouldn't recognize them. And they came into the tents at dawn when the people were sleeping, and they cleanly beat women, men, and everyone.

Afterwards, the next day, in the morning, they grabbed the women from the tents. They only did that in part of the camp, the back part of the camp. And they put them through everything, they took off their clothes, they stripped them, and they made them walk around the whole camp, in the middle of the whole camp, in the front part, like that, two by two, in a line on one side and a line on the other side. And they marched those stark naked women down the middle.

We Cubans threw, some people took off their shirts and threw them. Others threw them towels so they could cover up their bodies. Afterwards they took them naked to the dining room, and they sat them down at the dining room tables, and they put a breakfast tray [rapping on table] in front of them.

That's what it was [like a rape, in response to interviewer's question]. I wasn't from Camp Two, I was from Camp One. But when Camp One was destroyed, they got us and they went . . . they grabbed the people and they distributed them among Camps Two, Three, and Four. In Panama there were four camps. So, they redistributed the people from One. Camp Two was a family camp, where there were more families. They took everyone who was part of a family to Camp Two. Since I was with my daughter they sent me to Camp Two. When I got to Camp Two, I found myself in that phenomenon.

That was like three or four in the morning. And over there, they broke legs, feet, bones, and everything, they did away with everyone. There were people who, people who had all their teeth knocked out. They destroyed . . .

They jumped in there at dawn, when everyone was sleeping [knocks on table]. They grabbed various tents. They say that was ... to make an example [of them]. Like an exemplary action. And at dawn, they came in, eh, painted, you know and they came in [hits hand in palm] so much, but they wrecked the tents, they wrecked the tents, with sticks and everything. And they broke bones, heads, and everything. Clean beatings at night, beating, beating... beating, beating. They grabbed people like this [makes grabbing motion with fists], like sacks of potatoes. They grabbed people like this, like sacks of potatoes, and they ... threw them around. And they went around throwing everyone ... over to a hole, a little depression in the ground. And they kept them there until the next morning. All those people beaten there like that, without medical assistance or anything. They kept them there until the next day. So, the next day, they grab those women, they strip them and they parade them around ... the camp naked. Afterward they take them to the dining room, and they sit them down to eat, to eat breakfast.

It was a repression. Those last months that we spent there after the riots, until they took us back to Guantánamo again, I can't even talk about it. It was a horrible repression ... horrible, horrible.

And that was when the people began to fall into depressions again. A lot of military force, you know, they deployed a lot of military force, a lot of military force.

Part of the reprisals involved putting people in flexicuffs in Camp X-Ray for two weeks, in some cases on top of piles of rocks. Sylvia protested this by sitting outside of the camp on a chair every day until the prisoners were released. To my knowledge, the military has never investigated any of this as the clear abuse that it was.[25]

You know what? There was a moment in which many people arrived ... most Cubans who left, left Cuba to escape the Castro regime, you know. Hating, hating Fidel, hating the system, hating what ... in other words they left Cuba with the idea, you know, to never again stand on Cuban soil. So, when they found themselves in that, that maltreatment, with that situation that we had to live through, there were a lot of people who asked me, who commented to me in therapy ... in group therapy, "Well, it's what Fidel said, that imperialism is a monster." You know, they began to get, from all those trials ... what Fidel was constantly repeating in Cuba ... repeating, repeating, repeating, repeating, you know. A lot of them began to question, you know, "that this, what's happening, so Fidel was right. These people are beasts, these people are animals, they're domineering, they'll kill if they have to kill innocent beings." Because we were defenseless. And the people began to question all of those things. "They're assassins, they're assassins." Because they didn't have to treat us like that. There wasn't any reason, you know. We were stuck behind barricades, in the middle of barbed wire, surrounded by armed guards, what could we have done there? We had been thrown into the lion's mouth.

Eh ... I lived in the monster, in the belly of the beast, and I know his bowels. That was, you know. ... I told the people, remember that they are people, they're human beings like us, and they're completing a mission, you know. They're completing a mission, and they are representing the North American military, and they are receiving orders, but they're also receiving them from a human being. Many of them were acting on orders, not out of personal animosity.

When the residents of Camp Two in Panama were returned to Guantánamo two months later, they were placed mostly in camps Echo and Foxtrot. For the rest of the operation, both the military and civilian workers there had to deal with a high level of social dysfunction and individual behavior problems. There was no discussion that the residents had been thoroughly traumatized and no acknowledgment of the relationship between those problems and the beatings meted out after the riots.

Back in Guantánamo, while there had been no serious riots or reprisals after the September 9 protest in which people breached the camps, the stress on the women was unrelenting. In addition to the issues Sylvia mentioned, women faced sometimes overwhelming personal security problems for their entire stay on the base, and for that reason their experiences marked most of them more deeply than the men. In general, women were a clear minority among the population. Many reported not being able to use the latrines unescorted because some men would rip open the doors when the women entered alone. This became a big problem for the relatively few who did not arrive with a male companion. They faced other problems as well. Sylvia reported that the women in her camp often could not bathe without the specter of military men peeping at them as well. All of the women usually had male friends escort them to the showers and latrines. She describes how difficult the situation was for women.

Couples couldn't have sex there. I had to confront the issue in my practice [in the clinic] ... that the men would obligate their spouses to have sex because they didn't understand that in that situation the women couldn't do it. Men are different. Men's psychology is different. So, that was the source of the tensions. There were a lot of men who would hit the women, you know. There was domestic violence. It came from all of that, because the men wanted to have sex and the women didn't. They didn't feel like it under those conditions. And so that produced all of those ... situations ... that ... I'll tell you, there wasn't any, any ... I remember that it was a lot of work to bathe at the beginning, to go to the bathroom, to get water, because we had to walk very far. It was far from your tent, and you had to go get water in a pail to bring it back to

your tent, carrying those pails of water. It was a tremendous amount of
work, that was the situation. And it was dangerous too, you know, and
as time passed and passed sexual desires … men were crazy and then
the moment arrived when … so a lot of times one would hear that …
it was more than peering, you had to be careful, you had to be careful.
There were rapes, you know. There were a lot of situations, and you had
to be really careful.

This kind of constant stress and danger did long-term damage to many of
the women. Part of the problem with the operation was that despite the fact
that the military had fed, housed, and clothed thousands of Haitians a few
years prior to the rafter crisis, it had no training protocol in place to teach
the soldiers, sailors, and marines who rotated through the camps how to
deal with civilians appropriately. According to one of the camp commanders with whom I worked, the military was using the Marine Corps' *Small
Wars Manual* as a guide for the operation. A neocolonial relic emphasizing
psychological operations that the Corps updated from time to time, it might
have been better than nothing, but it certainly did not represent the kind of
awareness needed to care for civilians in a non-war situation.[26]

This meant two things. First, the military was not prepared to react to
some basic social problems because of the last-minute way in which the
operation had been thrown together. It often relied on the linguists to provide both interpreting services and a kind ear for troubled people. Only during the balseros' last few months on the base did the military, at the urging
of World Relief social workers, provide special daytime refuge tents where
women could really relax without peering eyes on them.

The second problem was that without training, each member of the military followed his or her own individual proclivities in interacting with the
balseros. So, on one hand, many people benefited from extremely compas-
sionate care and new friendships with members of the military, many of
whom would spend hours sitting and talking with people in their tents.
Some of the soldiers, sailors, and marines would even risk charges of fraternization by trying to vouch for their new friends with the INS or they would
send care packages after they rotated out of the camps. Sylvia, for example,
received care packages from one of the women with whom she had worked
in the clinic. Her problems came when she went back to her camp after work
and had to deal with the camp command.

The things that other members of the military did to some of the balseros undid the kindness of their compatriots. For much of the operation, instances of abuse were not systematic, but they took place systemwide. They were more common during the first eight months of the operation since a population under the stress of indefinite detention was potentially an enemy that brought out the worst in some people, and most base commanders did not expend much energy to systematically identify and rectify problematic behavior among their own personnel. Some soldiers and marines would do directly abusive things, like smashing someone's flip-flop-clad feet into the ground with their boots, or passive-aggressive things, like provoking anger in the men by insulting their wives or girlfriends in front of them.

Abusive military personal, usually a minority in the camps, created an unpredictable environment, which was detrimental to people's mental health given their experiences with trauma. Sylvia describes an incident that happened after they were returned to Guantánamo from the Panama camps.

One time my daughter and I were sitting outside the tent. And since it was like 6:00 or 6:30 at night because ... we were waiting for the long line to end, to go get food. You had two options, you went to get the food, you ate, you ate in the dining room, or you went to get the food and brought it back to the tent. We always went to get the food and we took it back to the tent and ate in the tent. So, that day we had gone to look for food and we were sitting there like that ... in the front of the tent ... eating. And suddenly they were all over us like this, like this, a deployment of soldiers surrounded us, *dududududud;* ... they came in like this, *rurururu* ... fast like that. We were with our plates of food in our hands, "What's happening, what's happening?" And what was happening was in our own tent. They caught us off guard [hitting hand in open palm]. Look, *muchacha,* they came into the tent and finished us off. They finished us off. And since we were sitting outside in front of the tent, the last thing they did was jump on top of us like this, and when they jumped on top of us, the plates of food went flying and ... I have the handcuffs here, I brought them with me [from the base].

They handcuffed the two of us, and they put us in a truck, and they took us to the command post. So, nothing . . . because, they say that somebody was drinking, that he had gone into our tent. So, they took us there, and when I arrived at the command post, go figure. I was about to lose it, my daughter was white as a piece of paper. She had just finished eating, and my daughter began to vomit . . . eh, and in a little while I began to vomit too. The food paralyzed us. Yes, so well . . . I asked him, how is this possible? The soldiers saw us outside eating, how can you treat us like this, how can you do this to us? So they let us go, the handcuffs, they gave us a glass of water to drink and they took us to the hospital to take our blood pressure, and, and they gave us some recognition. And afterwards they took us back to the camp. "Oh, sorry, very sorry, very sorry," but, already, I was like three days with diarrhea and my daughter was the same, and all of that because . . . the damage was already done. . . .

Like that, like that, like that, like that, those things, *mi hija*. How can I tell you all the things we went through there? It was constantly, constantly, constantly, constantly. . . . The more you were careful, the more you . . . and we were decent people, people who supported each other, people who didn't stick out. And we were always staying away from crowds. Look, we took our food back to the tent. We never ate in the dining room. So you know. It was like that, constantly like that. And when it wasn't with you, it was with the person next to you, and if not, with the person in front of you. In other words, you were constantly living with unpleasant things.

Humiliating things, you know. A hard, hard, hard situation. Really hard, really hard, really hard.

Being personally subjected to abuse was not the only potentially traumatizing element of camp life. Witnessing it also subjected people to vicarious traumatization. Sylvia describes another unforgettable incident of abuse, this time of a man, again for no obvious reason.

Yes, and there were beatings there, there were beatings, just so you know. There were beatings. . . . And abuse, you know, people tied hand and foot, they were handcuffed hand and foot, and they were beaten. You know, that's an abuse of power, an abuse of power.

I saw a soldier open up a wound in a man's foot with his boot that took five stitches [to close]. He stood on top of his foot . . . and he ground his boot like this [makes motion with foot] on, on, on, there, there, until . . . until he created a wound like this, standing on top of his foot like that, like an orange peel. I saw that right in front of me, just so you know. They filled the wound with dirt, and everything. Imagine, that man, he had to go [to the clinic] two times a day to heal that. I saw them do that right in front of me. He was handcuffed and thrown on the floor . . . they did that to him. They handcuffed him and they threw him on the floor, and they did that to him.

And the man hadn't done anything, he didn't do anything, or anything. The man was right next to me, he even had a sack of clothes, plus a sack of clothes from other people. He was carrying a sack of clothes from some women. They let him have it from above, they . . . took away the sacks of clothing, they threw him face down on the ground, they put handcuffs on him, on his feet and hands, and the soldier told him, "Ah, here you have a wound, here in your . . ." and he asked how it had happened, and the man said he got it playing on the football field in the camp. And he put his foot on it [making a grinding motion with her foot] and *tracaracaracaracar, sssssst* . . . until he opened it up and the blood flowed like this. That man, seized with such terrible pain like that. I'll never forget that, never. . . .

No, ah *hija*, what can I tell you *vieja*. What can I tell you, *hija*, what do I have to say? The things that I saw. A deployment of, an abuse of power is what there was there. A psychological war, you know.

Sylvia gives us a sense that "they" were always doing things to "them." Everyone had to be vigilant about the soldiers, for, as she indicates, even someone innocently carrying a woman's clothes for her could suddenly be attacked. Anyone who had arrived traumatized from the situation in Panama was subject to further traumatization at the hands of some members of the military in Guantánamo.

My experiences as an interviewer were consistent with some of the interviewees' descriptions of abuse. On my second day at work, when I entered one of the camps set up on the tarmac of the McCalla airstrip with the interview team, I noticed a man sitting under the blazing sun on a chair surrounded by a tangle of razor wire, as if he were in his own personal prison. When I asked the guard why he was there like that, he got defensive and told me that the man was being punished for having gotten on an inner tube to fish in the bay, in a tone of voice that suggested the man had committed a major crime. A few weeks later I witnessed a young soldier screaming in a pregnant woman's face because she had had to go to the bathroom too many times on the way back from the doctor. After I began working in the camps and could move freely among the people, I noticed that a few of the soldiers had arranged to have the gates to the camp close for the day in such a way that a group of gay men would arrive two minutes late and be subject to picking up cigarette butts and filling sandbags the next day as punishment. Because they were technically two minutes late according to the soldiers' watches, they could not be accused of doing anything against the men.

Miguel's observations illustrate just how vastly different the men's experiences were from the women's. He had been a medical student in Cuba, and while on the base he helped the military provide medical care. Like Sylvia, he worked hand in hand with them as a fellow professional and was treated very kindly at work. Unlike Sylvia, he did not experience abuse at the hands of the members of the military who ran his camp after getting back to his tent at the end of the day.

> I did like Guantánamo, and I got to know the American people better, and I knew how they thought. I had a close relationship with them, I was working eight hours a day treating sick people.... I think my life was a little bit easier when I got here because I understood them [the Americans].

Miguel had a positive experience because he worked with medical personnel who treated him as an equal and because he had consistently good members of the military in charge of the camp in which he lived so he was not subject to abuse after a hard day at work.

Women were not the only vulnerable population in the camps. Children were even more stressed and traumatized by the environment than the women were, and their presence affected the atmosphere in the camps in a number of ways, as parents became highly stressed from observing the impacts of the trauma they saw in in their children, often becoming frantic with guilt. The children all had dark sunken circles under their eyes, accenting what their parents were observing. Some of them even wondered out loud whether the houses in La Yuma (the United States) had razor wire and soldiers around them too.[27]

Every aspect of daily life was traumatic for the children. Their families shared living space with strangers, some of whom were unsavory individuals. They had to use portable toilets, which at first were communal for huge sections of the camp. People also bathed in them since there was little privacy elsewhere. Many children told me that they wet their beds because they were afraid to use the *baños plasticos,* the plastic bathrooms, at night. Sometimes children would go with one parent to queue up for water with hundreds of other people early in the morning. Eventually the military assigned latrines on a tent by tent or block basis and gave out locks, but security problems remained; some of the children saw men fling open the doors of the latrines when women were in there alone, or worse, they witnessed domestic and other interpersonal violence in the camp.

Volunteers soon began to organize activities that would help normalize the atmosphere for the children. This included creating schools or leading recreational activities including exercise and artwork. However, the volunteers could not change the conditions in the camps that frightened the children. Frantic parents witnessed symptoms ranging from voluntary muteness, aggression, and hiding in latrines to bed-wetting, insomnia, aggravated asthma, recurrent ear infections, and sore throats. The root of the asthma attacks were the chilly nights in the fall and winter combined with the heat from ten or twelve bodies, which warmed the tents and caused the inside of the roof to fill up with condensation that sprinkled down on its occupants throughout the night. Most asthma attacks among both children and adults occurred in the morning, when the tents were opened up and the cool morning air rushed in.

Children exercising on the McCalla airfield, January 1995.

Between the end of April and the beginning of May 1995, two major events occurred that completely changed the tenor of the operation, modifying the group narrative and improving relations between the balseros and the military in the process. First, in late April the military opened the gates to the front and back of the camps and officially allowed people to move freely among them. Second, it also let them use a small beach area located on the border with Cuban territory; the two sides were separated only by a chain-link fence that went out about ten feet into the water. It also allowed people to swim and fish off the cliffs in the back side of the Bulkeley camps.

Opening up the camps signaled that it would only be a matter of time before the balseros would be allowed into the United States and achieve their goal of finding freedom. It also facilitated communication among the balseros by letting them interact more freely. In fact, less than a week later, attorney general Janet Reno announced that the balseros would be admitted to the United States on a case-by-case basis. The INS would still screen out people who had criminal records or who had been confined to mental health facilities, but everyone else was eligible for admission. By that time, eight and a half months of uncertainty had taken its toll on some people. Shortly after the May 2 announcement, a man in Camp Delta committed suicide in one of the latrines.

Many of the balseros were being sent money from their relatives in the United States and were asking camp workers or military personnel to buy them things at the Navy Exchange, which was technically in violation of the rules. In June, the military installed a trailer along the cliffs that contained a little store offering, among other things, disposable cameras, basic snack items, and some clothing, which alleviated pressure on camp workers to buy supplies.

The change in policy to admit the balseros to the United States was accompanied by a change in attitude by the top command on the base, which it transmitted to the camp level. Prior to that, individual camp commanders, through their own attitudes and behaviors, which they passed down to the personnel in their units, determined whether the atmosphere of each camp was friendly and helpful, or hostile and damaging. The drastically different leadership styles in each camp seemed to be all the same to the top command until halfway through the operation.

When the US Navy put Rear Admiral Michael Haskins in charge of the operation in July 1995 he promptly demonstrated how the top command could influence the environment in all of the camps. Admiral Haskins publicly admonished the troops to treat the balseros as if they were members of their own families and reminded them openly on radio shows broadcast in the camps that the United States is composed of immigrants. He also sent his own people to walk around in all of the camps to hear complaints, which itself dramatically improved the environment in all of them. Admiral Haskins also spoke fluent Spanish and spent time inside the camps himself on a regular basis, which made everyone trust him. Though Admiral Haskins could not eliminate all the problems, and he was not truly in charge of bringing in art materials to the base, he made a huge and lasting difference in the operation. Subsequent base commanders implemented the same policy of no tolerance for abuse. The military obviously knew that many of its personnel were behaving inappropriately, to put it charitably, but it did not take concerted corrective action for months. Sylvia remembered:

Look, I would say that it alleviated things a lot. I would say that he resolved the problem, you know. Because he arrived with a completely different policy, diametrically opposite of the one that was in effect there up until that moment. He arrived with an open mind, you know. He received an order, I don't know what it was, but he didn't act like that because he wanted to act like that. He came with that mission. And he revolutionized everything there.

In other words, he made us feel human, because he began to treat us like human beings. He was aware of our situation, and he made us feel like that, you know. It wasn't only his words, but also his actions. So, well, let's say that last part, because really he was with us there for only a few months. But, I tell you, that if we had had an admiral like him from the beginning, a lot of things that happened there wouldn't have happened, understand?

Well, one of the first things that he did, as I just told you, was to respect us as human beings. Treat us like human beings. And he expected all of the military personnel there to treat us like human beings. He arrived to take some measures and had very direct contact with everyone.

[He was] the only admiral who you could see inside the camps, at whatever hour. But not only that, he created personnel who were inside the camps the entire day. And, the only work they had was to be inside the camps. Walking around over here, over there. They were listening, observing, informing him directly about all the things happening in the camps.

In other words, there were personnel inside the camps that were serving as intermediaries between us and him.

You know, and the troops knew that those personnel were there inside, and that those people were inside the camps, walking, walking, walking around the camps. They sat down to speak with the people. They came in, they sat down in the tents. It was a type of social work that those people were doing, no? Socializing there with the people. So, they began to gain the confidence of the people. Generally, they sat down, they arrived, and they said once, "How is everyone here? Is there a problem, do you have a need, is there something worrying you?" So, the people sat down and everybody told them what happened or what was happening, or what had happened, you know. And they took notes on all of that, and afterwards they left and told him about it. You know, in other words, it was another vision, another attitude towards us.

Ah, and another very important thing, he spoke Spanish and English. He spoke Spanish. He could communicate with us directly. He knew our culture, because he was Hispanic, so he understood a lot of our conduct. And he knew that it was normal, while many who passed through there, because the Americans thought that that was, you know . . . because, when Cubans get together, eh, you know that Cubans speak very loud. *So*, of course when a conversation gets loud, Cubans are speaking very passionately, and they gesticulate a lot and yell a lot. So the Americans thought that they were fighting. So they treated those persons as if they were fighting, and what those persons were doing was talking about a certain topic. Things like that, notice? So, imagine. They didn't understand. Because Cubans gesticulate a lot, and they [speak loudly] have a very loud mettle to their voice. They raise their voices.

He made himself very accessible, you know. So, the troops knew that if they abused one of us, he would find out immediately. Understand? Apart from that I am going to say that inside of the camps, there was an atmosphere that didn't let any soldier, you know ... commit any type of abuse, because as I already told you it was organized, they structured the camps internally in such a manner that they couldn't ... so the abuses disappeared quickly, all those things disappeared, things that, you know, that irritated us so much, that upset the people so much, you know, because a lot of the time, many times, no the majority of the time, there was a lot of injustice, much, much roving around, you know, a lot of unnecessary hanging around. One of the things that I saw them do a lot above all was to the married couples, to insult the woman in front of her husband by action or word. And you know, nobody likes that, you know, no man, whether he is Cuban or American, whatever he may be, if someone offends the woman at your side, you protest. You feel bad, you come out in defense of that woman ... it was a way of aggravating you too. And things like that, you know. All of those things came to an end, all of that. When he arrived all of that came to an end, and all of the camps returned to peace, and returned to normalcy.

And the people were fenced in, you know how it was with that barbed wire. He made them take all that down. You know. He opened the gates of all the camps. So you went to any camp you felt like, understand. You come back, you feel a certain amount of liberty. Because you couldn't go beyond a certain limit, but that limit was open. Until that moment, before he arrived, we were stuck inside of the camps, and you couldn't get out of there. He took all that away, and all of that barbed wire, everything, everything, everything, everything, he took away all of those things. And he opened it all up so that if you were in a McCalla camp and you could go to Camp Echo.

Or you could go to Alpha. You moved about freely, eh, for all of that over there, you see. And there was another thing. He fomented a lot of cultural exchanges among the camps. Of all types. Music, painting, or the plastic arts, he fomented a lot, and he began to help the people. He began to bring in materials, and things that the people could work with. With that, he began to bring in things to improve the conditions in the tents. Everything, even wood. Even wood, and sheets. He knew that, you know, that they make those dividers of cloth, of sheets ... and so, he began to, because there came a time when nobody provided anything, everything was, you know.... What is it that? They felt good with those dividers, you feel more independence, you feel more privacy with that ... ah well then. ...He facilitated things so the people did that, notice? He had a completely different attitude from his predecessors.

4

Coping in the Camps

Toward Individual and Collective Resilience

Psychologists have noted that working, re-establishing a feeling of normalcy, and telling trauma stories all promote emotional resilience and healing among refugees.[1] By the time the military dropped off the balseros at Gitmo and situated them in tents, they were already coping with the after-effects of a number of disturbing experiences, which left them vulnerable to being further traumatized by the difficult conditions they encountered on the base. Therefore, re-establishing a sense of safety and stability was imperative for them. Instead of sitting around numb and helpless, which would have been easy to do under the circumstances, large groups of people quickly joined forces to elect leaders and representatives whom they charged with improving communications with the military, helping organize the distribution of food and supplies, and establishing order among themselves. The balseros also re-created social institutions such as churches, schools, and libraries. These efforts came together to create a unique cultural environment in the camps, which also helped people answer the "why" and "what for" questions that are involved in re-ordering meaning systems and integrating traumatic experiences into their sense of self.[2]

After a traumatic experience, people need to create new meaning systems, adjust their identities to a new reality, and overcome confusion and disorientation. In his now-classic 1982 book, *Man's Search for Meaning*, Viktor Frankl discussed his experiences in a Nazi concentration camp during the Holocaust and what he learned about how people overcome trauma and despair by making meaning out of their experiences. Frankl noted that people create meaning in three ways: through creating something or doing a deed, by interacting with others in love relationships, and by suffering, becoming a victim of someone or something. He bore witness to the fact that "even the helpless victim of a hopeless situation, facing a fate he cannot change, may rise above himself, may grow beyond himself, and by so doing change himself. He may turn a personal tragedy into a triumph."[3] The process by which people change themselves after trauma in ways that reflect substantial emotional growth later became known as "posttraumatic growth," or PTG. People who have experienced PTG may have changes in their sense of self, develop healthier connections with other people, and undergo positive changes in their perspectives on their priorities and the meaning of their life.[4] Many of the activities that emerged organically in the camps were acts of self-healing that worked toward transforming various kinds of personal tragedies, creating PTG instead of PTSD (posttraumatic stress disorder).

Considering the extremely stressful circumstances the balseros had been through, it was remarkable that they could unite so quickly to organize themselves. Trauma is an overwhelming experience that threatens an individual's well-being and has severe emotional, cognitive, and physical impacts. Initial reactions of shock, disbelief, and numbness are very common because trauma affects the thought process as people struggle to understand what has happened to them. Trauma victims commonly experience guilt, anger, irritability, fear, anxiety, and depression. Some people withdraw from others, believing that no one can understand or help; they may feel numb, since the mind and emotions shut down to defend against further damage. Trauma also involves a confrontation with death, which was in high relief in Augustín's account of his rafting experience.[5]

Because trauma interrupts the cognitive processes, making people think that the world is no longer comprehensible, it also forces people to create new assumptions and beliefs. Survivors have a need to bear witness and have the crimes committed against them acknowledged. With all of these impacts, it is understandable that trauma victims typically struggle with meaning. As a result of all of these intense experiences, such victims have a changed experience of self.[6]

Among this population, psychologists have observed increases in drug and alcohol abuse and aggressive behavior. Trauma victims often have physical discomfort, which is related to the increased arousal of the autonomic nervous system. Many people experience fatigue, headaches, stomach upset, aches and pains, loss of appetite, and urinary problems, among other things.[7]

On a group level there is a tendency for people who feel threatened to form closer attachments to other people or communities; as the external threat becomes more terrifying, people's allegiance to the group becomes stronger. This intensified sense of belonging has been referred to as "the taming of terror" and the social support that the victims create for themselves as the "the trauma membrane."[8] When trauma victims are collected in one place, such as a detention center, individual psychic wounds can combine to create a mood or even a group culture that becomes more than the sum of its parts. This is why some sociologists have noted that trauma can create community.[9] This is certainly what was in evidence in the camps.

The ways in which the balseros approached the kinds of activities that increased their emotional resilience were related to their culture and upbringing under the Cuban Revolution. For example, they had a remarkable facility for organizing themselves, which was all the more impressive considering that many of them were still disoriented and in shock when they arrived at the base. Their capacity for community organizing reflected their experience in Cuba, as the majority of Cubans had participated in mass organizations in one way or another. Many served on neighborhood block watches organized by the neighborhood Committees for the Defense of the Revolution (CDRs) or were more actively involved in mass organizations such as the Union of Cuban Youth (UJC) or the Federation of Cuban Women (FEMUC). David explains how the CDR functioned.

The CDR was created to maintain the Revolution. The president of the CDR is someone who is very, very involved with the Revolution. Someone who is part of the Communist Party, someone who gets some benefits from being a communist, like vacations in hotels. So those people are very committed to the Revolution. In order to maintain that lifestyle they have to watch for people. They check what time you get in, what time you leave, who are your friends, if you are going to school or not. If not, they send social workers to see you. They check if you come back with a bag of a lot of stuff. If they can't see what's in it, they will visit to see what's in it. [When you are volunteering for the CDR] you have to be walking the streets from 10 pm until one in the morning. You have to; if you don't participate in the meetings, if you don't do the *vigilancia* [vigilance] you. ... The CDR also distributes materials like bricks and paint. Also, when you're applying for a position for a job, you need a letter from the CDR. It says who you are.

Under the revolutionary government, children were traditionally required to go to summer schools in the countryside to help harvest crops. This involved living in barracks-style housing and harvesting crops during the day, and participating in social activities, such as singing around campfires and going to dances at night. Not everyone had positive evaluations of their experiences in these camps (though most of the men told me that they had liked the unsupervised dating that the schools allowed), but their participation in these types of communal activities from a young age as well as involvement in mass organizations meant that they were accustomed to working together in groups for a common cause, despite individual differences of opinion or rapport. Miguel explains a little about the school in the countryside:

> There were two types of schools, elementary and high school. You go there just during vacation for thirty or forty-five days. You leave your family back home and they can go to visit you every weekend. It's a huge room with probably sixty to eighty students, it's like a barracks. At 6 am one of the professors comes in. . . . You go and eat breakfast. And then at 7 am everybody works until midday, and then you have an hour and hour and a half for lunch. Night is fun, somebody plays the guitar, you sing, you have your little things with the ladies and the girlfriends, it's fun. But it's fun when you are a little bit older. At the beginning you miss your family; you'd never been away from them before. I think [at that age] that's more educational, because there's no productivity; what can an eleven-year-old do? It's just to be prepared for later on, at the time you have to go to the army.
>
> There was a large room divided into three sections, and twenty girls slept in each section. I went there until I graduated from high school. It was the same thing with university. . . . I was used to communal living. [However,] when you get to the age of twenty-two you don't want to live with people without the same cultural formation that you have. Some people have problems. It's not the same thing to be university educated. There were many kinds of people in the tents, twenty-four hours [a day] with those people you don't know.

Of course it was one thing to live with dozens of other school children, and another thing to be thrown together in a tent with fifteen or twenty other people, some of whom were unsavory individuals, but in general they had grown up knowing what it meant to do things communally, and they had to expend less energy to organize themselves than other groups of people might have.

According to Juan, the collective organizing process was similar in all of the camps. He describes what occurred in Camp India, an all-male camp, which was later replaced by Camp Bravo, a family camp. After the tents were upgraded, the residents of Camp India were moved to a camp called Golf along the Cuban border.

The military played around with a lot of things. Psychologically they played around with a lot of things. Look, I remember that the camps organized themselves spontaneously. They let everyone out in there, in more or less those lines [of tents] like that . . . and so the people . . . the first few times that food arrived in the camp, it was, you know, embarrassing, you know. The people were desperate for food, and they thought that maybe there wasn't enough food for everyone, or that it would run out, that they were not going to get to eat. And so, there was a problem, there was a big fight for the food, and all of that. . . .

So, well, after a few days the people felt the need for some kind of order, and that we had to communicate with the military. We can't be a mass of more than 3,000 people without having a leader. And I remember that one afternoon a lot of people, a lot of people, a lot of people . . . more than a thousand people had a meeting under the only tree that there was in this case in my camp, to try to elect a camp jefe. So, well, imagine, a thousand people electing one person was so difficult that they couldn't do it. But we arrived at the conclusion that the best thing to do was go by our rows, by our rows . . . of tents, and elect a row jefe for each row of tents.

And later on those jefes would elect a camp jefe. And the mass, the only thing they wanted at that moment, the only expectation was that the camp jefe had to speak English and Spanish. No? . . . That was the only condition that the masses had, that the camp jefe had to speak English and Spanish. So, we went by rows, each one, and it got done very rapidly. A jefe was chosen for each row, and from among those people they chose a camp jefe. There were three candidates. Three supposed candidates . . . and they decided to choose the candidate that had those two characteristics, that he spoke English and Spanish, and that was also a professional. And one guy was all of that . . . an architect.

He was the camp jefe and they did a coup d'etat to him. They made him camp jefe, and he was the first one, you know . . . authorized by the mass, to go speak with the military, and all that.... And the military played around with him a lot, no? The people noticed that.

You know, for example, the people had a demand, for example ... there wasn't enough water. So, they go to him and they say, "Eloy, you have to speak with the military because there's not enough water, there is a big mess with the water. We need to get some order with the water, or there should be more water." So, he goes and tells the military something, and the military does exactly the opposite.

You know, they demoralized him a little in front of the rest of the people in the camp, no? And it happened like that a lot, a lot, a lot a lot ... of times, no? It happened so much that I remember one day, speaking with this person who was the camp jefe and he tells me, "I feel so bad right now that I don't want to go up there to tell them anything, that Captain. Because every time I tell her something, they do exactly the opposite." So, and you know, that began to create great tensions between the balseros and the military. Because we had already elected a leader to represent us and the result, to the thinking of the majority, was that the leader wasn't any good, that the leader didn't know how to do things, and he couldn't function, because there were so many bad results from his activities, you know?

The preceding passage hints at something almost everyone I interviewed mentioned: that at the outset of the Guantánamo operation, the military was implementing psychological operations on an experimental basis that were both obvious and oppressive, and the guards flaunted the fact that it all was a social experiment being carried out by the military. Since Cuban men must perform compulsory military service, they were familiar with these types of operations and had immediately suspected this anyway.

Sylvia described in more depth the techniques the military was using that provoked rioting in the Panama camps after a few months.

I noticed it all, you know. I noticed when they were doing psychological manipulations, I noticed it all. I told people what they were trying to achieve [getting them to go back to Cuba] and that they shouldn't let them do it. People became unhinged, it made them sick. Because if ... I come in every night, if every night ... when you are sleeping, you don't have to go to college to know that ... if I wait every night and one night I appear at one in the morning, the next night I appear at two in the morning, and I change the time on you ... so you can't get used to what time I'm coming in. Because the first day they did it at three in the morning, and so at three in the morning we were sitting waiting for ... but the next day they didn't do it at three in the morning, they waited to do it later. ... So, when we got to four, four thirty in the morning, "tonight they're not going to come," so we would lie down to go to sleep [snaps fingers in her open palm], and then they took advantage of that ... understand, so every night you do that, and you go into your house hitting poles against all of the walls, all of the furniture, you understand, and on top of that I lunge at you to throw a box of cigarettes at your face, tell me what you are going to achieve with that human being? What effect are you going to provoke in that human being? You don't have to be, you know ... very intelligent to notice that it makes people become unbalanced, completely unbalanced.

ELIZABETH: So, what you're telling me is that, I think, when there were riots—there was a disturbance in September of 1994 in Guantánamo, and later in Panama, the military provoked it.

SYLVIA: That's right. They provoked it.

ELIZABETH: With all those social experiments . . .

SYLVIA: No, no, no, forget it. That's not in question. They provoked those riots, of course.

ELIZABETH: And afterwards they blamed you all.

SYLVIA: Oh, of course, of course. Look, that was what I told everyone there, I told that to all of the military personnel who talked with me. You could see in one camp, where there were 2,000 people, let's say there were 2,000 people, you know. In a camp of 2,000 people, there could be one or two or three hundred who are crazy, unhinged, aggressive, delinquent, or whatever you want to call it. *Oye*, but pretty soon the whole camp revolted. Why? One camp was A1, A1 in obedience, in behavior, in everything, but it revolted. They provoked it, you know, they provoked it.

In the months before they rioted, the 8,600 people who had voluntarily gone to Panama were also employing coping mechanisms despite the vastly better living conditions and friendlier military personnel than at Guantánamo. Their strategies were similar to those that the population in Gitmo was using: community organizing and projects to make the environment more familiar and comfortable.

Pancho discusses how much better he felt in the Panama camps.

I chose to go to Panama because I saw it as one more way of leaving Cuba. I said, "Well, anything could happen if we stay on Cuban soil, so I'll go over there." We were leaving Cuba, we were in another country. In another country, another system. Whatever might happen, at least it's in Panama. I said, "Anything is better than being in Cuba. In Cuba, the way the Cuban system is, anything outside of Cuba is good. So, my brother and I decided that we would go to Panama, whatever. Whatever might happen in Panama, it was in another country, and we'll get there little by little, and we'll be in the United States one day. The hope was to get to the United States.

They told us that the conditions would be better, that the provisions would be better, and that everything was going to be a little more ... pleasant, and that over time there were going to be more amenities and everything.

There were guards on the plane to Panama. They took care of us. They told us how we had to do things. Imagine, I had never been on a plane. Many people, about 90 percent, had never been on a plane. So imagine, getting on the plane.... I felt cold, surprised. So the guards had to help us, understand. So they were very good to us, there weren't any problems, at least for me, I never had any problem with any of them.

There was a great reception for us when we arrived in Panama. There was a party so we could have fun. There was music, food, and everything. I felt great, perfect.

We began to make friends, make schools. We began to unite more, understand? People started getting to know each other, so we began to unite more.

Despite the improved physical conditions, there was the question of the Clinton administration policy of not allowing the balseros into the United

States. Military personnel in the camps were promoting the idea of the balseros returning to Cuba to apply for asylum.

Sylvia again describes what she saw as the root of the behavioral problems in the camps as a consequence of this, and how she personally tried to counteract the psychological strategy of the military.

The cause of all of the problems that happened there was the uncertainty that existed, that we didn't know what was going to happen to us. The people thought it was impossible that they were going to let us enter the United States. You know, when … I'll tell you this. Look, apart from the fact that I was experiencing the same thing, I was living with the people twenty-four hours a day. … And it was easy for me to notice that that was the cause of all that … conduct. I began to manage the situation. I'm going to tell you about the situation. … I knew that we were going to enter the United States. … I was convinced [by an astrological chart I had seen in Havana] that we were going to enter the United States. I brought that information from Cuba and I was certain about it. I was convinced. So, I began to transmit my conviction to the people. I began to transmit to people that faith that I had. I didn't always tell everyone why I knew, because I knew that it was less credible, no? I told some people, "No, because …" in other words, I told the story about the astrological chart I saw. That wasn't something that was well known when I left Cuba that wasn't a well-known thing in Cuba. No, no, no. So, I couldn't, I knew that I couldn't talk to them about something that they were unfamiliar with, but I began to transmit … I transmitted the emotional charge that I put on what I told them. That was sufficient, you know.

And they told me that I had a great power of conviction and that I transmitted a lot of peace to them, a lot of security. It was what I was feeling, understand. So that was how I began to help everyone around me to feel better. Understand, I transmitted that spirit to the others, and then to others and others, understand? Because I knew they weren't going to send us back. That it would be a little farther in the future, a little farther, but at the end, that's what I told them, "You have to try to arrive in the healthiest state possible, physically and mentally. We have to look for our energy, to do productive things, to improve the way we live here, to occupy our free time doing useful things, you know." That was how it occurred to me to make that garden in Panama.

> We converted the entire camp into a flower garden. We began to plant flowers, because there wasn't even one flower. Not even one little flower in the entire site. So, I gave the idea to the camp commander and they brought us flowers to plant. And we converted the whole camp into a garden. And that was how we began to fix up the whole camp. We began to paint. They got us paint, and we began to paint … to place rocks, to make little paths, to paint trees half way up, in the way they did in Cuba. We fixed them, you know, we fixed up the tents. And we began to improve the place in which we were.

From the accounts of people who stayed only in Guantánamo, the initial military strategy seemed to involve being as uncooperative as possible, hoping that the discomfort this created would make people want to return to Cuba. These tactics meant that the camp commanders would not comply with many or even most of the camp jefe's requests. When their situation did not improve, the camp population became angry and social tensions increased, as most of them did not understand that it was not usually the jefe's fault when the military refused to comply with his or her requests. If this happened often enough, though, one of the factions would remove the jefe (or *jefa* in the case of women) and install someone else. In Juan's camp, the replacement turned out to be a thug. In fact, many of the first jefes were people who had entered the United States during the Mariel Boatlift, the Marielitos, but had been deported back to Cuba for criminal activity in the United States. They had been selected as jefes because they spoke English. Additionally, until the distribution system became routinized, different factions would compete for the privilege of giving out food and donated clothing; they took advantage of these positions to procure extra supplies for their friends and family members, as they had done in their lives in Cuba. Skilled at stealing from the state from growing up in Cuba, the people were much more adept at filching supplies under the soldiers' and sailors' noses than the military initially realized.

People would become dissatisfied with the groups in charge of distributing supplies because the groups were corrupt or there were personality clashes—just as they had become dissatisfied with the jefes who could not convince the military to improve camp conditions. They would form new factions to support other people for camp leadership positions. In the end, the people sought the group they decided was the most honest. In Juan's camp, the honest group turned out to be Masons, known in Cuba for their integrity. He continues the story:

So, tensions were so high that one night a group of guys decided to remove him from his position. It was the Orientals [from the Eastern part of the island], remember the great group of Orientals [Raul]? They went, they fought, they even had a fist fight, and everything. And so one said to them, "Look this is the camp jefe," and they put in somebody else as camp jefe [named Carlos]. So, that one had thirty bodyguards around him. They were the ones who guarded him. It was a coup d'état, a classic coup d'état.

And so, another group of guys, who were the black guys, Carlos's brothers and all of that, they said they didn't agree with that. And that they were going to fight them, you know, because you know ... the majority of the people thought that they shouldn't have done that. But nobody wanted to have any problems with those people, because there were thirty or forty of them and they could have stabbed you.

So, those people, that group, in other words, the opposing force in this case, I remember that they went, and when the food arrived, they went and they took over the food distribution. You know, and so they said, ah, "You want to be camp jefe, we are the ones who are in charge in here. If you want, you can send him over the fence with the military but in here we're the ones in charge." And so, since the thing was balanced out, understand, it was just at that moment that I started the newsletter. Because I also felt, I didn't feel I had enough power to go and fight with the ones who did the coup d'état, and I wasn't in agreement with the attitude of that the other ones had, the ones who had taken the food for themselves.

We called them the boquete people. Boquete was to eat a lot. So, well, you know, it was already organized, and there was a kind of equilibrium, between the group of Orientals who were in that moment the camp jefe, and the group of Havaneros who were the food jefes. And the people in charge of the food were very clear about what they were doing, you know. They didn't go about doing bad things with the food, but that they knew that everyone was hungry and everyone needed to eat, and far from making a problem with that they were doing things very well, they did things very well.

On the other hand, the camp jefe wants to get a few perks for his group, you know? Like, for example, the people were desperate to get out of the camps, no? And he could convince the military to let him create a kind of cleaning brigade, or something like that ... which could clean up the camp, pick up little pieces of paper, and all of that, and afterward leave the camp and take us to the garbage dump, no? And so the people collected whatever they could find that was reusable and then they came back to the camp and then they recycled all of those things, and they were improving the quality of life like that.

Like, for example, you found a piece of carpet and you put it in your tent, and then you didn't have to sleep on a dirt floor, you slept on a rug, and of course there was less dust, no? So, those types of things were what the new camp jefe wanted to control, the one who had done the coup d'état, no? But the people from the kitchen, they had also grabbed another part, and they annulled his power a little bit.

The same kind of thing happened in all the camps. Because I spoke with a lot of people, and everyone explained that it was more or less the same process, understand. In one moment they elected a camp jefe with certain specific characteristics and afterwards, different power groups got together and they did a coup d'état and they did what they did *rara-rara*.... More or less it happened like that in all the camps that I had news about.

Definitely, at a certain moment I said, well, "This is part of democracy, you know, it's part of the exercise of democracy, no?" Because the jefes were elected by a minority, [in] this case it was the row jefes only, and the immense majority of the camp didn't agree with the activities of that person. The military also had a good portion of the fault because they didn't do what the person asked, understand? And well, another camp jefe came up through a coup d'état, practically, in this case, at the same time a political force, in parenthesis, speaking metaphorically, opposite of that person did.

Therefore, it was like a democracy, at least we had two parties, no? If you didn't like the food people you went over to the ... [laughing]. If you didn't like the Republicans you could go over to the Democrats. Understand? At that moment I said, "Well, what we lack the most now is a newspaper," so that there is a third force, understand. A third force. Because, when it was only that we all were in the same place, and you stayed right there [not being moved from camp to camp], understand? You stayed right there. So, it occurred to me to create a newspaper with the intention of, you know, to orient the people a little, with the intention to have what we say as a third position.

At first, the balseros also had difficulty getting adequate medical attention. Below, Juan describes what happened to a man with a severe kidney infection. He reveals his indignation at the camp commander's indifference and interprets the insufficient medical care as an attempt to get them to go home.

I remember one day at the very beginning a guy gets kidney pain, and it seemed very strong . . . it took him over, it gave him convulsions. And the people tried to do what they could, but at the end nobody could do anything, because there wasn't any medicine. At the end we grabbed him, we carried him on a cot, and we took him to the camp gate. There wasn't a door, it was a gate of that, you know [razor wire]. There wasn't any spot to enter or leave, they just threw things over the fence from one side to another, no? And we tried to speak with the captain of the camp, to get her to take care of him, no? To take him to the doctor or something. And they told us that they didn't want anything to do with him . . . that he should stay inside the camp. No? So, after a lot of arguing with the military, we decided to throw the little guy over the fence despite the kidney pain, and tell them that it was their responsibility, that we didn't have any responsibility for the life of that person. So, in effect that was what we did. We opened up the fence, put him outside and closed it up again, and we went back in and turned away from his body. So, in the end they called a military ambulance, they came they got him and they took him away. They treated him, and after like a week, they brought him back, without any problem, you know. But we had to go to that extreme, understand, to say to them that if he died it was their responsibility. And at that moment there wasn't medical parole or anything like that; in other words, getting sick was a real problem.

Aside from questioning the camp commander's motives, Juan is aware that together the people could solve a problem that could have dramatized their helplessness instead. He mentions death, which is a common element in the balseros' narratives, and suggests that the United States was not living up to its moral responsibility to provide medical care for the people it had interdicted at sea and taken to the base.

In addition to organizing themselves to distribute supplies more effectively and communicate their needs with the military, forcefully if necessary, there was also a need for internal security. They had to watch out for each other when they were sick as well as at other times. Relationships could be problematic, particularly in the beginning. Heightened social tensions were to be expected given the level of trauma everyone was experiencing, but aside from that, all types of people were thrown together: from professionals, to blue-collar workers, to Santería priests, to criminals. Additionally, some people tried to strong-arm their compatriots into participating in hunger strikes in the beginning of the operation, which caused more discord.

Below, Juan describes an incident that occurred when they discovered that a man had been stealing cigarettes from their tent mates. Juan begins by continuing with his theme of social solidarity.

> The people, the first thing that they did was, you know, like ants, unite. Because in unity there is more strength, more union, more love . . .

At this point, he tells a story about how people began to notice that their cigarettes were being stolen little by little, and what happened when they figured out who the thief was. It culminated with the passage below:

> Finally Cesar discovered who the thief was. I remember that more than 300 people grabbed him, picked him up, and threw him over the fence. And they told the military, "Take him back to Cuba, he's a thief and we don't want him." The military said, "No, we can't take him anywhere," and they opened up the fence and put him back in, and the people grabbed him again, *bmmmm*, and they threw him out again. They almost killed him. They threw him out more than three times. Finally, the military saw that the people could have done something to him, so finally they grabbed another small piece of fencing and made a little camp for him alone and they left him in there until the next day, and they took him I believe to another camp. Forget it. But that was, you know, a moral and civic action by the whole camp. Nobody wanted a thief inside. The unit of money was the cigarette, and therefore it was something important. And he was stealing just that. And the people threw him out of there. I was really content.

Here he repeats the theme of solidarity and agency and his satisfaction with the outcome comes across strongly. Instead of standing by helplessly, which can be the mark of some trauma victims, they organized themselves to demand medical care or remove a thief from their midst. The story is also notable for its use of rhetoric reminiscent of the Cuban Revolution. First, Juan describes what the people did, "uniting like ants" because of the strength and love in unity. Additionally, while the thief does not seem to have been beaten up, the action the camp took against him resembles an act of repudiation that Sylvia displayed when she resisted participating in beatings during the Mariel Boatlift. Finally, describing the incident as a "moral and civic action" also seems to be a use of popular political rhetoric common in Cuba.

Raul comments on what they achieved together through these types of acts:

> In Guantánamo, after a week, or a month, I'm not sure, when they began to give us the first assistance . . . we began to be able to get clothes and shoes . . . the people . . . that is . . . I know what I saw. . . . The people hung up their clothes, and put their sneakers in the door of their tents, and nobody lost anything. You know, or if somebody got up a little late, at nine in the morning, yes there was silence in the tent. So, we learned to respect each other, one another. We learned to respect your space, we learned to respect values, things, property; that was, I believe, what we achieved there.

The residents of Camp Alpha also got together to create a pleasant environment for themselves after having been through the hell of the rioting in the Panama camps that Sylvia has described. Camp Alpha was the last in a row of camps along a road called Bulkeley, which stretched from the border with sovereign Cuba to a recreation area called Windmill Beach. It stuck out from the rest of the camps because of the two large pieces of public art and a pleasant park, visible from the road, that the men in the camp had created after they arrived from the Panama camps. It was a good example of how the military worked with the balseros to facilitate projects, which then benefited camp personnel as well.

In Guantánamo, one of the camps whose residents had been in the middle of the rioting and subsequent military reprisals, Camp Alpha, came

Camp Alpha Street, 1995.

together and, with the assistance of the military, cleared the brush in front of the camp and created a large park, complete with a covered area and paths made from sandbags and gravel. It was a wise move on the part of the camp captain and his first sergeant to put the camp members to work on a large group project; the physical activity calmed down their nervous systems while the park they created gave them a distinctive sense of place.

Creating the park had taken a great deal of effort because a lot of vegetation had to be bulldozed by the military, and then paths had to be laid out with gravel and defined by sandbags, which needed to be filled. The wood left over from the clearing later served as raw material for sculptures. The result was a pleasant refuge from the monotonous camp environment that provided people with opportunities to socialize and relax in more normal surroundings. Eventually people from other camps would gather there as well.

Pancho describes what people did when they got to newly built Camp Alpha upon being sent back from the camps in Panama after rioting there in December of 1994.

We went back to Guantánamo with another mentality; we were prepared differently, we felt more comfortable, understand? It was already different, because we went back prepared, understand. So then, in Guantánamo there were more amenities waiting for us. They put in electricity and the entire camp was made of wood, the tents were made of wood and everything was very well prepared. They made a park, we made it ourselves.

Taking into account that when the riots happened the military ... sent all those people [who had rioted] to prison, all those people that didn't have any, in other words, even a little of an idea ... you know. ... And so, the people who were left were the people who were more educated, more intelligent. And so, what we did was unite. We created our own amenities with the help of the guards. In other words, we made a park. We made a basketball court. We made a barbershop. We made a school. We made a church, understand. We made a dining hall. We created *everything* for our own comfort, so there wouldn't be any problems with the guards. We helped the guards clean, we did everything, *vaya*.

We got together and created the park ourselves. The guards brought the equipment for cutting the brush, and the trucks, and we the balseros and the guards got to know each other. In my camp, there were never any more problems with the guards, because, well, we had been purified. Purified in the sense that they had taken out everyone who was no good. In other words, the people who remained were the people who were cultured, the people who wanted to progress, who wanted to feel good, to be comfortable, not to have any problems, understand.

We made a barbershop there with the help of the camp captain, Captain Coleman. He was very nice. I spoke with him. He was a good guy. I told him that I was a barber and I wanted a barbershop, understand, to have more amenities in the camp, because people were already waiting for me to cut their hair over in the camp. So the captain told us that "Oh, there is a cabana over there where you can make a barbershop, perfect, I'll help you."

And, well, we built a barbershop. They got us scissors and other things and gave them to us. After checking that the people in the camp didn't have any [behaviorial] problems, they gave us scissors, automatic shavers, and everything. They gave us all the amenities available. They gave us everything.

Additionally, Captain Coleman's right-hand man, Sergeant Carter, talked some of the Jamaican workers into getting a soda machine and some picnic tables for the park area. Some of his superior officers disapproved of this type of creativity, but he was not punished for his efforts. Carter also took the men who worked the hardest to the base's McDonalds in one of the military buses and treated them on a regular basis.

Even though its park was unique, Camp Alpha was typical of the other camps in that it had a high level of internal organization, some created by the military and some created by the balseros themselves. Each camp was broken down into numbered blocks, rows, and tents, and each tent labeled accordingly. This facilitated the distribution of supplies and locating individuals for appointments and mail delivery. Each row and tent had representatives who were the point people for the distribution of different supplies, such as cigarettes or donated clothing. Like the other upgraded camps on the Bulkeley side of the base, Alpha also had three *globos* (globe-shaped fabric structures). One served as a cafeteria, one as a World Relief school/TV room, and the other as a chapel and library. The same small group of men always watched TV or music videos for hours on end, and after a few months they learned English almost by osmosis. Banks of large sinks where people could go to wash their clothing had also been constructed toward the back of the camp.

Many of the men in the camp also played on intramural baseball teams and went to English classes at the World Relief school to pass the time. Roberto, a World Relief camp worker who spent a lot of time holding support groups and walking around chatting with people, had helped set up a tent with painting supplies for people who either already knew how to paint or wanted to learn. Many men also spent time lifting weights. One group in particular had outstanding muscles from spending a large part of each day lifting weights. Some of the weights had obviously been provided by either World Relief or the military, but others were improvised (with military help) from concrete slabs formed by putting concrete into pails and then connecting them with tent stakes. Men also sat in the area in between their tents playing cards or dominos, using cigarettes as money for betting.

In addition to the group-level coping and social solidarity that was commonplace in the camps, individuals also coped by identifying and mobilizing social networks. They had become adept at this while growing up with the chronic material shortages that have characterized the Cuban Revolution, and by creating meaning from their trauma.

Despite the initial tensions, the military, often with the help of World Relief, supported the balseros in creating smaller organizations/activities such as clubs when asked. These ranged from establishing schools and churches to newsletters, art galleries, and libraries, to a tent outside Camp Echo for practicing Rastafarians, to a rock and roll club, which Guillermo describes. Having to improvise to overcome the deprivations of the Special Period and chronic shortages before that had taught the balseros coping skills in the form of the linked concepts of *inventar* (to invent) and *resolver* (to resolve). Not only could they modify and re-combine objects in ingenious ways, but they were extremely adept at using social networks to get resources they lacked and at manipulating the bureaucracy.

Guillermo's story provides a good example of the skill of mobilizing social networks. He lists all the different camps he was moved around to during the first couple of months of the operation, which heightened everyone's feelings of destabilization, and then describes how he manipulated the system to move himself and his friends out of the all-male camps and into a more stable and interesting environment in a family camp. Soon he found that he could do the same thing to get material resources he wanted.

> We created a rock and roll club. Apart from having the club, we wanted to get out of the camp, when those camps were still closed. So, we made it on the outskirts of the camp; they gave us a tent. It was just for us, the rock and roll club. And all our friends met and began to create [it], and after that people from other camps went.
>
> The people from World Relief, everyone began to find out and so they started to take people who liked rock and roll there. People from the military began to get in, and all that, they began to leave music for us there, music or videos. They began to bring things, and that was it. We achieved it, me and Albertico, the club. With the help from the guy from the library, we had a library, a bookstore, with the help from people from World Relief it was what we made. But the idea was ours the whole time. And so we made a rock and roll club.
>
> We were in the art gallery, I don't know how that popped up. There were a lot of art galleries, a lot of people made art. And so the McCalla 6 gallery, it was left without artists, the last ones left were already ready to go [to the United States on medical parole]. And so, well, we decided to get into the art gallery, me and Albertico. We went to the art gallery and we began to paint ... but soon we didn't paint anymore, we began to fool around instead [laughs]. What mattered to us was that

we passed the whole day outside of the camp there, in the art gallery, and that we were there, in that story ... nobody bothered us, not the soldiers, nobody. The soldiers even began to talk with us and the girls from World Relief and we all slept in the tent together and all that, but we didn't have any [sexual] relations, we just did it because we were friends and all that. But the military didn't like it and so they began to complain, and things like that.

There was one bad thing. I had some sunglasses, some Ray Bans, they were good, and a soldier tried to play around with me, and he robbed me. And he ripped the art gallery [tent], they ripped the [section of the] roof between the ceiling and the roof, he ripped that place, so he could take the sunglasses. And he took them, and at the end some people saw him with them, and they had told him, and they told him, but anyway we couldn't prove anything, and besides, I wasn't interested in it anyway. To me, what I liked was that we went there, we went downtown, to the Navy Exchange, all that, yeah, and I don't remember what it was called, that was where we did those expositions. That was where we went.

We made artwork, but, for art people it wasn't anything, for us it was a way to pass the time there, yes. We painted ourselves, we have photos, look I'm going to show you the photos. We painted ourselves, hair or goatee, all painted, in colors, right? And we liked to fool around, we were playful, we were jokers.

One of the reasons Guillermo was so successful was that he had a skill that was in demand by both the military and the balseros: tattooing. He parlayed this skill into getting supplies to make himself and his tent mates more comfortable. This kind of sharing was also characteristic of social relations in Cuba. Guillermo also demonstrated another common skill that developed under the conditions of scarcity of the Cuban Revolution: modifying an object for a new use. In this case, he turned an electric razor into a tattoo machine. These kinds of individual situations were occurring throughout the camps in different configurations.

The story also illustrates an element that the military operation had in common with Cuban society under the Revolution: underneath the surface discipline and strictness, an informal social system operated in which people violated the bureaucratic rules to get what they wanted, even if it was prohibited. In Guillermo's case, alcohol was strictly prohibited in the camps, but the soldiers gladly provided it to him in exchange for his tattooing services.[10] This type of rule breaking probably felt familiar to Guillermo and his companions.

Additionally, the passage reveals another interesting element of the camp culture present early in the operation: a monetary system, which Juan also referred to in his story about getting rid of the cigarette thief. This occurred because at first there were many, many fewer cigarettes available than the tobacco-addicted portion of the population needed, especially in the context of high levels of stress. Therefore, the few cigarettes that were available immediately became the camps' currency, as they do in prisons elsewhere in the world. In general, Guillermo is describing the re-creation of a social system based on favors, but with a much greater availability of material resources than under the Cuban Revolution:

From Mike I went to Kilo, from Kilo they sent me to India, and I escaped from India to the McCallas. Yes, we escaped for the McCallas, me, Albertico, and Migue. We left. We were tired of being there among men and that whole story, and we ... I made tattoos. And so, it was funny because everybody in the tent worked for me. She made me the dye, she made everything for me in the tent. And everyone smoked cigarettes because ... or they charged cigarettes during that stage. And so, this was a tremendous business, making tattoos, understand? In Cuba I had made two or three, I studied design, right? I knew how to draw and all that. And afterwards, over there in Cuba I had done two or three, and after I got there [to the camps] I said, "Good, this is my solution." For more or less resolving two or three stupid little things that I needed, among those things were cigarettes.

And then I began to make tattoos, and I liked that whole story. I began to make tattoos, and afterwards I made myself a tattooing machine. I always had the idea for the machine, what happened was that I didn't have the conditions. I bought a little [electric] shaving machine for twelve cigarettes. It wasn't good for shaving anymore, but it still worked. It had a little motor, and I made myself a machine ... a machine. And I began to make tattoos. I had begun making tattoos by hand, with a needle and afterwards, I moved on to the machine.

And there I was. I made tattoos for everybody, a soldier, everybody, everybody, everybody. The tattoos gave us a little control over certain things, right? Among other things, many people came to get tattoos. The person who didn't smoke saved up his cigarettes. He already knew, for example, if I told him "I'll give you three tattoos for twenty cigarettes," he knew that he had to be saving twenty cigarettes to get the tattoos, right? Because they gave out one cigarette per day, and things like that. And so, the one who smoked didn't have cigarettes, and always did you a favor, understand? Or whatever we might need.

And one day we got together and decided we needed a doctor's appointment, the three of us. They gave us a doctor's appointment and we went to the hospital. When the bus got there it left us at the hospital. We didn't do anything in the hospital. We waited for the return bus, but instead of getting the bus that went to our camp, we got the one that went back to the other camp, McCalla. And from there I don't remember how we got in. I know that we went into the camp, and after we were in the camp, to continue, the only thing that came to me was the tattooing machine, when I got there with the tattooing machine, right way I began to make tattoos, and I found somebody, the camp jefe of the place, of McCalla 6, he got me a DMPIT, he got the three of us new DMPITS [ID bracelets].

Everything, everything, everything, everything was for tattoos. Everything for a tattoo. Yes, and afterward they looked for me, the police looked for me. They looked, they looked for me. Yes, because they already knew that there was someone using the machine that did tattoos. And so, I made tattoos for the soldiers too.

And so, when they looked for me I got the machine and I threw it over to another camp, [the one] in the front. I had friends. I threw the machine over with the dye and I hid over next to there. The soldiers brought me the dye. Yes, the soldiers themselves brought me the dye. At the beginning we made it, and afterwards they got it for me. Because they knew that a tattoo here cost $15 to $300 or better. And I did it for them right there for a bottle of Jack Daniels or something like that [laughs]. We got everything, everything we were lacking. Almost always it was drink. And I didn't drink. That was the cutest thing, that I got it for everybody inside. And that, because of that, what more could I have asked for? Understand. What interest did I have in that? Nothing, yes, that didn't interest me there, but that was the best thing they could give me. And so, nothing mattered to me. I asked for it for everyone else. But, that was all of it there. And we were there for a tremendous amount of time.

Guillermo's concluding sentence indicates not only the amount of time during which they were forced to employ various coping mechanisms, but also that there was enough time for a camp culture to develop through the daily practice of new routines.

Maria's case illustrates how individuals actively imposed meaning on a traumatic experience that had its genesis in the camps. One day in Camp Delta I found that Maria was HIV positive when her name came up with a flashing red bar across it on a computer screen in the command post. The soldiers were confusing her with a woman with the same name who was in a leadership position in the camp and gossiping about it. But that had been only the latest breach of her privacy. Maria was a single woman in her twenties and traveling with her mother, who had gotten a medical parole but had stayed behind with her daughter instead of leaving her alone in the camps. Maria explained that she had had a boyfriend in Cuba who had gone to fight in the war in Angola. Neither one of them had realized that he had been infected with HIV there.

Maria told me that there were two terrible things about her life in the camps as an HIV-positive person. One was the way the military told her of her status, and the other was the way they purposely compromised her privacy. Her mother had gotten a medical parole and they both had mandatory blood tests. When Maria's HIV test came back positive, the military sent an ambulance into her camp on the McCalla airstrip, lights blazing and sirens blaring. A group of medics got out of the ambulance, now surrounded by a group of curious onlookers, and proceeded to tell her about her status in public, in an insensitive, brusque manner.

That was traumatic enough but it was not the end of the story. When she found out that she was HIV positive, the immigration policy in effect at the time would have precluded her admittance to the United States. However, the International Organization for Migration had facilitated her inclusion on a legal challenge to that policy and had won. After the government was forced to admit her on the condition that she find an institutional sponsor, the military translators assigned to her during hospital visits suddenly vanished. They were replaced by other balseros who had volunteered to serve as translators, guaranteeing that her privacy would be compromised yet again.

The day I found Maria in her tent she was alone with her mother. Her most pressing issue was keeping track of her t-cell count and trying to stay healthy, since no anti-retroviral medication was available in the camps. Her face was also broken out from the coral dust, which was common. The only thing I could think to do was buy vitamins for her and visit on a regular basis.

However, instead of succumbing to depression and despair, Maria had instinctively done the thing that would help her heal from trauma: search for meaning. Maria's way of doing that was to find religion, and she had become quite devoutly Catholic as a result. While this fact made her case no less tragic, it was also intriguing. She prayed every day for strength and felt that God had given it to her. Eventually, she also found an institutional sponsor in Miami and was able to enter the United States as well.

As Maria was finding God, another tragedy was brewing around a gay man's religious experiences in Camp Delta/Charlie. Because that camp came out last in the lottery, its residents spent about sixteen months on the base before being admitted to the United States. I got to know him because he had been involved in creating the camp's art gallery. Within a few weeks after the first art show there he had begun to be very argumentative and disruptive. Toward the end of December, the decline seemed to become steeper, so I started asking the people in the camp for their view of the situation. They thought that the decline started after he began to attend evangelical church services in earnest.

This man had not found peace in religious belief but had instead become increasingly disturbed.

According to his friends, he had some serious unresolved identity issues around being gay that had been exacerbated by the condemning attitude of his new church toward homosexuality. His friends told me that he had attempted to "cleanse" himself of his sexual orientation by going to church a lot but had only become more and more unstable. Eventually, he was removed from the camp and the World Relief social worker determined that he had had a break with reality. She reported that she was having a difficult time getting him to develop the will to come back to a more stable state. Sadly, he was repatriated as a mental patient. I felt his instability had just as much to do with the fact that he was in the last camp to leave as it did with the church services.

In addition to people who had found religion for the first time, with both good and bad results, others were becoming more heavily involved in already familiar religious practices. This meant to some extent Catholicism, but always Santería. Catholic masses were conducted in the chapel on a regular basis, and they were well attended. Special services took place during

Art gallery, Camp Charlie-Delta, late 1995.

Advent season. Many people in the camp were also devotees of San Lázaro, or Saint Lazarus, the patron saint of the sick and injured, and asked that candles be provided for his day, December 15. A statue of Saint Lazarus also appeared propped against a telephone pole in the camp.

One day, after I had been in the Camp Alpha. A month, a man everyone called the soda jefe, whom I had to stop and talk with each day or face a hurt scolding the next, invited me to a picnic lunch in the park (thereby illustrating what I later found out was a Cuban talent for making seemingly impossible resources appear out of nowhere). After I agreed to stay in the camp for my lunch hour the next day, I arrived at the park to find a fried chicken picnic. The picnic table was covered with a white tablecloth made out of a sheet, and the chicken and French fries, which they had cooked in the park, were fresh from the Navy Exchange. Dessert consisted of Tootsie Rolls and other candy from the Meals Ready to Eat (MRE) pouches. While we were eating, the man showed me a package he had received from a nun he had studied with in the Panama camps; she had sent it to him from her trip to Medjugorje, Bosnia-Herzegovina, a town famous for sightings of the Virgin Mary. Among the things in the package was a letter that went into detail about a message that she had received from the Virgin Mary. Among other things, it warned people to take care of the current generation of young

San Làzaro statue, Camp Delta-Charlie, late 1995.

people because they were in particular danger of being led astray. The package also contained a dozen small medallions of the Virgin Mary. He gave me one of them, which I put on a silver chain and wore around my neck for the rest of my time on the base. While we were examining the contents of the package, the man told me that he thought his new faith had shielded him from the riots in the Panama camps. During the time when rocks were flying and tents were burning, he had stayed alone in his tent on his cot, and in the end found that everything around him was burned or damaged except for his cot.

On an individual level, people developed ways to cope with the stress of being detained up to eight months without knowing their fate, and then with waiting the long months until they could get on a flight to leave the base. Many went to the World Relief school to learn English or vocational skills. Others played on softball leagues or participated in physical training every morning alongside the members of the military in their camp. Some spent their days at the beach after the camps were opened up while others did artwork or busied themselves decorating their tents.

In Camp Alpha, a group of three men regularly walked around with two guitars singing in beautiful three-part harmony. Another man had gotten some semblance of a Cuban military uniform together and had obtained a fake gray beard and walked around the camp doing Fidel Castro impersonations.

The people who lived in the gay man's tent were mostly cross-dressers, which is a common practice among gay men in Havana. They were extremely friendly, usually wore skirts or spandex pants, and often had bows in their hair and red polish on their fingernails. They went to great lengths to decorate their tent. Like the people in the family camps, they put up dividers, which they had made from white sheets that they had meticulously sewn together (World Relief provided sewing machines for each camp). The cots all had bedspreads and neatly sewn pillows on them, some of blue satin. The dressers, made from plywood and the boxes the Meals Ready to Eat came in, with plastic utensils for handles, had many toiletries lined up neatly on top of them. Part of the reason for the dividers was to give privacy to night visitors, some of whom did not self-identify as gay.

One day, three of the men from that tent invited me to a cliff-top croquette lunch. To make the croquettes, they would take the ham from an MRE pouch and coat it with breadcrumbs that they had made by drying the bread from their meals on the roof of their tent. Then they would make a fire in a small pit, and fry them in a small amount of oil on a flattened can. Usually they did this in the park, but they wanted to have lunch with me by the ocean. That day they had dressed up a little for lunch: two of them had taffeta bows in their shoulder-length hair, which they had pushed up on top of their heads, and all of them wore red nail polish. Frying up croquettes along the coral cliffs was a pleasant break from walking around in the camp under the broiling Caribbean sun. We were having a nice time eating the first batch of croquettes when a guard came by and made the men put out the fire, putting an end to my only cliff-top croquette meal.

Sylvia coped by doing physical exercise on returning to the camps after working with the military as a psychologist. Below, she discusses how she helped a group of women, and then describes her own strategies. The number of times she says the words "scream" and "problems" reminds us of the amount of tension she was carrying around, and the extent to which other people's problems piled up on her every day since she was living with the extra burden of helping people cope with their own trauma.

> I walked. And I did groups, I did therapy groups, and I took groups to the ocean at the times when everyone was going back to the camps, and the shore was empty, and we went there, and we . . . screamed. Scream therapy. Screaming. We did relaxation. I did relaxation exercises with people, and I did meditation. Well, just so you know, when they finished in the gyms, I went every night, every night I went to the gym, every night. And I walked and everything. In other words . . . I took care of myself, you know. Besides the fact that all day I was hearing people's problems, people's problems, people's problems, so I had to look for some way to relax myself, and also let go of that load a little.

Posttraumatic growth is evident in the balseros' narratives and may be responsible for many people's positive evaluations of their experiences on the base. For example, below Raul describes the process of creating a moral order in the camps, which helped people re-establish a sense of safety and predictability. After that, his discussion of what they gained out of the experience, which he felt was worth it, exemplified posttraumatic growth. A likely reason for the positive evaluations of the camp experience among many of the men who stayed on the base for more than a year was that they had had ample time to develop new meaning systems. A couple of the all-male camps also were lucky enough to have had consistently sympathetic and calm members of the military overseeing them, so they were able to begin the healing immediately instead of undergoing new traumatic experiences.

> A person who would leave maybe from Havana on a plane, and they put him here in Miami. . . . This society suffers when people arrive without any kind of preparation, no type of discipline. So as I was saying at the beginning, I believe that in relation to people, I believe it was an achievement because after a year ... in Guantánamo, everything that took place, one knew why he came, why he came to this country, what he wanted, one learned to respect his fellow humans, respect what is around them, and isn't achieved in a week, that isn't achieved

in a month.... The people didn't justify thefts, they didn't understand them, compadre. They *repudiated* them. In Guantánamo it was difficult to separate it. In Guantánamo it was difficult to separate it. So, when we arrived at Guantánamo we were full of vices, full of things. After spending many months we began to purify ourselves, we began to see, you know, we began . . .

5

Creative Expression in the Camps

In addition to mobilizing their individual and collective organizing skills to cope with the camp environment, the balseros engaged in so much creative activity that art became one of the salient features of the camps. Army cots became armchairs and rockers, caps from miniature Tabasco sauce bottles became chandeliers, sheets of plywood became billiard tables, and plastic spoon collections became "beaded" curtains. People who had never before created any kind of art made paintings, drawings, sculptures, tattoos, and even monuments expressing different aspects of their stories. They also got together to create art galleries and organize poetry readings and variety shows. The talent and industriousness the balseros displayed in doing those things impressed the military so much that it allowed some of them to paint permanent murals on base buildings, such as the Windjammer, and to redecorate the base's day care center.

Researchers have noted that people undergoing collective trauma or social change create artwork that is a vehicle for expressing their personal and collective identity. It contains a narrative, bears witness to and helps process collective suffering or social change, and can be read together with life histories.[1] All of these elements were plainly evident in the balseros' artwork. There were several reasons that the artwork came together in a particular way in the Guantánamo and Panama camps. First, people feel a psychological imperative to create new meanings and identities in the wake of trauma. Creative expression provides a vehicle for this process. Second, while growing up in Cuba certainly was fraught with what some call the "errors and horrors" of the Revolution, it did leave the balseros with a lot of tools from which to draw in creating new meanings. Third, everyone had a lot of time

Early art gallery, McCalla airstrip.

on their hands and tended to worry about their fate, and creating things helped them relax.

The balseros had an abundance of cultural tools at their disposal because the Cuban Revolution sought to expose people to the arts from its outset. For example, in 1960, the government created a number of national organizations including the National Film Institute, a national publishing house, and the Casa de las Americas, which promotes cultural exchanges with other Latin American countries. It also created Popular Councils of Culture as an arm of the People's Power political structure and imported the idea of the Casa de Cultura (Culture House) from the Soviet Union. The Casas are local cultural centers usually set up in old mansions that contain things including libraries, art galleries, auditoriums, conference rooms, music rooms, and art studios. Mass organizations and unions also promoted folk song festivals, art contests, writing circles, and amateur theater, among other activities. Professional artists and musicians from major urban centers were often involved in advising amateur groups from rural areas, ensuring that the arts did not remain only in Havana and other urban areas.[2] Because the Revolution also focused on literacy and education, the balseros were more educated than other people from the region might have been. Some of the Revolution's major accomplishments in this area included a huge literacy campaign in the countryside in the 1960s that dramatically increased literacy rates and was partially responsible for a tenfold increase in the number of university students, many of whom then became involved in cultural research or community-based artistic activities.[3]

Carlos thought that the artistic activity in the camps also reflected the natural creativity of the Cubans as a people.

> Cubans are like that—Cubans are creative people. Of course I was impressed by it, but it didn't surprise me that they were like that, using creativity as a resource. . . . They are well-prepared people. The composer composes, in other words, the musician plays music, the painter paints, the poet writes. I wrote a poem to my daughter while I was there. It was a present for her second birthday when I was in Guantánamo.

Although their educational and cultural backgrounds and a psychological imperative for self-expression were the main sources of creativity in the camps, two of the interviewees, Juan and Raul, gave an additional reason for its prevalence. They relate what they experienced as they became conscious of throwing off the yoke of oppression and self-censorship. The account suggests that part of the group-level anxiety that was so palpable to outsiders during the early days of the camp operation was the product not only of indefinite detention but also, ironically, of new feelings that arose when they began to find out that they could express themselves freely, even though they were in detention. Juan and Raul segued into the topic after talking about the problem of the *doble moral* (double moral) in Cuba, which refers to the requirement that people project a public face in support of the Revolution no matter what their true feelings. Both of them laughed a great deal when they told the story, suggesting how odd the process seemed to them in retrospect. They also noted that not everyone had thrown off the habit of self-censorship even after residing in the United States for a few years.

> RAUL: The double moral. In Guantánamo, after some time passed, the people didn't have to hide themselves when they were saying anything. If they wanted to say anything, they said it.
>
> ELIZABETH: Yes, a mediator from Washington told me, because I went after you all had been there for four or five months, that initially the

Cubans in the camps talked like this, behind their hands, very low, like everything was a secret.

RAUL: [laughs]

ELIZABETH: And was it like that?

RAUL: It was like that. No actually, it's still like that right now in this country [the United States, five years later].

ELIZABETH: Still?

RAUL: No because that was a . . .

JUAN: The people stayed like that, it stays with them.

ELIZABETH: When they came here?

JUAN: No, no, no, with our companions, our companions just like us are still like that.

RAUL: Yes, sometimes we're going to talk about President Clinton and [speaking softly] "*Oye*, did you hear what happened to Clinton?" And you know [laughing], they are . . .

ELIZABETH: [laughing] They are habits that . . .

RAUL: They're habits [laughing].

JUAN: They're habits [laughing], that you can't talk bad about the president.

RAUL: Or no, that . . .

JUAN: Or, now that they're here, they can't talk bad about Clinton [laughing].

RAUL: Where it's not even prohibited [laughing], they prohibit it themselves; it's that Cubans before were afraid; well, I know it's already a question of habit, but people should have already gotten rid of those habits.

ELIZABETH: But, how did they go about changing like that, because, they saw some things in the Americans who were, with, working there, or . . . ?

JUAN: No, there were people who, the Americans who were working there . . .

RAUL: Aghhhh . . .

ELIZABETH: That could express themselves freely.

JUAN: That could express themselves in another way, and the people, there were also people who in Cuba, you know, at least when you know liberty in one way, you know that, at least you had read about it, and you knew that everything is different in liberty.

ELIZABETH: Oh, OK.

JUAN: Besides, liberty is something that you feel; it's palpable, you know, it has a flavor.

RAUL: It's difficult to explain it.

ELIZABETH: What?

JUAN: That it has a flavor.

ELIZABETH: Ohhhh . . .

JUAN: It has an odor, it has a flavor, and you feel sometimes that it's cold, sometimes hot, but it's something different. It's palpable in your spirit. You feel it physically, understand?

RAUL: It's something very strange.

JUAN: It's something very strange.

ELIZABETH: Really?

RAUL: Yes, something peculiar.

JUAN: Very peculiar.

RAUL: Yes, and we went about discovering it in Guantánamo little by little. But little by little, we noticed what we had.

ELIZABETH: Yes, but from the beginning you were going on strike, and all of that screaming.

RAUL: [laughing]

ELIZABETH: No . . . there was a strike in September of 1994.[4]

RAUL: [laughing] That's the anxiety, the anxiety of liberty, that hit them . . . [laughing] . . . all of that, I believe, you know.

ELIZABETH: Before feeling it, you had to try to . . .

JUAN: No, I don't believe that the people felt it afterward; they had a horrible necessity to express the fact that they were already free.

RAUL: Yes.

JUAN: Understand, and doing that type of . . .

RAUL: And to speak or to dress however you wanted, and to eat whatever you would want.

ELIZABETH: That's why there were so many . . . things, artwork, well, art, that said "libertad, libertad," all over the place?

RAUL: Yes, because in Cuba we lived so, so, so repressed, in . . .

JUAN: It was a necessity to express it. . . .

RAUL: So big . . .

JUAN: To express what the people were feeling, you know.

ELIZABETH: A friend of mine told me that when they left on the raft, once they saw the shores of Havana, the ocean shore, everyone began to scream, "liberty, liberty," like that.

JUAN: Ya.

RAUL: That, that, . . . when you have it, as Juan said so well, it's incredible [laughing], it's incredible, and one doesn't just discover it from one day to the next, but little by little you go about noticing that, you go about noticing your rights. Also, your responsibilities, but one goes about noticing all of . . .

JUAN: The exercise of liberty.

RAUL: One also goes . . .

JUAN: That's what the people went on learning, you know, every day.

ELIZABETH: Oh, yes.

JUAN: Yes, the exercise of democracy, the exercise of liberty.

RAUL: To demand, to demand, to demand your rights, beginning with the responsibility . . . let me explain. So, at the beginning, at the beginning it was a little bit comical, because . . .

JUAN: For example . . .

RAUL: The same thing, because, excuse me, Juan. That same thing that you said, that strike. Cubans had never had that [laughing] courage . . .

ELIZABETH: Really?

RAUL: And well, when one first arrived in Guantánamo, one felt the right [laughing] . . . that was very comical, to tell you the truth. One felt the right that, that [laughing] . . . that we deserved a lot of things.

JUAN: Ha ha ha ha [laughs hard].

ELIZABETH: Yes?

RAUL: We deserved a lot of things [laughing], you know, without having earned them for ourselves, without . . .

JUAN: Without anything . . .

RAUL: Without anything [still laughing], and saying, "I want my son to become a doctor, I want a plate of food for myself, for those that, that . . . " And so, the problems were terrible, you know, because the person who had stood with two fingers up and said "but look at that Cuban, look at what he's saying!" but, you know, "he's crazy!"

JUAN: I couldn't believe it.

RAUL: "But what's going on here, why yell?" [laughing]. So, the Cuban, that behavior, the shock of liberty, saying things like that, it's really terrible. It's terrible because from one day to the next, they're telling you you had everything, everything that was prohibited for you, for good or bad, they're telling you that you can do everything, that you can do what you wanted to do, that you can ask for what you want with your own mouth. So, that was something shocking in the first month. In those first days, in those first weeks, because the Cuban had it and he didn't know it, he didn't utilize it, he didn't utilize it well. They even went up to the military and they didn't express themselves, they didn't express themselves.

JUAN: The military played around with a lot of things.

ELIZABETH: Psychologically, no?

JUAN: Psychologically.

Together with the impacts of trauma, this habit of self-censorship could have left them feeling extremely helpless, but engaging in self-expression was healing for both of those things. Marcos discusses how he and a group of friends began doing art themselves and then began giving classes.

Um hum, not too long, after about a month and a half or two we were doing that. And after fifteen days of being in Guantánamo I was designing ... a flag for the painters. After fifteen days, and after a month and a half, we began with the schools. And from there they moved us ... people went to Panama. Right there I began to form a group of artists. We grouped ourselves together and we made a little tent outside, and we went and painted and gave classes. We took children there too.

Roberto comments on why he thought people made so much art.

I don't know, to my imagination, it seems to me that it was also the length of the stay. Not having anything to do. To see somebody doing something, you wanted to try it also. And I saw a lot of people there who surely discovered talent that they didn't know they had, artistic talent that they didn't know about before.

Pancho's discussion about why he made art combines the idea of having a lot of time to think while they were on the base and the fact that many people in the camps had had some art education.

I put the painting I did of my daughter up on the wall [in the tent]. I sent it to my daughter in Cuba [at the end of the operation] and she still has it in a place in her house.

I made it because ... imagine, when one has a lot of time, and you don't have a job, you get to thinking. So, in my life in Cuba, when I was young I studied painting at the San Alejandro [art] school. I went to that school for like a year, studying painting. I was about fifteen years old. I was really young. Afterwards, I left because it was really, really far away from my house. I lived in Regla and it's in Marianao, at the far end of Marianao, so it was really far and the transportation was really bad, and sometimes I couldn't get there on time. And so, I have some idea of what it is to paint, to create art, understand.

So I was thinking about my family, and so I had a little tiny photo of my daughter. So I made the photo into a larger painting while I was there. There was a lot, a lot of art in the camp, a lot of people who painted, a lot of people who made sculptures, who made ... eh, who composed music, or things like that; it was beautiful. There was a very high level of culture, really high.

There were really beautiful things. They even make things from cots, broken cots. They made couches, chairs, different things. Fishing spears and other things from saws ... they made different things, like fishing spears. They made twenty things there, things that you would never have imagined making. We made everything, we performed in *peñas* [informal gatherings where participants give music and theater performances], we made houses of culture [*casas de cultura* in Spanish], they formed musical groups, they did activities in other camps, and things like that.

They formed teams for baseball, basketball, and soccer, everything. Sometimes I miss all of those things, I miss that. I really miss the tranquility that I had there, understand? The environment was very tranquil. I had a lot of friends there, understand.

People who painted and sculpted usually did not pick random themes but chose subjects that were either in their physical environment or on their minds. This meant that the art was just as changeable as the Clinton administration policy toward admitting them. It tended to contain major themes or subjects that revealed how threatening the physical environment was and how they felt about Clinton administration policy toward them. In the beginning of the operation, images of barbed wire, sharks, and visual suggestions of an impeded search for liberty, such as the Statue of Liberty blindfolded, predominated in the paintings, drawings, and sculptures. By late 1995, after the physical conditions had improved and the people knew they would be admitted to the United States, they tended to make things such as ships in bottles, carvings of dolphins, shell ornaments, and paintings without political content or the images of razor wire. The paintings in an art exhibition I attended in Camp Delta in December 1995, a month before the last flight left the base, had mostly pastoral themes, along with ocean or dolphin images. Several weeks prior to that, a craze to make ships in a bottle or models of eighteenth- and nineteenth-century ships had swept the camps, and they became ubiquitous in the environment. A few images of American and Cuban flags continued to be scattered throughout the artwork. Images of Fidel Castro as the devil also remained the same; that much did not change.

Many of the paintings were very engaging, with themes that made a lasting impression on people who saw them, whether they were balseros, members of the military, or civilian camp workers. Miguel and the author discuss a couple of paintings that made impressions on them.

ELIZABETH: One of the things that was really impressive to us too was all the creative expression, all the artwork. What impressed you most about all of that?

MIGUEL: I saw a painting of the Statue of Liberty with a cloth tied on her face.

ELIZABETH: And all the little naked people climbing up it. That was my favorite. Was that how you felt?

MIGUEL: Yes, but I saw another one. It was Castro's hand on one side of a chess game, and Clinton on the other side, like making deals.

ELIZABETH: And that's how you felt.

MIGUEL: Exactly, and that's what was happening, you know. Castro was using us for his own purpose, and Clinton then didn't know what to do.

ELIZABETH: So then, what about the inside of the tent? Did your group decorate inside the tent?

MIGUEL: We had a very nice guy. He made a rocking chair out of a cot. That was the most impressive thing I saw.

The paintings that were so remarkable were only seen by individuals in each camp or at times by people visiting other camps or going to a World Relief–sponsored art show. The newsletter, on the other hand, circulated throughout all of the camps. It was one of the most important ways in which the balseros communicated, modified, and commented on their group story and their experiences in the camps. The official camp newsletter was called *¿Qué Pasa?* Although there were other newsletters created in some of the individual camps, *¿Qué Pasa?* was the only one that the military distributed to the entire camp population. The newsletter was actually a Psychological Operations (PsyOps) project whose purpose was to alleviate camp tensions, but it was staffed by balseros who chose the specific content. Perhaps it was for that reason that there was a disclaimer at the bottom of each issue asserting that its contents did not reflect the views of the military.

The newsletter usually contained articles reprinted from newspapers such as the *Miami Herald*, *El Nuevo Herald*, and *USA Today*. Occasionally, articles from other papers such as *El Diario*, *Prensa Latina*, and the *New York Times* would appear. The editorial staff chose articles that had to do with Cuba, rafters, sports, and certain world events, such as the war in Bosnia. The amount of space dedicated to current events could never have alleviated their feelings of isolation, but the articles did give residents some general idea of what was going on in the world.

In addition to choosing articles, newspaper staff went to individual camps to interview other balseros, and they reported on what they were saying about different aspects of camp life, such as the living conditions and medical parole issues. The social work staff of World Relief often contributed articles on psychosocial issues, and military personnel sometimes provided information on public health or announcements about things such as mail distribution. Each issue also included an update on the number of people who flew out of the camps on medical parole, and later, on how many people flew out under the lottery. Occasionally, the staff wrote about new balseros arriving on the base, usually mentioning the ongoing deprivations of the Special Period that continued to drive Cubans out of the country. The paper also had an entertainment section, which included exercises in the English language, word puzzles, and comic strips.[5]

The comics page was one of the most creative and funny sections of the paper. Much of it was drawn by Dámaso Pérez Busquet, who became the camps' political cartoonist until he left for the United States later in the operation. His comics usually poked fun at different aspects of the balse-ros' situation on the base and always ridiculed Fidel Castro. The cartoons before the May 2 announcement that the balseros would be allowed into the United States tended to focus on elements of the parole process, includ-ing INS bureaucrats, while the ones afterward mostly poked fun at different elements of camp life.

The first comic strip, from the April 1, 1995, *¿Qué Pasa?* is part of the *Picanticos* (Little Spicy Ones) series. An INS officer stands in front of a desk with a tall pile of paper on one side and holds up a bat as if he is about to take a swing. The caption reads, "The next one is for the Miami Medical Team." This is a reference to the fact that the Miami Medical Team doctors recommended so many people for medical parole that it became a problem for the INS because other base doctors often refused to agree with many of the parole recommendations. The balseros usually were left with the impres-sion that they had gotten a valid parole recommendation that was not acted on, which caused a lot of tension in the camps.

In the next panel, two men are sitting on beach chairs made out of cots, and little rolls of razor wire are in the background. They are both wearing DMPITS bracelets. One man says to the other, "I've never had a vacation that was so long and so well paid," to which the other one replies, "They say that it costs a million dollars a day." This is a reference to the high cost of keep-ing the balseros in Guantánamo and to how ridiculous the situation was.

The next set of strips from that issue is called "Cuentos Cubanos," or "Cuban Stories." In the first one, a little boy is asking a little girl what she wants to be when she grows up. The girl replies that she wants to be a singer like Madonna. When she asks him the same question, he replies, "A func-tionary of Immigration to give parole to everybody." The strip below that one envisions the balseros being sent back to Cuba. One friend asks another how it was in Guantánamo. He replies, "It wasn't so bad; at least I got to know the famous liberty." His friend then asks, "Tell me, what's liberty like?" The man replies, "Nothing, some tents, some plastic bathrooms, and a lot of barbed wire." The strip at the bottom of the page, always reserved for Fidel Castro, has him say, "I have no choice but to get rid of all the satellite dishes. Capitalism and its propaganda are really affecting us a lot." He finishes, "Of course, I'll keep watching it to inform all of you. It doesn't affect me at all, of course you've already seen what I looked like in Paris." This strip begins with an allusion to TV Martí, the US television station aimed at Cuba that the Cuban government blocks, as well as to other stations Cubans can pick up from Miami with illegal satellite dishes. The last scene seems to be an allusion to Castro's hypocrisy as well as his vanity.

The second group, from May 20, focuses on the material conditions in the camps. Notably, there is no mention of razor wire, since by that time it had been replaced with fencing. This time, there is a bag of bread talking to a lunchbox full of food, teasing, "So hot and nobody wants you," to which the food replies, "Don't talk, they don't even take you out of the bag." Obviously, people were tired of the food, but many of them had six to eight more months to go. The issue of the material conditions continues in the next strip, where two latrines are speaking with each other. One says, "I don't

Comic strip by Dámaso Pérez Busquet, April 1, 1995, edition of *¿Qué Pasa?* newsletter.

lack desire to be converted into something else," to which the other replies, "and we still have a lot of [fecal] extractions to go through." This refers to the way the latrines were cleaned, with what everyone called "shit suckers." The smell produced when the latrines were cleaned was another source of stress in the camps.

In the next strip, a DMPITS scanner says to a bracelet, "Are you going to the beach or not?" and the bracelet replies, "That's envy or racism." The author may be making a reference to the soldiers guarding the entrances to the camps. In the strip below this one, one DMPITS bracelet says to the other, "I've been waiting to leave for thirty days." The other one replies, "Cheer up, not everyone has your luck." This reflects some of the conversations that occurred in the camps. People who were waiting for their flights

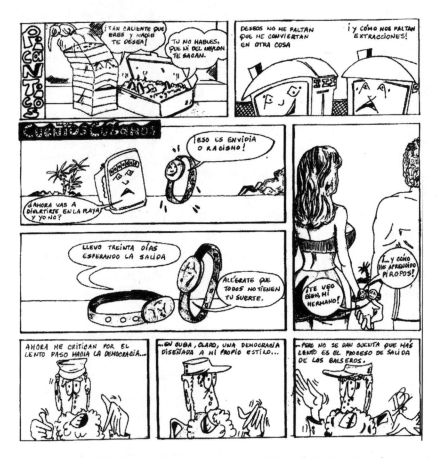

Comic strip by Dámaso Pérez Busquet, May 20, 1995, edition of *¿Qué Pasa?* newsletter.

were often delayed by the slowness of the bureaucracy or by lost paperwork, and many became obsessed over how long they had been waiting, which annoyed some of their compatriots. At the time this issue came out, even though the balseros all knew that they would be let in to the United States, the only people who were leaving the camps were those with medical parole, and the military had not yet announced how or when the rest of the population would be taken to the United States.

Next, on the right side, was the spot where Dámaso put in a series called "Papo y Nena," which was always a couple whose bantering was full of sexual innuendo. Here, a very shapely woman and a man are holding hands and their DMPITS bracelets are talking to each other. The one on the woman's wrist says, "You're looking good, my brother," to which the other replies, "Ooh, I've learned to flirt." They had been in the camps for so long that even their ID bracelets were learning pickup lines. The next comic is the familiar one that pokes fun at Fidel Castro. In the row of three panes, Fidel is saying "Now they criticize me for the slow steps toward democracy in Cuba, of course a democracy designed my way, but they don't notice that the balseros' process for leaving is even slower." Though this strip usually mocks Castro in some way, here Dámaso uses it to comment on how long the government was taking to get them out of the camps.

Another way in which the balseros communicated their story to everyone on the base was by creating the monuments that dotted the camps. Two of them were commemorative. One was a large, wooden model of a tugboat, which was a memorial to the people who drowned after the Cuban Coast Guard attacked a hijacked tugboat called *March 13*. A second one was a tall concrete monument honoring a female soldier who was killed in a traffic accident on the base. Although it did not make a direct reference to the balseros, it acknowledged the role of the military in their lives. A third expressed the balseros' demands for liberty. It was built in an originally all-male camp, Camp Kilo, which was renamed Camp Bravo after it became a family camp, at around the same time the memorial to the *March 13* tugboat victims was constructed. Both of the commemorative monuments could be seen by people from more than one camp and therefore could influence the group narrative at the same time they reflected it. Another monument, actually a large sculpture, sat outside the entrance to Camp Alpha to thank the military for rescuing the balseros from the dangers of the sea.

Wooden monument to *March 13* tugboat incident.

The monument to those aboard the *March 13* tugboat, which the Cuban Coast Guard sank with water cannons in mid-1994, consisted of a large wooden replica of a tugboat on which the balseros had painted shadows of people whose body language, hands held in the air out of either panic or surrender, revealed a crisis situation. The style is reminiscent of socialist realism. For a few months, the monument sat along the road that led from the downtown area to the camps on the Bulkeley side of the base. The front of the boat had steps on each side, so that it was actually possible for people to walk around on it, but people never seemed to be doing so, possibly because it was quite a distance from the side of the road. It did not remain in its original spot for the entire operation and may have been stored to protect it from fading under the Caribbean sun. Located far from the camps, it really seemed to speak more to the American staff than to most of the balseros, but anyone on a bus going from one side of the base to another could also see it.

The *March 13* tugboat incident seemed very important to the balseros' identity and connected the past to the present. The incident apparently was not covered by Cuban news but spread quickly by word of mouth in Havana. It was evident that the people's repulsion at the Cuban government's attack on the boat's occupants caused one of those "Aha" moments that cemented many people's disaffection with the Revolution. Two elements of the incident were particularly repugnant. First, since the boat was hijacked and therefore full of innocent people, attacking it was inherently unjust. Second, after sinking it, the Cuban Coast Guard did not even try to rescue anyone, which added to everyone's horror.

Marcos's description of the *March 13* incident is representative of the balseros' interpretation. He interjects a commentary about the Cuban government as a way to highlight the contradictions between the Cuban government's rhetoric and its actual actions before returning to the story.

[The] *March 13* [incident] is a day I will never ever forget. *March 13* meant a lot to the balseros. For two things. The *March 13* [incident], I'll tell you, it was a catastrophe in Cuba. There are ways in which the Revolution has made decisions transparently. I think that Cuba spends *a lot* of money for world public opinion for an image, a good public image. It's sometimes an image that isn't real. It's very romantic. They show Cuba as a paradise, that reality, that truth. Cuba seems like a paradise . . . in all respects. But socially, Cuba isn't a paradise. I think that all governments that try to enclose people in one idea are going to have that problem. They all do it differently, they all have a lot of ideas.

So, more than that, they sink a tugboat in Havana and it was carrying people that weren't leaving Cuba; the boat was hijacked. Well, the Border Guard has boats that are really powerful and fast. A tugboat is a slow boat and they tried to detain the tugboat, and when they couldn't stop it, they began to shoot pressurized water at it.

I believe the tugboat was from Regla. It was the one that went from Havana. In other words, the people leave from there to the island [Regla] because they live there, others because they are going to the sanctuary of the Virgin of Regla. And all that time that little boat is full of people. People in many cases aren't leaving Cuba, they . . . weren't leaving Cuba, according to my understanding; I was still in jail. According to my understanding, they broke up the tugboat in plain sight. In other words they ripped it apart.

And it begins to sink. And they didn't save the people. They don't do anything to save the people. That's really ugly. Because, I look at it from the point of view of neither good nor bad, I tell you this from the point of being Cuban. We are all Cuban. But on top of that, even including being Cuban, we're all human. I think that if I were a member of the military, if I were in a situation like that, well, if at best I can't disobey an order to detain a ship, but what I can do is to help the people who are drowning survive. And innocent children. Those things are what have made many people disaffected, many people who saw in the Revolution a just system for the whole world.

Because we have a card so that everyone goes to work. It gives privileges to people, even though there were those who were always problematic, but it was important because they gave it to everyone. A black is equal to me. I loved a black as much as I loved a white. Eh, we helped each other. That was a *very* good custom in Cuba. To say, "Neighbor, give me some salt … neighbor, give me some salt." "Neighbor, I don't have rice." "Neighbor, give me beans." "Grab some beans." That's to say that there was even a custom in Cuba to cook, and to give a sample to your neighbor of what you made. Every day he gave you what he made. Understand. It was beautiful how I lived, with Cuban customs and how I grew up, and how, I told you. For me things like that, it was the same thing with Mariel. To grab eggs, good food that the people needed, to see them thrown at the people who left. No, what I saw, what I saw wasn't good in that respect.

Marcos also draws a contrast between the Cuban government's actions and the people's mores. He portrays a communal spirit that was actually more in line with the rhetoric of the Revolution than killing the people aboard the tugboat was. By bringing up another contradiction, the act of throwing good food at people who wanted to leave during the Mariel Boatlift, at a time when many people did not have enough to eat, he connects disaffection to both the balsero crisis and the Mariel Boatlift.

Augustín also talked about the *March 13* tugboat incident.

The *March 13* is a tugboat that leaves full of people, women, children, many children were among the people and many women. A Cuban [government] boat starts [to chase] it and sinks [it] five miles from the bay [of Havana], where everyone dies. That is the tragedy of the *March 13*. Fidel orders it sunk, he orders that, the order is his, the Cuban boat didn't fire a shot, but went to sea. . . .

I spoke with one of the survivors who was in Guantánamo with me. It was an old wooden tugboat, from the Second World War. There were two tugboats. The tugboat that they followed, and another tugboat. The other tugboat was an iron tugboat. And they assault it [fist smashing hand], they began to assault it, the new tugboat begins to assault the older one, the one that had the old wood, against the steel. Before that they sprayed jets of water, and water and jets of water until they sink the tugboat, full of children, seventy-three people. In Cuba, news runs by word of mouth. Unofficially. I heard the official news after I arrived in Guantánamo. I knew people who were in the tugboat, who survived.

A group of men in an all-male camp originally called Kilo constructed the second monument, to liberty, before the military moved them to Camp Golf near the border with sovereign Cuba and turned Kilo into a family camp called Bravo. This meant that even before people could move freely among the camps, the monument reinforced the balseros' story among the few thousand people who first came into contact with it. It was basically a proclamation of their claims to freedom. The men inscribed it in Spanish on one side and English on the other. It read: "Brothers: everyone listen to his voice, from the depth of the sea, rises a giant wave, and the crest will take the claim of our people. FREEDOM FREEDOM." This statement directly associated the balsero identity with the claim to freedom and their experiences on the ocean. The fact that the flags were included in the monument also indicates the degree to which the military facilitated the creation of the camp culture by providing the materials.

Juan and Raul were both involved in making the monument. Juan describes the collaborative process and how individual members of the military in his camp also assisted them in the endeavor.

There was a guy who came to give me the paper [for the camp newsletter] and he said, "Why don't we make a monument?" So, I tell him OK, good, perfect, how do we do it? So, there was one guy who said we should make it out of rock. There was a guy who said we should make it out of wood, and there were a lot of ideas at the beginning, but in the end a man came and said that he was a professional carpenter and that we should make it out of concrete if the military would get the cement and water and plywood for it. So, we went to the military and they told us that they were in agreement, that it was all right with them, but that they couldn't supply the cement. . . . So we took up a collection and were able to get $25 together, and the soldiers put in the other part of the money, from their own pockets. And it cost about $120, or something like that. Once the monument began ... they saw the goodwill, and more materials appeared ... even a hand-cranked concrete mixer.

The process was rather simple: someone came up with an idea and then asked the military if it would help. The story also shows goodwill on the part of many members of the military who contributed their own money for the concrete.

At first glance, the third monument does not seem to reinforce the balseros' story of a search for freedom. After a female soldier was killed in a traffic accident on the base, the balseros wanted to commemorate her service, and, by extension, the service of all the military personnel who had taken care of them in the camps. It was no accident that it was built after Rear Admiral Haskins dramatically improved relations between the military and the balseros.

Like the monument to the *March 13* tugboat, the design is reminiscent of Soviet-style socialist realism. It is the silhouette of a female soldier in a

Monument to liberty, Camp Bravo.

forward-thrusting position with a gun in her left hand and an anvil in her right. She sits on top of what perhaps is a small boat. The inscription reads, "In honor to the US armed forces." Although it does not contain a reference to the past or to freedom, the effort formally included the military in the balseros' story.

After all the Cubans were moved back from Panama to Guantánamo in the wake of rioting in the Panama camps in December of 1994, the military moved some of the men into a camp called Alpha, where the commander immediately began to work with them to create large projects, including a pleasant park and several large pieces of public art. The first thing that was evident on approach to the camp was a large model of a raft that a group of men had built out of green polyester tarp, tires covered in blue tarp, wood, and sandbags, behind which they had placed a huge sign that read, "Liberty." In front of the raft they had spelled out a message using sandbags: "American friends, we the Cuban rafters want to thank you for rescuing us from the dangers of the sea."

Monument to a fallen female soldier, Camps Echo
and Foxtrot.
Photo courtesy of Kari Wickenheiser

Monument to liberty and rescuers, Camp Alpha.

The men in Camp Alpha embraced creative projects so much that artwork permeated the environment. About fifty yards from the monument was a large model of the camp in a huge plywood frame topped by a sign with its official name, Villa Alpha. The men who had created it continued their work together in a tent near the park, where they went on to make a series of smaller models of all of the camps. Some of these were eventually shipped to a US Navy museum in San Diego. Behind the command post was a rest area for the members of the military, dug into the side of a small hill and lined with white sandbags. It was complete with homemade tables shaded by round, thatched roofs. With the help of military bulldozers to clear the prickly underbrush, the men had also created a large park, lined with sandbags, for general use.

A group of teachers in Camp Delta created a large piece of public art and nailed it to their tent, which faced the road. They cut a large piece of plywood into the form of the Statue of Liberty and then painted the details onto it. Next to the Statue of Liberty, they placed a sheet over one of the windows on which they painted a raft with oars coming out of it. Putting the painting of the raft next to the Statue of Liberty created an association between the two, reinforcing the connection between the search for freedom and the balsero identity and broadcasting it to anyone passing by.

Rafter identity images on tent, Camp Bravo.

The staff of the World Relief Corporation was also impressed by the ubiquity of the artistic expression and facilitated it whenever possible. A married artist couple from that organization volunteered to paint a World Relief truck with their version of the balseros' story. The artists had become known for painting images of bodies with disembodied hands and heads, and they continued to use that style on the truck. They painted one side of it with waves, underneath which were coral-like bodies planted into the ocean floor, a reference to the balseros who died at sea. Three naked people with disembodied hands adorned the door. They looked off into the distance at the silhouette of a jet enclosed in a white bubble. A decorative flower and a black and red flag covered the hood. On the other side, an elongated raft took up most of the length of the truck. Underneath the raft, which had oars in it, were choppy seas. As if all this were not traumatic enough, razor wire wove around the raised oars. Three white doves on the front of the raft suggest hope, even though the terrible razor wire was present behind them. The flag of Cuba covering the hood associated the scene with Cubans.

World Relief provided enough art materials after the first few months of the operation for most people who were interested to try their skill at painting or some other kind of artwork. Initially, some of the materials had been scarce and people had been painting with things like rake tines or

World Relief truck with balsero symbols.

their fingertips, but so many people were painting anyway that at least three galleries sprang up in the McCalla camps within the first few months of the operation. When the military closed the McCalla camps and moved the population to the Bulkeley side of the base, more art galleries appeared. Eventually, there was such a large volume of paintings and carvings that World Relief and the military worked together to do an art exhibition at the Navy Exchange mall, where a few of the young men who liked grunge music also gave guitar performances.

The common symbols the balseros used in their identity work were rafts, oars, sharks, and, occasionally, flags. There was such a fad of balsero logos in Camp Alpha that the military held a contest to decide on the best logo. The winning one would be used in camp ceremonies and a smaller version was reproduced on a ceiling tile and installed in the Officers Club. Two basic logo designs came out of the competition. One included the common elements in the balsero identity. However, Gerardo Alfonso Piquera, who had studied architecture, took that basic concept and designed a logo that was not only more artistic but also more overt in the way it tied together the search for freedom and the confrontation with death. The Piquera logo consisted of a large double circle that says "exodus-rafter-liberty" along the bottom half and the dates "1994–1996" along the top. Inside the circle is a skeletal figure, which at first glance seems to be a headless eagle with its wings open. However, upon closer examination, the breast and arms are human and they meld into the wings. The body is in fact human, but it has disappeared, revealing that it had been lashed to a cross, thereby evoking the martyrdom of a Christ figure. Piquera explained to me that the figure represents the fact that many people die in search of liberty. As in the other artwork, the projected identity revolves around the narrative of an impeded search for liberty, and it also resonates with a traditional Cuban political theme of death or martyrdom for a cause. The words on the logo are mostly in English, and this may have meant that the logo was aimed at having the military and civilian camp workers understand the balseros' sacrifices. The most common logos contained a raft with a shark coming out of it, oars, and Cuban and American flags, and appeared on things like T-shirts and tattoos.

Another art form that was popular in the camps was carving. People made carvings and sculptures out of both found wood and melted plastic. The wood, often two-toned, was freely available from the bulldozing of

Piquera logo, Camp Alpha.

shrubbery that the military had done to prepare the ground for the camps. Carving tools had to be obtained through World Relief or the military and were kept in safe, centralized locations. People melted the thick MRE (Meals Ready to Eat) bags into molten balls, which were easy to carve. People who had not tried any kind of artwork before found themselves making impressive carvings, which they often displayed outside their tents. As with everything else, there were common forms and themes in most of the carvings. The ones that appeared most often were sharks and other images that suggested rescue at sea and the stretched human figures common in Caribbean sculpture. People also made carvings that referenced incarceration by using carved DMPITS bracelets or razor wire dipped in plastic. The balseros also made carvings of Fidel Castro as the devil on a fairly regular basis.

One of the interviewees, Roberto, carved a wooden self-portrait while he spent time in the tent that World Relief had created for a group of Rastafarians in an area between Camps Echo and Foxtrot. The figure actually did resemble him, but it was bent over to one side. He has a cuff around his neck, which he told me symbolized his feeling that he was in jail in the camps. His mouth is open while his eyes are downcast, suggesting that the figure is in pain. However, the mouth and the way the eyes are set are also somewhat reminiscent of the cowry shells that Santería practitioners use to indicate the orisha Eleggua, who opens paths for people. This could be an accident or an unconscious reference related to his social environment in Cuba. The cuff and the fact that the figure is in shorts are an expression of Roberto's experience after the riots in Panama, when the military roughed him up and made him sit flexicuffed on a pile of rocks for two weeks in Panama's Camp X-Ray in nothing but his underwear. Roberto told me that he had not participated in the riots but had merely been a resident of the camp in which they started, Moreover, he did not relate the story of being imprisoned in X-Ray easily. I had to re-interview him to learn of it after Sylvia told me about the military reprisals following the December 1994 riots. Roberto's carving thus reflected his own experiences even though it also contained a theme common to the group, the idea that the balseros were in jail.

The paintings and drawings provided some of the most poignant indications of what the balseros were feeling, in addition to being statements of identity and illustrations of their story of a search for freedom.

Wooden self-portrait carved by Roberto.

One of the paintings shows two men sitting dejectedly at a table. It is obvious that the men are in despair about their situation. They have taken old inner tubes out of the attic, but one is still not inflated. The entire atmosphere is bleak. The painting is dark, save for some lightened portions in the plaster near each of the men. The refrigerator door is open, revealing nothing inside. One man holds a fan in his hands, a reference to the blackouts, or *apagones*, of the Special Period. This theme is reinforced by the kerosene lamp on the table. On the wall is also a tourist poster that says "Cuba te espera" ("Cuba is waiting for you"). This painting seems to say that the Cuba waiting for you is a depressing one. The men seem to want to fly away, as they have wings on their backs, but the feathers on them have become scarce and are falling off, perhaps from all the waiting or just due to the decrepit state of all things in general.

The artist Reynaldo Gonzalez, explained his concept of the painting:

In September of '94 the government closed the Cuban coast; many stayed behind and couldn't flee. That's why I painted a pair of wings with feathers falling off, it was where they began to suffer from total hopelessness. There was an epic in which a poster was sold in Cuba that said, "Cuba awaits you." It was for tourism, but I wanted to say that it meant that what awaited Cubans who remained behind wasn't going to be easy, and that has been true even now. That painting was selected for the cover of the catalogue "Colors of Liberty, One Year of Artistic Creation," which was made in Guantánamo [to accompany an art show]. The continuation of this series of paintings is *"Los Que Se Quedaron."*

The painting *Los Que Se Quedaron*, in fact, has a similar theme, but focuses more on the wanting and waiting to leave than on the material conditions of life. In it, a young black man is sitting on a sea wall, probably the Malecón in Havana, looking off into the horizon. A transparent clock is barely visible on the horizon, an indication of waiting. On the ground near the wall is a small dog that looks as if it is about to attempt to jump up on the wall, perhaps to join the young man. A bicycle leans against the wall, a reference to the prevalent mode of transportation at the time. The low storm clouds and the choppy seas hint at the underlying emotions.

Malas Noticias by Reynaldo Gonzalez. Courtesy of the artist.

Los Que Se Quedaron by Reynaldo Gonzalez. Courtesy of the artist.

The artist explains:

I dedicated this to those who couldn't leave Cuba for whatever reason. Those Cubans felt like I felt for years. Every time someone I knew or a friend of mine left, I asked myself, "When will I leave?" The years passed and everything stayed the same or got worse, and the time passed very slowly, without hopes or dreams. I felt very limited and in a very critical emotional state. The only way out I saw was to throw myself into the ocean. What Cuban didn't sit on the wall of the Malecón [Havana's sea wall] with a bottle of alcohol looking towards the north, dreaming and asking themselves, "When will it be my turn?" The other question was, "Will I ever get there?" That sad painting, with a gray, stormy sky, [expresses] much loneliness, frustration. The dog represented hunger, the wall the deterioration of a lot of things, etc. The painting is acrylic on linen. I took one of the sheets that they gave us in the camps. I painted so much that sometimes we ran out of canvas.

In addition to being inspired by their feelings about Cuba, their detention, and the passing of time on the base, the balseros were also buoyed by Cuban and Cuban American musicians, actors, and sports figures who visited the bases in Guantánamo and Panama to show their solidarity with the balseros' cause. During 1995, the jazz trumpeter Arturo Sandoval, the pop singer Gloria Estefan and her husband, Emilio, and the actor Andy Garcia, who played conga drums in Estefan's band, all performed for the balseros in Guantánamo. By the time the entertainers went to the base, the camp residents had organized themselves to make reciprocal gestures in the form of artwork and performances.

Arturo Sandoval gave a concert in June. The balseros decorated his stage with many pieces of artwork, and afterward, they put on a peña, a traditional community showcase for local talent, which involved singing and doing satirical skits about Justice Department employees and bureaucrats. Two skits in particular illustrated issues that were salient to the balseros at the time of Sandoval's concert. One satirized the young CRS employee who had read them the statement on the Coast Guard cutter when they arrived on the base. She was actually a college student who was the daughter of one of the permanent CRS employees in the United States and had worked in the camps for two short periods of time. The second skit combined CRS and INS personnel into one person in the form of a man in a wig and black army boots. This was an imitation of Maria T., whose signature look was long blonde hair and tall army boots. She was a beloved and talented social worker who had worked for CRS in both Panama and Guantánamo. The man played an INS officer who was interrogating a balsero in a rude fashion. Since the performances were meant for both the camp residents and Arturo Sandoval, they served as both an outlet for tension and a way to communicate salient elements of camp life to an outsider.

Before their concert, Gloria Estefan and Andy García visited a few camps, including Camp Alpha, where the military had arranged for representatives of the camp to present some carvings to them. At the presentation ceremony, Gloria voiced her solidarity with them for escaping Fidel Castro, further reinforcing the balseros' story of a search for freedom.

In December 1995, the balseros put on two shows for combined Cuban and American audiences. The first one, a fashion show, was performed against a backdrop of a stylized Havana skyline that was straight out of the 1950s. Most of the show consisted of models showing off different humorous pieces of clothing that had been created out of sheets. The balseros included their symbols of their identity at the end by having a staff member from World Relief come out dressed as the Statue of Liberty, while

Arturo Sandoval concert, June 1995.

surrounded by men in guayaberas and black bow ties, again evocative of 1950s club life in Cuba (even though Cuba was also ruled by a dictator at that time).

Another aspect of the show revealed a nascent Cuban American identity: two balseros brought a sheet onstage at the end of the show that had been painted with merged Cuban and American flags, on top of which was written "Proud to Be a Cuban American." The show was in a sense inaugurating that new identity.

The Christmas show combined Cuban culture with American Christmas traditions, which were reflected in the stage backdrop. On a large panel on one side was a snow-covered Christmas tree with gifts under it. The panel in the center left section was painted with the words "Happy New Year." The center panel had the only hint of Cuban culture, with what seemed to be part of the front of a colonial home in Havana with stained glass at the top. A tropical countryside was visible through the door. Next to this was a panel that said, "Merry Christmas," and next to that was a panel with a huge figure of Santa Claus. Although these images are known by many Cubans, especially those with relatives in Miami, they are not as popular in Cuba as they are in the United States. Christmas was not a major holiday period either. In fact, Cubans were not even given a day off from work at the time. The performers danced rumba, played carnival music, and did an elaborate presentation of the dances of the main *orishas* (gods) in Santería, an African-derived religion in the Americas that has a Catholic overlay.

The final stage of the operation took place about a month after the Christmas show, with the last flight of balseros from the rafter crisis leaving on January 31, 1996. Throughout the operation, each person had typically been filled with nervous anxiety as he or she took the final steps off the base, and the balseros had ritualized this action. The night before their flight out of Guantánamo, people slept in a special small camp; the military contributed to the ritualistic feeling by calling it "Villa Feliz," which they translated as Happy Camp. As they left their camps, their friends who were staying behind would squirt them with shaving cream. At 7:30 on the morning of each flight, the ones who were leaving were loaded into blue buses and taken to the ferry landing, where they would wait in an area cordoned off by an orange snow fence. Any workers, whether military or civilian, who wanted to see their friends leave for the United States could go there to see them off. When the McCalla camps had been in operation, a small group of people faithfully gathered each morning on the cliff that overlooked the ferry landing to wave brown MRE bags, white T-shirts, and an American flag as a sendoff.

Augustín wrote the following entries in his diary about this process.

October 9, 1995 (Mon)

It's 9 in the morning, and they still haven't released the list to leave tomorrow, and my anxiety has increased so much that I'm not even hungry. Today I woke up with the sun and last night it didn't rain; I hope it stays like this. Finally, cojones!

At 1:45 pm they release the flight list for Wednesday, for [lottery numbers] 1238 to 1415.

1415–1238 = 197 Numbers [of people] on the list [and thereby the flight].

This is the way we'll go to Villa Feliz tomorrow and on Wednesday we get to liberty! There will be eighty-one people left in the camp for the flight on Thursday. Everyone who is leaving tomorrow is going to "Villa Feliz" and we have to move to Globe 2 (the movie globe), everyone except for [my brother] Pupy and I, because we are going to stay in another tent. A hurricane called Roxana is threatening Puerto Rico and Havana; I hope that it turns to the west and doesn't hit Cuba. In the afternoon, Albert invited us for a toast to say goodbye to us, but I don't go. This is the last night that we are going to spend in camp Golf; tomorrow we go to "Villa Feliz."

Augustín created this drawing that merges the idea of freedom and being detained on the base as the cover of that diary.

Liberty drawing by Augustín.

Over time, World Relief helped the balseros decorate the waiting area at the ferry, which they called Camp Josefina after a Cuban exile woman from Miami; in addition to working as an interviewer on the resettlement team, Josefina was in charge of collecting preliminary information for INS medical parole interviews and then coordinating the process of getting people onto the flights to the United States. She had quickly become a beloved figure for the kindness she showed in the course of doing her job. They fashioned a plywood door to Camp Josefina, and labeled it the "Gateway to Freedom." Eventually they decorated it with a logo that had elements common with other balsero logos: a raft, wings, elements of the Cuban flag, and oars. Above the door was the name "Camp Josefina" and a map of the island of Cuba. The names of the different branches of the armed services were written around the sides, which integrated the military into the idea of getting to freedom.

Toward the end of the operation a group of artists painted a series of murals on pieces of plywood and set them up so that they formed a border along the holding area. Together the murals made a visual depiction of the balseros' story: leaving Cuba, staying in the camps and dealing with uncertainty, and then heading for the United States, represented by the Statue of Liberty. The first panel showed a family with a child leaving on a raft, with a dove behind the woman's head that made it appear as if she had angel wings protecting her. The next panel showed a dark night on stormy seas and a Coast Guard ship. Subsequent panels depicted uncertainty symbolized by question marks in the air, with a caged-in feeling achieved by prominently featured razor wire and ominous shadows of soldiers. The last two panels show the resolution of the situation, with the old environment destroyed and the razor wire turned into confetti as the Americans work together with the Cubans to create upgraded camps, symbolized by the merging of the two flags in the middle. The final one showed a racially diverse group of Cubans happy together in a group, waiting to be carried on the ferry to the airstrip, and then to the land of liberty, symbolized by the Statue of Liberty far in the distance.

By placing the set of murals in front of the holding area and creating a door to the area, the artists forced the groups leaving to cross the threshold out of the camps and walk past their story as they boarded the ferry for the other side of the base. The whole routine was a rite of passage in which they left incarceration behind and went toward a new, Cuban American identity.

Although it was not meant to be artwork, on the very last day of the operation two people with the last numbers in the lottery created a sheet to commemorate the occasion. It read, in English, "End of the 1994–1996 Exodus" down the front and "Guantánamo Bay" down the side. The way people signed it revealed an identity issue that really marked the end of their incarceration. Signing their names on a T-shirt was common during people's last days or weeks on the base, as mementos of the experience. In this case people wrote only their DMPITS numbers on it. They were literally leaving behind the aspect of their identity that was associated with being imprisoned.

6

Resolving A Different Kind of Rafter Crisis

The arrival of the last flight of balseros at the Homestead Air Force Base on January 31, 1996, signaled that the rafter crisis was officially over. The last people to leave the camps were more emotionally and physically exhausted than those who had left on medical parole earlier in the operation. They had made it through a number of traumatic experiences, including the scarcity and repression of the Special Period, the risky rafting trip through the Florida Straits, and the extreme environment and uncertainty involved in their stay in the camps at Guantánamo. This was a recipe for posttraumatic stress disorder (PTSD).[1] After all of that, the resettlement system expected them to dust themselves off, adjust to a new country and economic system, get a job, and become independent within eight months. People who resettled in Miami would also have unexpected, and sometimes hurtful, exchanges with some of the older exiles who considered anyone growing up under the Revolution to be contaminated and were resentful that the balseros had not tried to overthrow Fidel Castro themselves. This was surprising to people who had lived for more than a year with a firm belief that by staying in the camps they were making the sacrifices necessary to achieve freedom. It was also ironic considering that the people criticizing them had themselves fled instead of overthrowing Castro. However, this experience was not universal. Other groups of older exiles welcomed the balseros with open arms and did all they could to help them adjust to their new lives.

Augustín describes in his diary the process of leaving the base and his first days in Miami. He was eventually resettled in a northern state but after a few years made his way back to south Florida.

October 11, 1995 (Wednesday)

I get up at 2:30 and I can't sleep anymore because there were already people bathing and visiting each other. I start to get ready at 5 am they call us to give us breakfast, one little brown box, but neither I nor Pupy [brother] grab one. I'm not hungry because I'm too nervous and I decide to walk around the camp one last time to reflect, and I have to smoke a cigarette. At 6 am they take us to the (DMPITS) office and check our watches; they give us our photos and cut off the watch. We are finally free! They cut off our fetters! We get on the bus for the port, and we arrive at the other side of the bay at 7:10; a little while later we get on another bus to the airport, where we see the plane waiting for us on the runway, a Boeing 727 from Air Miami, with a Florida Marlins logo on the tail. We go directly to the plane and wait in line to get on. At exactly 8:10 we take off from our homeland; we don't know how long it will be before we can stand on it again. The voice of the stewardess says it's flight 290 to Homestead.

In the middle of the flight I take out my camera and we take a photo on the plane and when we see Miami from the air we take another one. Ah! They give us bread with ham and cheese and a Pepsi-Cola on the plane. At 9:30 am we touch down on the land of the free. Before we land the stewardess tells us, "Put on your seatbelts because in a few minutes we will be landing in Havana!" The screams that went up were incredible, and afterwards she said, "No, Homestead!" When we land in Miami they put us on some buses and take us to a room inside of the base, but not without taking our bags to inspect them. In that room they call us one by one to do our paperwork for legal entry into the USA and assign us to a church group [resettlement agency].

We finish at exactly 4:30. After six hours! They take us out of there and put us on a General Motors bus to Miami. It seems like a lie that I could write that but yes, I'm not dreaming. For Miami! Our eyes pop out when we see the spectacle of so many cars on these highways. When we arrive in Miami they take us to a hotel called Travelodge at 1170 NW 11th St., Miami, FL. Tel: (305) 324-0800. At almost midnight they take us to room 302. Ah! When I had just arrived they ran to see me when I was still in the front of hotel; [my friends] Julito and Simón invite me to my first beer in freedom! A Coors Lite. We get to our room on the first floor (air conditioning, two double beds, hot and cold water and color TV with cable).

I feel strange sleeping in a bed for the first time in more than a year. After we bathe, a shower with hot water, ah! Julito takes us out for a drive.

To that thought, the last entry in his journal, he added the following, marked with an asterisk:

* On this day, the 31st of January of 1996 the last flight leaves from the naval base at Gitmo with 125 balseros. The balseros' nightmare is over!

To honor the last flight to Miami, members of the Cuban American community working in the local resettlement agencies prepared a ceremony that was attended by a few former camp workers who lived in the Miami area. The ceremony was delayed for about an hour as soldiers wearing latex gloves went through everyone's luggage to remove prohibited items, which included Cuban flora and fauna. Among other things, they found three dead Cuban finches that had been hidden in toilet paper rolls. When the event finally got under way, it involved resettlement workers and Cuban exile leaders making long, self-congratulatory presentations about who they were and how they had been helping the balseros. The balseros, all from Camp Delta/Charlie, listened politely.

The ceremony did have a few poignant moments, especially one that involved twelve-year-old violinist Lisbet Martinez. Lisbet had taken her violin with her on the raft and played the "Star Spangled Banner" to her Coast Guard rescuers while they were still in the middle of the ocean. This had brought them to tears. Once in the camps, she also serenaded people there. As a minor, she had been able to leave after five months under a parole protocol but had sworn to keep her DMPITS bracelet on until the last balsero left the base. She took the spotlight by playing the "Star Spangled Banner" again, and then extending her wrist for someone to cut off her DMPITS bracelet, ritually formalizing the end of the rafter crisis.

After the ceremony was over, the admissions procedure began. The resettlement agencies distributed stickers with the initials of the agencies to which each person had been assigned, instructing everyone to place them on their shirts. People without sponsors were sent to a few hotels in the seedier sections of Miami, where they would stay for the first two weeks while arrangements were completed for travel to other sections of the country. One of the interviewees suffered a heart attack and had to have surgery during this period, after which he was resettled in a northern state.

Augustín and the others who remained after the medical parole system ended left the base under a lottery system. Although this was an efficient and seemingly fair way to determine the order in which people would leave, it made no special accommodations for families to leave together. Some people were able to change places with other camp members, but others were not. Sylvia was one of the people who could not arrange to leave with her daughter. This was extremely upsetting to her because her daughter was having a difficult pregnancy and had not been able to leave during the medical parole phase of the operation. She describes how she coped with the situation.

I left in December '96. My daughter got one number in the lottery and I got another number, of course. That was something really painful for me. That was one of the things that marked me in Guantánamo. We really were there for a year and a half; we were almost the last ones to leave. There was only one camp after ours, Delta-Charlie. And they were smaller as well. And they were very, very exhausted already, you know that. And we were very, very tense. And our nerves, you felt like you couldn't take it anymore.

So, I left my daughter in those conditions [moving from tent to tent] when she was eight months pregnant, with a very bad pregnancy. She had a very bad pregnancy because she had a sugar level of 440. It was the sugar level ... and she didn't know it. She was constantly vomiting, vomiting, vomiting. She didn't lose hair but she got so skinny she looked like a little noodle. So, I had to leave her in that condition. Apart from that, you know, when I saw myself on that bus, they took me out of the camps the day before, óyeme [long pause, about to cry].

She got there twelve days later. Almost two weeks after me. That wasn't one day or two, it was weeks that I had to leave her alone in there. All alone without knowing. They didn't let us change flights. They let people change, me for example, I got number 400. And my daughter got number 1,800. So, what do you think the change was? It was me for my daughter's number. Understand? Because, what happened? It was a decision that we made between ourselves. Because, each one looks at her conditions, no? We decided that I wouldn't change the turn, no, the number. I wouldn't change it, because it was better for me to get there before she did. Because, I'm going to tell you what happened. I sponsored myself, but there wasn't anybody to sponsor her. So, they had assigned me to stay in Miami, because I had a sponsor in Miami. But we couldn't get a sponsor for her. And they were sending her to Albuquerque.

So, I left first with the mission and with the certainty that when she [knocking on the table] arrived, I would already have gotten her a sponsor, you see. Because if I had stayed there with her, because yes, we had been there for a year and a half already, that to arrive fifteen days later, what was that going to be for me? It was harder for me to leave her than if I had stayed myself. But I came with the mission that I had to get her a sponsor before she arrived [knocking on table] so that they didn't take her to Albuquerque on me.

So it was like that. When she arrived, I had a sponsor for her already. I got a sponsor because what wouldn't a mother get for her daughter? I almost sponsored her myself, *muchacha*, without being able to communicate with her. I didn't know anything about her until the day she got here. I didn't have a way of communicating with her. Well, imagine, it was very bad. It was very bad, and she was alone there. I felt bad that I had to leave; imagine when she told me to go first and she stayed there, that wasn't anything easy, you know. That wasn't anything easy, but well.

When my daughter arrived I had already completed all of the paperwork that one does when one gets here, so she was easier, because we already knew everything, you know. We began to make her arrangements, since she got here pregnant, and she had so little time. So her medical condition was prioritized, and that's where the diabetes came out, and she had to be hospitalized.

Although many of the men would remember Guantánamo with nostalgia, Sylvia's description of the impact of the camps represented many, perhaps the majority, of the women's experiences there.

I think the effect [of being in Guantánamo] wasn't good. It left the mark of something that happened in your life that was very disagreeable. I'm describing that to you right now. You know, the person who arrived in Guantánamo and the person who left Guantánamo wasn't the same in any respect. It left a mark on me, even though I've gone on overcoming it;

at the beginning I couldn't talk about it, and that was the stage in which one is overcoming it. But the mark is still there, in one's memory. It's an experience you don't forget. And I'll tell you sincerely, that I would not like, you know, to repeat an experience like that again in my life, if they told me, "Look, I would like to work like that, as a collective effort." For example, I think that if I were to have been here in Miami or another part of the United States when the exodus happened, I would have been one of the people who would have volunteered to work there because I like that kind of work. Today I tell you that never in my life do I want to see a situation like that again.

I'll give you an example. Every time that I see something like a disaster in El Salvador, at times I catch myself thinking that I can go back into a situation more or less like that, because it's said that when one finds oneself in a situation like that, one develops a series of abilities and capacities that permit one to learn how to adapt under those kinds of situations. I don't doubt that. But, you know, want to know something.... I wouldn't want to see myself having to use those capacities that *supposedly* I developed there by having to have been in a situation like that. Because I wouldn't want to see myself in a situation like that again, even voluntarily, notice? Not even as a volunteer. No, no, no. Not even as a volunteer. That leaves a deep mark, very, very, very deep.

It left a deep mark on my daughter as well because she saw the same things I did. And you know why? Because she was only twenty years old, no more, you know, and she had never been in any kind of situation like that. Nothing like that, understand. She left her house, *pon*, and pretty soon she finds herself in that phenomenon. It was very hard for her, you know. And however it may have been for me, I was forty-four. You know, I was already mature, and I had a different perspective on life, but not her.

Yes, she had had posttraumatic stress disorder. A week after she got here I had to put her in the hospital for a month. She was in the hospital for a month. She had diabetes. Her blood sugar level went up. I had to put her in the hospital for *one month* to control her blood sugar. She still has diabetes. She also had nightmares and flashbacks and everything. So did I.

Children were particularly vulnerable to developing PTSD. A group of psychologists and psychiatrists from the University of Miami did a study to evaluate its prevalence among the Cuban children who had been held in

Guantánamo. It provided disturbing evidence of how traumatic the camps and the rafting journeys had been for the children. The group evaluated eighty-seven children in Miami four and six months after their arrival from the camps and found that the majority experienced moderate to severe symptoms of PTSD. Sixty-seven percent experienced avoidance of reminders of the experience, 64 percent displayed regressive behaviors, 60 percent re-experienced the traumatic events, 52 percent had somatic symptoms, and 51 percent had problems with hyper-arousal.[2]

Although the incidence of PTSD among the adults held in the camps has never been formally studied, the symptoms Sylvia describes reveal a severe case of it. As a psychologist, she had more emotional resources and coping methods to deal with it than others, whose ability to work may have been severely affected.

The first month, my first month in the United States, I lost thirty pounds. I lost a pound a day. I lost a *pound* a day. After I was here for a month. [rapping on table] I was thirty pounds lighter. The diarrhea wouldn't stop. I don't know how long, I can tell you it was diarrhea, diarrhea, diarrhea. I had to live on Pepto-Bismol. If I finished a bottle, I bought another one, prssst, the diarrhea came. No, no, no, no, no, what can I say, what can I say.

My son took me to see a physical therapist. Because when that happened he had already graduated from massage school. And when he examined me, you see I had my whole spinal column out of alignment. . . . I had my hips out of alignment also. So, he took me to the specialist he worked with. When they put me up onto the table to examine me, the first manipulation he did, I wet the bed and went on the bed. Well, you know, he couldn't give me any kind of adjustment. He had to begin with light, infrared light I think it was. He had to begin the first three sessions with infrared light, you know. So later he could little by little, you know, doing the manipulation, giving me the adjustment, relaxation, muscular relaxation and all of that. He says that all my pelvic zone was all, all, all, all backwards. Because many women, we concentrate our stress there, tension in the pelvic region. That's frequent with women. I never noticed. Because I was there for a year and a half, almost two years. And we started there, one day, yes, one day, no. There, there, therapy, therapy, therapy, there, there, there, there, there, there. Imagine people who arrived here and didn't have that service. This spot here on me [pointing to shoulders and neck] was like a rock. My neck, was a rock, I couldn't even touch it.

After six months, one day I sat down and analyzed myself, I was already here in this country for six months, and I horrified myself, I horrified myself. Because after six months I was still having nightmares. I couldn't sleep well. I didn't sleep. I woke up. I would sleep for a while and wake up suddenly. I felt those knocks, and all those noises, all those sounds I heard there, I heard them as if I were, eh, I woke up like that. After six months I did a self-analysis. I said, "My God, I'm never going to get out of this, this is going to stay with me tremendously for my whole life." Yes.

I got destroyed a lot physically in Guantánamo. A lot. You have no idea. Look, when I arrived at Guantánamo I didn't use glasses. I had twenty twenty vision. And when I got here they did a medical check, mmm … a visual check, and I was 275. I was completely blind. Blind. In a year and a half. I became conscious of the blindness after I got here. I couldn't see anything. Nothing, nothing, nothing, nothing. However, in Guantánamo, one day I began to try on glasses that came in the donations, because I felt a certain level of discomfort, no? I found a pair of glasses so I saw better. And I got by with them until I got here. But I thought it was not so, so, so [bad]. Now I'm better; I use contact lenses. And it was like that, you know; a lot of time went by, for example, visual, auditory stimulus, olfactory stimulus, and taste also, yes, yes. How could it not be?

The effects of living in the camps lingered in Sylvia's psyche for years. When I first met her, Sylvia told me that it had only been three weeks since she had been able to speak about Guantánamo without crying and since she had stopped bursting into tears over little things. She still teared up while talking about having to leave her pregnant daughter behind in the camps. This was nearly five years after her arrival in Miami.

Whether or not they had symptoms of PTSD, all the newcomers found themselves in completely novel situations in a market economy to which they had to adjust very quickly. Sylvia continues:

That whole process was a very brusque thing, very accelerated, because everything happened so quickly. I had to begin to learn how to drive and go through that whole process, get my license, buy myself a car, and begin a job quickly. I began to work after being here for one month. I was working by the eighteenth of January. I began working for a private company that did therapy in a nursing home. I was one of the ones who did therapy in different nursing homes. I notice now that it was work that was, mmm, let's say it in these terms, brusque, no? for a person who just got to this country, who hadn't had any orientation.

I was very disoriented. And it was the first time I had driven ... now I see the streets as normal. But notice that what is a street here is an avenue in Cuba. You've been in Cuba. The expressways, you don't see them in Cuba like that. The streets are very wide in Cuba and all that, no? There isn't this volume of vehicles in the street. Or, that speed, muchacha, right? Imagine, the maximum speed limit in Cuba is the minimum here. That's what I saw, the minimum here [knocking on table] is the maximum speed in Cuba! Yes, yes, yes.

When you get here, the cars here seem like missiles [laughs]. You know, they seem like missiles, and the cleanliness, the amplitude, because Cuba is like a new little shell. Here you see everything big. When you arrive it seems to you like you're never, never, never going to be able to get away from it. I saw Miami, and for me it was as if it was the whole world, vaya, you know. Because when a person has been, in this case I had lived in Cuba and I had never left Cuba, eh, it doesn't make any sense, you don't have ... that amplitude, you don't have that.

The first time I went to Publix [supermarket] it didn't do anything to me, I felt normal, it was if I had lived here all my life, don't you know? It never gave me a headache or gave me. On the contrary, I loved to go, I loved to go. I didn't have any trouble deciding what clothes to buy either, and I'm going to explain why.

Look, when I got here, I was, how can I tell you, I thought a lot, you know. I managed my money very well. Look, from the beginning, I'm going to tell you this. To me everything that, I'll tell you like this, the rags that they gave me in Guantánamo, I could tell that everything they gave me was from the Dollar Store, you know. But, well, that was what they gave me, and that was what I knew. And I was fine with that. You understand, I didn't have any problem using it. With the help they gave me, and everything, I invested everything in concrete things. The people would go to the stores to buy clothes and buy baskets of things, not me. I came with my underwear from the Dollar Store, and I continued with the underwear from the Dollar Store, you know. Some very small little things that the people gave me, but don't think they were big things. I brought everything they gave me in Guantánamo with me, the shampoo, the deodorant, the powder, the sheets, the blankets, I brought everything, everything they gave me. Because I heard a lot from the counselors that went there to advise us about the United States, they told us, "Don't throw away anything, take everything all of these things there, because the beginning is very hard, and those things are money that you don't have to spend. Afterward, little by little you will go along buying things according to your taste, and your budget." No?

That's what I did. So, look, I got the money, first of all what I did was revalidate my degree, in other words, to make my degree be accepted on the same level as a US degree. Immediately afterward what I did was, well, of course, was pay for my things, for example, to pass the theoretical exam. I had to pay for it; we had to pay for all of those steps. So I paid for all of those things from the assistance that they gave me.

My son already had been here for a year and a half. At the same time we were in Guantánamo, he was here. He wasn't doing really well, really, really, but he already had a little car, a little pickup, and only two people fit in the cabin in the front and all of us got in behind. So, we got by like that, we went all over like that. He already had rented a four-room apartment with two bathrooms, and we lived together there like gypsies, you know. All of us together inside of that apartment.

So, the other part of the money, I got together, of course that wasn't in a month or anything, no? The first little car was a loan that broke down, it was transportation, it broke down all over the place, whatever. The first car that I bought myself cost $300, I tell everyone the same thing—$300, that little $300 car, stopping at every corner, and spewing fumes all over. It was like that until I could buy a $650 car; I had that car for a year. I had to get rid of it because they crashed into it from behind, and it was a total loss.

They destroyed it. It was a Dodge, an '84 whatever. But with that little car I ... and a car comes up behind and *fuácata*. It crashed into me. That little car went for like a year. In other words, I, you know, I economized a lot. Yes, that craziness of buying and buying, no, not me, you know, not me. I didn't get into that, thank God.

One of the valuable things about Sylvia's story is that she uses comparison with her own story to shed light on other people's experiences. In my conversations with the balseros in Miami, many of them talked about their difficulty coping with the material abundance and the materialism in the United States. Many people did not manage their money well on first arrival, going on buying sprees with the small amount of money they were given for subsistence during their first few months in the country (this assistance had some of them writing to their friends back in the camps that the United States was like "Comunismo con cosas," or "Communism with things"). Others mentioned being overwhelmed by all the choices in the stores. Some also talked about having difficulty accepting the fact that a lot of social status is conferred on people merely for the number of possessions they can accumulate. Most were also overwhelmed by the physical differences between the two countries. Like the other interviewees, Sylvia talked about the speed of the cars. Others spoke about the brightness of the street lights, and how at first they felt intimidated by the sounds of sirens at night.

According to a group of former colleagues who worked for Catholic Community Services in Miami doing resettlement work after their job in Guantánamo was over, the newcomers found that adjusting to capitalist labor markets was also a big shock. Some of the balseros found completely overwhelming the idea of having to look for a job instead of being assigned one, and for that reason they missed interview appointments. Others had been used to passively rebelling against authority by not showing up for work, and they had problems when they repeated that behavior in a new context. Because of these kinds of issues, Cubans in general face their own set of challenges in adapting to the United States, and the balseros in particular had these kinds of troubles compounded by high levels of long-term stress and trauma.[3]

People also reported another experience related to the oppression they had escaped in Cuba, which one interviewee called "the dream." Fernando told me that he had had a particular dream about Cuba, and that whenever he had asked his friends from the camps if they had had a similar one they had all responded affirmatively. When I asked others about it, most of them indeed had also had "the dream." The basic story line was that the person goes back to visit Cuba and is happy and comfortable visiting family and friends. He or she knows that it is a visit only, and not a return for good. However, when the time comes to leave for the United States, the person is prevented from leaving, usually by the government, on the grounds that it would be illegal to leave the country, or because the person has already left the country illegally. So, the person becomes stuck in Cuba, unable to leave.

Although this originally seemed to be another indication of how much the balseros had internalized oppression, when I asked Augustín whether he had had the dream, he vaguely told me yes, but then went on in detail to describe how the Cuban State Security had indeed interrogated him for hours the first time he returned to Cuba. Although he was released, he told me that he had felt intimidated and had feared that he would not be allowed to leave the country. Thus, while the oppression has indeed been internalized, there was actually a continuing basis in reality for at least part of the balseros' fears. It also reminds us that the camps and the Florida Straits were not the only sources of trauma in the balseros' journeys. Although many balseros, such as Marcos, had been sent to jail for openly opposing the government in one way or another, others had lived in fear of being caught merely for disagreeing with the Revolution.

While many people had difficulties adjusting to their new country because of after-effects of trauma, others, mostly men, felt nostalgic about the social solidarity and personal growth they experienced on the base, and their memories of those things were much more prominent than the more difficult aspects of being held there. This was particularly true for many of the men who had lived in all-male camps such as Camp Golf, which had consistently been run by kind military commanders, even before Admiral Haskins arrived on the base. These men had derived a great deal of strength and inspiration from their shared purpose, finding freedom, so the question arose of how their shared story of a search for freedom fared once they were resettled in Miami. During the interviews, many people talked about the importance of knowing why they were here, and a few voiced the opinion that people who were having trouble adjusting to their new lives had forgotten why they were here. Could they have been implying that the Cubans had forgotten the story that had come together in the camps? Raul describes what seemed to have been a process of internalizing the conversations the balseros had among themselves in the camps.

So, like I was saying in the beginning, I believe that on a personal level it was an accomplishment, because after a year in Guantánamo, everyone who made it here knew why they came, what they were coming to in this country, what they wanted. One learned how to respect his fellow beings, to respect the surroundings, and that isn't achieved in a week, that isn't achieved in a month.

He made this comment during a longer conversation about the consequences of having lived in a society that seemed to be degenerating and the psychological effects of discovering that, once in the camps, they were no longer oppressed. But Raul generally noted how people began to think differently after they had been in the camps for a while, and that this had a positive impact on their adjustment to life in the United States. The implication that they *had* to have stayed in the camps for some length of time to accomplish this was a bit extreme, but it points to his belief that the process he described usually takes some time to develop. He may also have meant that many balseros felt such joy even in the limited freedom they had in the camps that those positive feelings became associated with the place.

In describing the existential angst he was experiencing at the time, Roberto also mentioned this topic right after he talked about his disillusionment with his life in the United States. Whereas Roberto could get by in Havana being what Cubans call a *jinetero* (a Cuban who has sex or other types of trade with tourists), in Miami he had to become part of the formal economy. This would have been a huge adjustment for anyone, let alone someone with his low literacy level and no experience in a capitalist economy. However, based on what I observed and was told during my fieldwork in Miami, his feelings were not unique.

One comes from Cuba, one thinks that the idea is to get here and enjoy everything. Let's go dance, let's eat, let's drink. And yes you can do that here, you can do that, but within limits. Because you have to work, so that's the part we didn't understand in Cuba. So here we see the part we didn't have. It's a total contradiction, understand. Because they look a lot alike. In Cuba one aspect was that you had more fun. You had more fun, no? Eh, you didn't have that weight on your shoulders, that you have to pay the rent, things like that that you have to pay for, the water, the lights, the electricity, whatever. And, it was easier, it was easier, you understand, life. Because when you are having fun you forget everything. Even if there's no food.

It's true. It's true because everyone has subsisted on that, right, all those years people who live in Cuba. So, here it's different, right? Here, yes you can subsist, you can have food, you can have a new car if you want, you can have a house made of … what you want. The material things here, yes it's easy, because you get it yourself, for your own benefit, with your own hands, by what you can do, understand? But enough already. This is a country of work, eat, sleep, get old, retire, and then begin to live. That's the truth, understand. Yes, I believe it, I say it, and I sustain it. I don't know what I'm doing here, I don't know. I don't know what I'm doing here. Me, I don't want to go back to Cuba … because I don't want to, understand. But I want to know other things. This isn't what I thought it was going to be and it wasn't what I was looking for. I have to keep looking.

While many people seem to have had similar feelings, at least initially, I suspect that the less educated people who had more difficulty finding work that paid a living wage were more likely to have felt this kind of culture shock in their first months and years in the United States. In addition to the difficulties Roberto describes, Augustín voiced another source of unease, which he called *la añoranza*, the longing to see friends and family, which is common among all immigrants. Augustín was missing his family terribly when I interviewed him five years after his arrival.

At the time, he was obviously sad about not having been able to return to Cuba to see his father before he died of cancer (he died before Augustín was legally eligible to revisit the island), and he talked at length about his daughters and how he longed to see them. Augustin was also one of two balseros I interviewed outside Miami—in his case, Lancaster, Pennsylvania. In typical fashion, within two years of the interview he made his way back to Florida and had been successful in getting one of his daughters out of Cuba. His longing for home and family was somewhat alleviated by being with one of his daughters and living among his compatriots in south Florida. Eventually he was able to get both of his daughters and even his ex-wife into the United States.

Aside from the predictable adjustment issues, many of the balseros who resettled in the Cuban enclave in Miami had another issue to face. Some of the older members of the exile community aggressively asserted an idea about who the balseros were and why they left Cuba that was in direct conflict with the balseros' idea of who they were and why they had left. Nearly everyone I interviewed, and many more with whom I interacted, made reference to confrontations with older exiles who asked why, if they had really been so unhappy under Fidel Castro, they had not overthrown him themselves.[4] Some of the confrontations ended on a friendly note and some did not. This fact came out in interesting ways in the balseros' narratives. When they were talking about their lives in Cuba or Miami, some of them suddenly seemed to feel that they had to defend their passivity toward the Revolution or their reasons for escaping the island. I also thought that two other interviewees consciously set out to portray all aspects of life in Cuba as negative, to the point that it dominated their stories about their lives in Cuba, and I surmised that this was related to the fact that they had lived solely among the older exiles.

A piece of Miguel life narrative illustrates this point. While he was talking about how he chose to study medicine and his feelings about compulsory military service, he suddenly veered off into a justification of why he did not try to do anything to bring down the government. He had been discussing how he served in the military before attending the University of Havana, and the fact that people who refused military service were not allowed to attend college at all. While he was talking about all of that, it seemed as if the conversation he had had with older exiles began to intrude into his thoughts, and that this produced a need to talk about why he did not take part in protests against the government.

So, then, people behave, people go with the wave. I went with the wave. You have to, if you want to survive. If you have goals, if you want to be somebody, if you want to have a profession, if you want to have a family, children, to be somebody, then you have to follow the rules. You don't have to say anything, you don't have to say "Viva Fidel," you don't have to say that, just keep going. "Why do we have to do this?" Just do it. Because you don't know how long you have to be there [in the country]. And your life is going to be miserable if you don't do it.

Even the exiles, the exiles they see things differently; they don't see things the same way. They say, "If you don't like Castro, why didn't you fight against him?" That's not easy. We don't have any organizations, we don't have weapons, we don't have anything to fight against Castro.

Miguel reported that he would not discuss politics with the exiles because of the kinds of accusations they had leveled against him. By the way he excluded himself when he referred to "the exiles" it was clear that he did not identify with them at all. The truth was that Miguel had left Cuba because of an incident that occurred when he was finishing medical school. He had been one of seven students who refused to be assigned to the army. Thus, he had indeed protested against the system, and he knew his career would be destroyed because of it, so he left. Instead of validating his experiences, which would have been healing for both sides, the exiles seemed to imply that the balseros' motives for escaping to Miami were impure or strictly financial, which, to them, was not a valid reason for leaving the country. Similarly, when Roberto discussed the reasons he left Cuba, which were obviously economic, he suddenly seemed to be reacting to dialogue he had had with older exiles in Hialeah, a blue-collar city next to Miami that is home to another Cuban enclave.

Roberto seems to plead for some compassion for those who left due to the deprivations of the Special Period:

> That thing with the food is bad, but if one doesn't eat, one can't live, or think, or walk, or anything. Food is something important to the human being, no? Nutrition. So, sometimes you say to somebody, "No, we left because of the food," don't criticize that, because it's doesn't look bad, it doesn't look bad. Human nutrition is an important thing. If you say it because you live here, it's bad. Because stop eating and see how you feel. Understand, as much as you fault the political or the economic system, whatever form, human beings always try to look for the best. Where you feel better, where you feel ... where you feel yourself. Because, you have, if it's your country, you were born there, because, "why don't you overthrow Fidel?" It's that it's not like that. It's not about overthrowing Fidel, understand? Because you don't think about it like that, you don't do it like that, understand?

It is obvious that Roberto had had a confrontation similar to David's in which he had been accused of not doing anything to get rid of Castro. At the end of the interview, Roberto told me that he had had a number of arguments with his neighbors about why the balseros had left the country instead of overthrowing Fidel, and for being an "económico." The pre-Mariel exiles were negating the balseros' identity as a group of people in search of liberty, which had served them so well in coping with life in the camps.

Since the first waves of exiles in fact had done the same thing—escape the Revolution rather than stay and overthrow it—they were actually projecting their own guilt and unacknowledged trauma onto the balseros, who, having had their own trauma to contend with, were in an emotionally vulnerable state. When I discussed this with Sylvia, she told me that she thought that emotions and politics were overly intertwined in the Miami community, and because of that many of the older exiles had not grown emotionally over the years. In her view as a psychologist, they had focused so much on the political reasons for their own pain instead of dealing with impacts of their own exile trauma that they had not healed. In other words, the members of the community expressing aggression toward the balseros had not experienced posttraumatic growth. Sylvia had taken it upon herself to convince her elderly neighbors, who were still talking about going back to Cuba to recover the property that had been confiscated early in the Revolution, that they should not keep their lives on hold. She told them that even if they got it back the next day, they were already too old and unhealthy to become farmers again. She reported that as a result of those conversations, they started focusing more on the present, which, she felt, was evident in the fact that they had started taking better care of their apartment.

Sylvia's efforts to assist her neighbors in accepting the permanence of their exile reflected a common sentiment among the balseros as a group. Rather than obsess on Cuba, Fidel Castro, and when they would be able to return to their old homes, the balseros focused on creating new lives for themselves in the United States and remaining in communication with their relatives on the island. Most of the people I interviewed or spoke with were also pointedly apolitical.

The balseros were soon subsumed by an influx of people who immigrated under the lottery system created to resolve the rafter crisis. After the end of the rafter crisis in 1996, the Cuban government held three national visa lotteries under the Special Cuban Migration Program, known as *el bombo* (the lottery) on the island, to determine who would be allowed to apply for one of the allotted visas at two-year intervals, 1994, 1996, and 1998. Cubans eligible for the program had to be between eighteen and fifty-five years of age and be able to answer "yes" to two of the following questions: "Have you completed secondary school or higher level of education? Do you have at least three years of work experience? Do you have any relatives residing in the United States?" People who were selected in the lottery were given parole status and a visa good for six months, and they could be accompanied by spouses and minor children. In 1994, 189,000 registrants qualified. The number increased to 433,000 in 1996 and 541,000 in 1998. Since the actual number of visas reserved for this group was far lower than the numbers who qualified for admission, Cubans who could legally obtain visas under the 1998 lottery were still being admitted to the country in 2009, even though the United States Interests Section had formally suspended the program two years before that.[5]

Since the May 2 1995 accords mandated that people interdicted at sea be sent back to Cuba, or at best sent to Guantánamo while the government investigated their asylum claims, most Cubans have been arriving clandestinely, paying smugglers with speedboats to take them to Miami instead of attempting to cross on rafts, or hiring smugglers to take them to the Mexican border. By 2015 a new tactic had emerged in which thousands of Cubans flew to Central America and then attempted to make their way through Mexico from there. These new tactics are the result of the "wet foot, dry foot" policy that developed out of the rafter crisis. Under this policy, the United States still admits Cubans if they make it to dry land, but returns them to Cuba if they are intercepted with even one foot still in the water.[6]

Like the Cubans in the Mariel Boatlift before them, in the end the balseros were thankful to have been admitted to the United States and adjusted to their new country. Most became productive citizens, with or without PTSD. They certainly were less controversial as a group than the Marielitos had been, but this has meant that the stories of their journeys have not been widely told, despite the fact that they were held in what later became one of the world's most infamous prison camps.

In looking back on his time in Guantánamo, Miguel remembered another impact of being held on the base:

> I can say that we all changed. I can say that we knew the American culture, we knew how to treat the American people, and we knew how the American people treat other people. And we all changed I think. Cubans talk loud, they gesticulate a lot. And you found a very quiet, smooth, nice American big, tall guy. And you changed a little bit. You know you don't have to talk loud, you lower the volume. You don't have to gesticulate. And then you got here and you knew already how you had to behave and then you start taking care of your own things, and you change.

Pancho evaluated his experiences on the base in a manner similar to the way Mario did:

> For me, it was a very interesting fifteen months, a story, a nice experience. I had nice experiences there, and that's what one has for history, to tell the story. That's really beautiful. I had nice experiences like you, learning things, to be able to get through all those problems, and to learn the American system. To get to know the American military also, how they worked, how they functioned, understand. So, I don't know, living among so many different kinds of people, that's really beautiful, understand. And trying to reach an agreement to get along, that was really beautiful. It was really interesting to feel united, with a purpose. Our proposal was to arrive to this country, it was our dream, to arrive to this country, understand, to be free.

As a woman, Maria's more terse statement about her relatively more brief stay on the base suggests she was less sanguine about her experience than her male compatriots.

> [Being held in Guantánamo] was a sacrifice that was worth it. And I wasn't there that long. We left after four months on medical parole because my husband Fernando had prostate cancer.

As with the Marielitos, after varying periods of adjustment to the new culture and economic system, and recovery from their experiences on sea and at the base, the balseros as a group were indeed happy. In the words of Fernando: "I feel super happy in this country. The United States is my second country. I will defend this country. . . . I love the United States as much as I love Cuba."

Epilogue

The Cuban rafter crisis was one consequence of tensions between the U.S. and Cuba that stubbornly persisted until well after the Cold War was over. In fact, the relationship between the two countries did not improve appreciably with the end of the rafter crisis, and in the five years after the balseros arrived in the United States, Cuba and the exile community were often in the news. Shortly after the last flight of Cubans from Guantánamo landed at the Homestead Airforce Base outside of Miami on January 31, 1996, the Cuban government shot down a plane flown by members of the exile group Brothers to the Rescue after it ignored warnings not to fly into Cuban airspace. Congress responded by passing the Helms-Burton Act, also known as the Cuban Liberty and Democratic Solidarity [Libertad] Act* which President Clinton quickly signed. The law codified the embargo, making it impossible for subsequent presidents to remove it through executive order. Even worse, both the legislative and executive branches would have to be in agreement to repeal the law and the Cuban American Congressional delegation remained strong enough politically to derail all attempts to do so. Ironically, even though President Clinton tightened the embargo during the rafter crisis and then signed the Helms Burton Act after it was over, a major crack developed in it at the end of his administration. In 2000, farm groups and agribusiness interests successfully lobbied for the enactment of the Trade Sanctions and Export Enhancement Act, which allowed companies to export agricultural commodities, food and medical products to Cuba. Even though the law did not allow Cuba to procure international loans to obtain those items, since that time U.S. firms have been able to export millions of dollars of worth of goods to the island each year.[1]

* PUBLIC LAW 104-114—MAR. 12, 1996

Unfortunately, the next president, George W. Bush, ushered in a darker era for U.S.- Cuba relations. He adopted a series of measures to tighten the embargo, including further restricting travel and severely limiting the amount of remittances Cuban Americans were allowed to send to the island.[2] These new policies created a great deal of consternation in the Cuban American community, partly because they made it difficult or impossible to make emergency visits to sick or dying family members on the island. Clearly, then, the embargo has been damaging to Cubans on both sides of the Florida Straits. Regardless of who has been president, the embargo has made it difficult for Cuban exiles to reunite with and send remittances to their relatives, has further impoverished the population on the island, and has encouraged irregular departures from Cuba through shark-infested waters. It also helped set the stage for the rafter crisis.

While the embargo exacerbated the economic conditions on the island that eventually led to mass exodus, politicians in the United States did not anticipate one aspect of the human element involved in the rafter crisis that eventually had a great impact on its trajectory. As stressful as the camps in Guantánamo (and Panama) were, the balseros' identity was so firmly rooted in their search for freedom that the vast majority of them were determined to stick it out on the base no matter how many times they were told that they would have to go back to Havana to apply for asylum. This determination and the strong sense of social solidarity among the balseros are two things they will remember for the rest of their lives, along with the creativity inherent in the camp culture that developed on the base.

Trauma theory suggests that the creative activity in the camps was partly driven by psychological imperatives related to recovery from trauma, particularly those involved in reworking prior meaning systems. It also helps explain why new cultural features emerged in the Cuban camps. If culture can be considered to be a shared system of meanings, when groups of people undergo traumatic experiences together, the new meaning systems, interior dialogues, and daily routines that develop in those social contexts come together to drive the development of distinct cultural forms. In this case, social and individual experiences of trauma, along with an unbottling of self-censorship particular to the Cuban experience, created a collective need for self- expression as a vehicle for meaning making in the camps.

Those who were forced to spend many months on the base also had a lot of time to think about where they had come from, compare the way they were thinking with the way they saw the camp workers (Americans) expressing themselves, and then re-interpret their own culture using this new information. This suggests that the people who were held in the camps for an extended period of time experienced a cultural shift. A man in Camp Alpha who told me that Guantánamo had been a decompression chamber and Juan and Raul's description of learning that they had free speech but had to respect each other both hint at this. At the very least, the balseros were bearers of both Cuban and the camp culture, which means that they arrived in the United States with understandings that prior groups of émigrés did not. This kind of thing probably also happens in areas such as the Mexican border when people stay in border towns for long periods of time before making it to the United States, as well as in other refugee-camp situations, but further research is needed on this issue.

Trauma was the elephant in the room among the exiles living in Miami at the time of the rafter crisis. Apart from one study on the incidence of PTSD among the children held at Guantánamo, we do not know much about trauma among adult Cuban exiles. We do not know what the prevalence of PTSD is among the older generations who fled during the early days of the Cuban Revolution, or how it has affected their lives. Moreover, some community leaders, and even academics, have tended to deny the extent to which unresolved trauma helped shape both the private and public spheres in Cuban Miami.

An incident that occurred in Miami five years after the rafter crisis ended revealed that many of these old traumas were still boiling just under the surface. On Thanksgiving Day in 2000, a five-year-old boy, Elián Gonzalez, was found floating alone on a raft near Miami. After it became apparent that his mother and step-father had perished during a rafting journey across the Florida Straits, a custody battle ensued. The boy was initially sent to stay with relatives who refused to turn him over to his father when they found out he that did not want to leave Cuba. This caused a standoff between the Justice Department and the community that lasted for weeks. During that time, hundreds of people would gather in front of the family's house in Little Havana, among them some of the balseros, and thousands of people on the island staged mass protests in response. The Miami exiles' behavior seemed hysterical and irrational to a nation watching the drama unfold on the nightly news, causing horror instead of sympathy throughout the country. When the Justice Department finally spirited the boy out of the house and returned him to his father, the community suffered a huge public relations defeat. Afterward, exile leaders had to tone down their rhetoric, at least at the national level.[3]

The significance of the Elián episode was not limited to public relations or politics. Based on the stories I was told about what some people felt as they gathered outside of the "Elián house," the situation provoked flashbacks to the traumas involved in their process of exile, lancing some old wounds. One woman told me that as she was standing in front of the house yelling she had a vivid memory from the Mariel Boatlift. She had been ten years old when the Boatlift occurred, and her mother had loaded her onto a bus headed for the Peruvian embassy. The bus had been designated for women and children only but as it was en route to the embassy a group of men tried to climb in through the windows. Ana remembered that her mother had grabbed a soda bottle, broken it, and began stabbing the men in their arms to force them to let go. She ended the story by exclaiming, "it was right there that I realized that my mother would kill for me." Although she was a happy thirty-year-old professional, who did not normally get involved in politics and would never have considered herself a traumatized individual, Ana somehow felt compelled to stand in front of that house and scream along with her fellow exiles, and had had a cathartic experience as a result. These are the kinds of stories that are not well-known outside of Miami. A thawing of relations between the two countries would create opportunities for healing a myriad of wounds created by separation, exile and transnational family hostility.

In fact, over time, enthusiasm for continuing the hostilities that the trade embargo exemplifies has waned among everyone but the staunchest of the hardliners. By early 2015, this provided a political opening for President Barack Obama to begin the process of dismantling the embargo piece by piece through a series of executive orders aimed at making it irrelevant. With the goal of reestablishing commercial and diplomatic relations between the two countries, he began by relaxing travel restrictions and quadrupling the amount of money Cuban Americans could send to the island each month. These efforts culminated with Cuba being removed from the list of state sponsors of terrorism, and the renewal of diplomatic relations between the two countries, which were officially reestablished on July 20, 2015, and followed by the first visit by a US president to the island in 88 years in late March of 2016.[4]

While President Obama's actions heartened those frustrated with the decades-long standoff between the U.S. and Cuba, the country also needs to face some serious issues related to the uses of the Navy base at Guantánamo Bay. Specifically, how does the nontraditional use of the base as an extraterritorial detention center align with the basic precepts on which the United States was founded? Why does a country that holds itself up as a worldwide beacon for human rights and the rule of law continue to insist on taking advantage of the base's liminal situation to deny due process rights to asylum seekers and to evade Geneva Conventions standards for the treatment of prisoners?

In the fall of 1995, during the last few months of the balseros' stay on the base, members of the military started to talk about Guantánamo as the new Ellis Island. This suggested that the government intended to continue to send migrants, refugees, and other inconvenient populations to the base. Since the rafter crisis ended in 1996, the government has housed an average of 30 Cubans at Guantánamo while it investigates their asylum claims,[5] but it has also shown a willingness to send other groups of refugees and migrants there. In late 1996, the U.S. Coast Guard picked up two groups of Chinese migrants and took them to the base for a brief period before denying them asylum. Since then, Chinese migrants have largely found alternate routes to the United States.[6] A few years later, in the spring of 1999, the U.S. began erecting another tent city in preparation for 20,000 refugees from Kosovo, drawing immediate protests from many quarters. The plan was quickly scrapped. In 2007, the Bush Administration, worried about another mass migration after Fidel Castro became seriously ill, signaled the government's continued willingness to house large numbers of Cubans (and Haitians) on the base by awarding a $16.5 million contract to build an "immigrant reception center" to house up to 10,000 Cubans.[7]

The use of the base for legally- and politically-inconvenient populations took a decidedly darker turn after the September 11, 2001 terrorist attacks. On January 11, 2002, with the arrival of the first prisoners who had been labeled illegal "enemy combatants," the U.S. moved from using the base as an extraterritorial immigration detention center to deploying it as an extraterritorial prison camp. The two types of operations were connected in a number of ways. First, the military retained the naming scheme for the camps: Camps X-Ray, Delta, Echo, etc. Camp X-Ray had been the prison section of the camps for the balseros, and then it became the first prison erected for the "unlawful combatants." Like the balseros, they were to be held indefinitely. Unlike the balseros, the Bush Administration did not change its mind about that fact. Second, a legal precedent for denying the prisoners their rights on the base had been established during the rafter crisis, in a January 1995 ruling by the United States Court of Appeals for the 11th Circuit, which stated that constitutional rights "bind the government only when the refugees are at or within the borders of the United States."[8] While the "unlawful combatants" were not refugees, this was a precedent for declaring that all people held outside of its borders could be denied the constitutional rights enjoyed by people on U.S. soil. The prisoners subsequently made various legal claims challenging the conditions in which they were held, and asserting their right to challenge their detention in court. Substantiated claims of abuse, torture and other human rights violations have caused people around the world to associate the naval base at Guantánamo Bay with human rights violations, which has greatly stained the country's reputation.[9]

As a candidate for president, Barack Obama made a campaign promise to close the prison camps in Guantánamo. Although he attempted to fulfil that pledge soon after he became President, he encountered surprisingly vehement opposition in Congress and would not press the issue again until near the end of his term, when negotiations over the thaw in relations between the two countries were underway. Over time, it became evident that the cases against the vast majority of prisoners were flimsy or non-existent, and they began to be released back to their homes or to third countries, although many remained behind due to a variety of legal difficulties. However, difficulties including where to house the few prisoners deemed too dangerous to release, present continuing political problems.[10] They will make closing the prison a complicated endeavor unless Congress suddenly summons the political will to confront these issues in a productive way. The fact that there even is a controversy around using the base as a prison camp reflects the extent to which the notion that the base can or should be used to skirt international law has become entrenched in the U.S. political system. As long as the U.S. continues to operate a military base that is so easily repurposed as an extraterritorial detention center, future presidents will certainly continue to succumb to the temptation to send politically-inconvenient populations there.

One of my main motivations for documenting the camps and the balseros' admirable resilience was to highlight the human costs of the tensions between the U.S. and Cuba, and, more specifically of using the base as an extraterritorial immigration center. President Clinton's decision to send people fleeing extremely difficult conditions in their country to camps in Guantánamo had a high human cost in addition to huge monetary one. Additionally, holding tens of thousands of people who were only following historical migration patterns in indefinite detention for more than eight and a half months, while blaming them for being "illegal migrants," was inhumane at best. The fact that the people held in the camps did not have consistent experiences with the military, with some being traumatized by abuse while others were extremely comforted by a level of kindness that was far above and beyond the call of duty should be unacceptable. Worse, the INS never disciplined any of its officers for the amount of verbal abuse that a few of them meted out to people whose only crime was launching themselves into the middle of the ocean in search of freedom. Instead it returned to Washington D.C. the only Officer in Charge who actually cared whether or not his personnel were abusive on some absurd, trumped-up charges of fraternization.

By recounting the balseros' stories, particularly by letting them tell much of their stories in their own voices, I hope to have sensitized people to the trauma inherent in these types of operations, particularly since no government official involved has ever publicly expressed any kind of remorse for traumatizing tens of thousands of people by holding them in indefinite detention in difficult conditions, for reasons related to political expediency rather than compassion.

I have not even broached the story of the Haitians in Guantánamo, who were never provided with the type of material conditions or political consideration the Cubans were. Perhaps the worst part of that story involves how the U.S. government somehow saw fit to drop off unaccompanied minors in Port Au Prince without even attempting to find their parents. The story of how some of those children became street urchins in the poorest country in the hemisphere would break anyone's heart, but that will have to be fleshed out in more depth at another time. The fact that immigration officials continue to refer to these types of operations, which are really extraterritorial immigration detention centers, as "safe havens" adds insult to injury for both Cubans and Haitians alike.

With its more recent infamy as the site of abuse and torture of so-called terrorist suspects rounded up in the wake of the September 11, 2001 attacks, the naval station in Guantánamo has become an albatross around the country's neck. When the entire value of the base is reduced to the fact that it is easier to deny inconvenient populations legal rights there due to its extraterritorial nature, it is time for the country to take a long, hard look in the mirror. Any modern relationship with the island would automatically involve returning the base to sovereign Cuba, just as any modern respect for human rights would automatically preclude holding future groups of people fleeing terrible conditions in circumstances that preclude their ability to assert those rights in a legal system that adheres to common rules of international law.

Appendix: The Interviews

Compared with the general population of Cuba, the balseros were over-represented by people under thirty, men, professionals, and residents of Havana. Women comprised 27 percent of the total population held on the base and usually traveled with a male partner or relative.[1] Helping to produce this demographic were a number of factors, including the restrictions of Cuba's political economy and the daring nature of embarking on a dangerous journey in the Florida Straits on rafts constructed out of everyday objects such as Styrofoam and inner tubes, a risk that younger men would be more willing to take. As Havana is the cultural, political, and economic center of Cuba, it was no coincidence that Havana was the location of the riots that sparked the exodus and the source of more balseros than other parts of the island, and that a majority of the balseros were young men.

The population of balseros had undergone trauma, and this also influenced my ability to interview them, since even years after the crisis many people did not want to think about their raft journeys or their stay on the base. To obtain my pool of interviewees, I did a snowball sample (where one interviewee suggests another person who would be willing to be interviewed) and networked in the community. One of my interviews resulted from a chance encounter at the beach with a man I had known in the camps, and another was the brother-in-law of my taxi driver during my trip to Havana. The interview pool also over-represented white-collar professionals and was slightly older than the average balsero. Among those interviewed, their professions in Cuba had been engineer, lawyer, geographer, computer programmer, medical student, and art student. I also interviewed a barber, a self-taught artist, and a sixth grade–educated tourism worker. To maintain the male/female ratio from the camps I should have interviewed three women instead of two. However, on arriving in Miami I found that the women had been much more traumatized by the camp experience than the men and were therefore more difficult to recruit for interviews that included talking about the camps. Nonetheless, all of the people I interviewed had the same cultural references, shared the same types of experiences of escape and detention, and were subject to the same stressors and existential angst as the rest of the population.

I also found that the people who remained traumatized by their experiences, whether these incidents had occurred in Cuba, the Florida Straits, or the camps, or who were completely maladjusted to life in the United States, were not good choices to interview. It is possible, then, that the people who did allow me to interview them had experienced greater healing or had been less traumatized than the larger balsero population. Since no studies have been done on the incidence of PTSD in the adult balsero population, this was impossible to determine in advance.

Only one of the male interviewees, whom I call Roberto, had undergone an acutely traumatizing experience in the camps, and he was also not very happy with his life in the United States at the time. Since he was very honest in how he felt about his new life (which contradicted the community narrative), and since I was aware that some other balseros shared several of his opinions, I believe his story speaks for a number of them during their first years in their new country, even though they were clearly a minority. Roberto did have a great deal of emotional support from a former World Relief worker from Miami, which I believe affected his ability and desire to talk about the camps. He also shared one opinion with the rest of my interviewees: namely, that Guantánamo was an important chapter in history, and that it was important to have the detainees' experiences documented. I felt that this was the reason most of the people allowed me to interview them even though talking about their journeys was bound to bring back memories of extremely unpleasant experiences and emotions.

I chose to focus my interviews mainly on the balseros who had resettled in Miami since 66 percent of Cuban émigrés who left the island during the 1990s resettled there. In fact, Cubans are the most demographically concentrated new immigrant group in the United States.[2] Thus, ten of the interviews took place in Miami; one was held in Lancaster, Pennsylvania, and one in Rochester, New York. Most of the interviews required at least three sessions, each covering a different period: Cuba, Guantánamo, and the United States. I then transcribed and translated key sections of the interviews.

In addition to conducting life history interviews in Miami, I did participant observation with some of the interviewees over the course of six months. Two of them, Juan and Raul, were a gay couple with whom I spent a considerable amount of time after the interviews. I attended social gatherings at their home, and they took me to the house where Elián Gonzalez[3] was kept during the controversy surrounding him and told me how they reacted to it. Spending time with them outside an interview context allowed me to catch some of the contradictions between the stories Juan told me about life in Cuba while I was interviewing him and the ones he told when he was not being recorded, particularly in regard to his experiences at the summer schools in the countryside. I also spent a great deal of time at the art studio of another interviewee, a self-taught artist who was trying to create a community arts organization with a group of Cuban exiles and another artist whom he knew from the camps. I observed what he was painting and how he interacted with different members of the community, and I met one of his mentors, a *babalawo* (Santería priest), who had also been an ethnographer in Cuba. Additionally, I spent a few days observing one interviewee in his barbershop.

I chose to interview two people outside of Miami so I could ascertain whether the Miami community narrative influenced the balseros' stories about life in Cuba and the camps. Judging by those interviews, being part of Cuban Miami did influence descriptions of life in Cuba, but not stories about the camps.

The Interviewees

- **Augustín**: a computer programmer from Havana in his forties. He initially resettled in Pennsylvania but moved to Florida after five years to be closer to his compatriots and to avoid Northeastern winters. He was in Guantánamo for a total of fifteen months.
- **Fernando**: an engineer from Villa Clara in his thirties who resettled with his wife Maria south of Miami. He was detained for six months in Guantánamo.

- **Guillermo:** a design student from Havana in his twenties. He resettled in Miami, where he was attending Miami-Dade Community College when I interviewed him. He was detained for fifteen months in Guantánamo.
- **Juan:** a geographer from a fishing village in his thirties who resettled in Miami. He was detained for twelve months in Guantánamo.
- **Marcos:** a self-taught artist from Pinar del Rio in his thirties who resettled in Miami. He was detained for seven months in Guantánamo.
- **Maria:** an engineer from Villa Clara in her thirties, married to Fernando. She and her husband resettled south of Miami. She was detained for one month in Guantánamo.
- **Mario:** a former government official from Havana in his forties who resettled in the Northeast. He spent eight months in Guantánamo.
- **Miguel:** a medical student from Havana in his twenties. Although he initially resettled in Miami, he was on his way to a medical residency in the Midwest when I interviewed him. He was detained for ten months in the camps.
- **Pancho:** a barber from Havana in his thirties who briefly attended art school. He left Cuba with his brother, who had been jailed as a political prisoner for twenty years. He was detained for fifteen months, partly in Guantánamo and partly in Panama, and resettled in Miami.
- **Raul:** a sound engineer from Havana in his thirties who resettled in Miami. He was detained for twelve months in Guantánamo.
- **Roberto:** what Cubans would describe as a *jinetero* (one who makes a living from hustling tourists), who has a sixth-grade education. In his late twenties, he is from Havana and resettled in Miami. He was detained for a total of fourteen months, divided between Guantánamo and Panama.
- **Sylvia:** a psychologist from Havana in her forties who resettled in Miami. She and her daughter were detained for fourteen months, split between the Panama and Guantánamo camps.

Notes

Introduction

1. For example, see *Castro's Final Hour* by journalist Andres Oppenheimer (New York: Touchstone, 1993).

2. Norman Zucker and Naomi Flink Zucker, *Desperate Crossing: Seeking Refuge in America* (Armonk, NY: M. E. Sharpe, 1996), 58, 60–66; Kelly Greenhill, *Weapons of Mass Migration: Forced Displacement, Coercion and Foreign Policy* (Ithaca, NY: Cornell University Press, 2010).

3. Carroll Doherty, "Presidential News Conference: Clinton Changes Policy on Cuba, Describes View of Crime Bill," *Congressional Quarterly Weekly Report* 52, no. 33 (August 20, 1994): 2472.

4. Felix Raul Masud-Piloto, *From Welcomed Exiles to Illegal Immigrants: Cuban Migration to the U.S., 1959–1995* (Lanham, MD: Rowman & Littlefield, 1996).

5. See Ruth Behar, *The Vulnerable Observer: An Anthropology That Breaks Your Heart* (Boston: Beacon Press, 1996).

Chapter 1

1. Amy Kaplan,"Where Is Guantanamo?" *American Quarterly* 57, no. 7 (September 2005): 831–858.

2. Jonathan Hansen, *Guantánamo: An American History* (New York: Hill and Wang, 2011), 77.

3. Roger Ricardo, *Guantánamo: Bay of Discord* (Melbourne, Australia: Ocean Press, 1994), 11.

4. Louis Pérez, *Cuba: Between Reform and Revolution* (New York: Oxford University Press, 1996), 133–134.

5. Thomas Skidmore and Peter Smith, *Modern Latin America* (New York: Oxford University Press, 1989), 249. See also Pérez, *Cuba*, 136–137.

6. Skidmore and Smith, *Modern Latin America*, 250.

7. Skidmore and Smith, *Modern Latin America*, 250–256; Pérez, *Cuba*, 338.

8. Emily Hatchwell and Simon Calder, *Cuba: A Guide to the People, Politics and Culture* (London: Latin America Bureau, 1995), 11; Pérez, *Cuba*, 147, 341; Hansen, *Guantánamo*, 155; Marifeli Perez-Stable, *The Cuban Revolution: Origins, Course, Legacy* (New York: Oxford University Press, 1993), 7; Samuel Farber, *The Origins of the Cuban Revolution Reconsidered* (Chapel Hill: University of North Carolina Press, 2006), 73.

9. Pérez, *Cuba*, 341; Liz Balmseda, "Now-Grown 'Pedro Pan' Seeks to Unravel CIA Mystery," *Miami Herald*, May 19, 1998, 1B.

10. Louis A. Pérez Jr., *On Becoming Cuban: Identity, Nationality and Culture* (Chapel Hill: University of North Carolina Press, 1999); Gerald Poyo, "The Cuban Experience in the United States, 1865–1940: Migration, Community and Identity," *Cuban Studies/Estudios Cubanos* 21 (1991): 19–36.

11. Norman Zucker and Naomi Flink Zucker, *Desperate Crossing: Seeking Refuge in America* (Armonk, NY: M. E. Sharpe, 1996), 30; Maria de los Angeles Torres, "Elian and the Tale of Pedro Pan," *Nation* 270, no. 12 (March 27, 2000): 21–24.

12. Luisa Yanez, "Pedro Pan Was Born of Fear, Human Instinct to Protect Children," *Miami Herald*, May 16, 2009. http://www.miamiherald.com/2009/05/14/1050851/pedro-pan-was-born-of-fear-human.html, accessed July 4, 2012.

13. Yanez, "Pedro Pan Was Born of Fear."

14. Torres, "Elian and the Tale of Pedro Pan," 21.

15. Skidmore and Smith, *Modern Latin America*, 343; Ted Henken, *Cuba: A Global Studies Handbook* (Santa Barbara, CA: ABC-CLIO, 2008), 133.

16. Felix Raul Masud-Piloto, *From Welcomed Exiles to Illegal Immigrants: Cuban Migration to the U.S., 1959–1995* (Lanham, MD: Rowman and Littlefield, 1996), 52, 54.

17. Masud-Piloto, *From Welcomed Exiles to Illegal Immigrants*, 50–51.

18. Masud-Piloto, *From Welcomed Exiles to Illegal Immigrants*, 59; Torres, "Elian and the Tale of Pedro Pan," 21.

19. Jorge Dominguez, "Immigration as Foreign Policy in U.S.-Latin American Relations," in *Immigration and U.S. Foreign Policy*, R. W. Tucker, C. B. Keely, and L. Wrigley, eds. (Boulder: Westview Press, 1990), 153–154; Piloto, *From Welcomed Exiles to Illegal Immigrants*, 57–58; Zucker and Zucker, *Desperate Crossings*, 32–33; Kelly Greenhill, *Weapons of Mass Migration: Forced Displacement, Coercion and Foreign Policy* (Ithaca, NY: Cornell University Press, 2010), 86–87.

20. Pérez, *On Becoming Cuban*, 200.

21. Ruth Ellen Wasem, "Cuban Migration to the United States: Policy and Trends," 7–5700, R40566 (Washington, DC: Congressional Research Service, June 2, 2009).

22. Pérez, *Cuba*, 344; Gil Scanlon and John A. Loescher, *Calculated Kindness: Refugees and America's Half Open Door, 1945 to Present* (New York: Free Press, 1986), 181.

23. Zucker and Zucker, *Desperate Crossings*, 47.

24. Zucker and Zucker, *Desperate Crossings*, 48.

25. Zucker and Zucker, *Desperate Crossings*, 48; Scanlon and Loescher, *Calculated Kindness*, 182.

26. Maria Cristina Garcia, *Havana USA: Cuban Exiles and Cuban Americans in South Florida* (Berkeley: University of California Press, 1996), 70–73; Pérez, *On Becoming Cuban*, 199; Dominguez, "Immigration as Foreign Policy," 156; Scanlon and Loescher, *Calculated Kindness*.

27. Charles B. Keely, "The United States of America: Retaining a Fair Immigration Policy," in *The Politics of Migration Policies: Settlement and Integration, the First World in the 1990s*, Daniel Dubat, ed. (New York: Center for Migration Studies, 1993), 73.

28. Zucker and Zucker, *Desperate Crossings*, 58, 60–66; Greenhill, *Weapons of Mass Migration*, 112–113.

29. Steven Greenhouse, "The Flight from Cuba: The Policy; Cuba Strategy: Reactive or Planned?" *New York Times*, August 23, 1994, A16.

30. Greenhill, *Weapons of Mass Migration*, 110–112; Lisandro Pérez, "The End of Exile? A New Era in U.S. Immigration Policy toward Cuba," in *Free Markets, Open Societies, Closed Borders? Trends in International Migration and Immigration Policy in the Americas*, Max J. Castro, ed. (Miami: North/South Center Press, 1999), 202–203.

31. Greenhill, *Weapons of Mass Migration*, 110–112.

32. Pérez, "The End of Exile," 202–203; Greenhill, *Weapons of Mass Migration*, 113–114.

33. Pérez, "The End of Exile," 204. The political clout of the Cuban exile community was also evident when their treatment is compared to that of the Haitians who

were also being held at the base; there is no evidence that Clinton gave representatives of the Haitian community the consideration he gave the Cuban Americans.

34. Pérez, "The End of Exile," 205; Masud-Piloto, *From Welcomed Exiles to Illegal Immigrants.*

35. Carroll J. Doherty, "Presidential News Conference: Clinton Changes Policy on Cuba, Describes View of Crime Bill," *Congressional Quarterly Weekly Report* 52, no. 2 (August 20, 1994): 2472–2473.

36. Masud-Piloto, *From Welcomed Exiles to Illegal Immigrants*, 141.

37. Doherty, "Presidential News Conference," 2472.

38. Pérez, "The End of Exile," 203–205; Max J. Castro, *The Cubans Are (Still) Coming: U.S. Immigration and Foreign Policy* (Washington, DC: Georgetown University Center for Latin American Studies, 2001), 5; US Coast Guard, "Alien Migrant Interdiction," US Department of Homeland Security, www.uscg.mil/hq/cg5/cg531/AMIO/amio.asp, accessed May 7, 2012; Human Rights Watch, "Cuba: Stifling Dissent in the Midst of Crisis," *Human Rights Watch/Americas* 6, no. 2 (1994); United States Coast Guard, "Operation Able Vigil: Service Participates in Its Largest Peacetime Efforts Ever, Keeping Cuban Rafters Alive," *Commandant's Bulletin* (November 1994): 4–5; United States Coast Guard, "Alien Migrant Interdiction," http://www.uscg.mil/hq/cg5/cg531/amio/amio.asp, accessed January 12, 2014.

39. Zucker and Zucker, *Desperate Crossings*, 127; United States Department of State, "U.S.–Cuba Joint Communiqué on Migration," *U.S Department of State Dispatch* 5, no. 37 (September 12, 1994): 603.

40. Masud-Piloto, *From Welcomed Exiles to Illegal Immigrants*, 128.

41. As the operation wore on, for example, the military replaced the tents with elevated, hard-backed ones, which were much more comfortable and cooler. It also facilitated the procurement of resources for artistic activity. It did neither of these for the Haitians, which disappointed some of the officers toward the end of the operation.

42. See the Hermanos al Rescate (Brothers to the Rescue) website for more information: www.hermanos.org.

43. During the first few weeks of the operation, 8,600 people were sent voluntarily to a US military installation in the Panama Canal Zone to alleviate some of the stress on the Guantánamo base's facilities. Conditions were initially much more comfortable and friendly there.

44. David Bentley, "Operation Sea Signal: U.S. Military Support for Caribbean Migration Emergencies, May 1994 to February 1996," *National Defense University Strategic Forum*, 73 (May 1996): 2.

45. Pérez, "The End of Exile," 206.

Chapter 2

1. Ana Julia Jatar-Hausmann, *The Cuban Way: Capitalism, Communism and Confrontation* (West Hartford, CT: Kumarian Press, 1999), 38–39, 57; Miriam Uriarte, *Cuba: Social Policy at the Crossroads: Maintaining Priorities, Transforming Practice* (Boston: Oxfam America, 2002), 19.

2. Jatar-Hausmann, *The Cuban Way*, 38; Uriarte, *Cuba: Social Policy at the Crossroads*, 20.

3. Susan Eva Eckstein, *Back from the Future: Cuba under Castro* (Princeton, NJ: Princeton University Press, 1994), 94–99, 226.

4. Eckstein, *Back from the Future*, 99, 134.

5. Jatar-Housmann, *The Cuban Way*, 51.

6. Not only is nickel processing energy intensive, but at the time, two thirds of Cuba's nickel output went to the Soviet Union to pay for its investments on the

island. Closing the factory may also have been a message to the Soviets that Cuba needed continuing oil supplies. See Carmelo Mesa-Lago, "Cuba and the Downfall of Soviet and Eastern European Socialism," in *Cuba after the Cold War*, Carmelo Mesa-Lago, ed. (Pittsburgh, PA: University of Pittsburgh Press, 1993), 165.

7. Jatar-Hausmann, *The Cuban Way*, 41; Eckstein, *Back from the Future*, 96–97, 124–125.

8. Cf. Jatar-Hausmann, *The Cuban Way*, 63.

9. Eckstein, *Back from the Future*, 97; Jatar-Hausmann, *The Cuban Way*, 112, 123.

10. Jatar-Hausmann, *The Cuban Way*, 52.

11. Jatar-Hausmann, *The Cuban Way*, 119–120.

12. I have changed all of the names of the balseros who provided interviews for this book to protect their privacy in the United States and to protect their families in Cuba from possible retribution.

13. Human Rights Watch/Americas, "Cuba: Repression, the Exodus of August 1994, and the US Response," *Human Rights Watch/Americas* 6, no. 2 (1994): 3–5.

14. Jatar-Hausmann, *The Cuban Way*, 119–120.

15. Jatar-Hausmann, *The Cuban Way*, 122–125; Antoni Kapcia, *Cuba: Isle of Dreams* (New York: Berg, 2000), 217.

16. Human Rights Watch, "Cuba: Repression, the Exodus of August of 1994, and the US Response."

17. Other accounts of that incident cite forty occupants drowning and thirty-one passengers returned to the island. See Lisandro Pérez, "The End of Exile? A New Era in U.S. Immigration Policy toward Cuba," in *Free Markets, Open Societies, Closed Borders? Trends in International Migration and Immigration Policy in the Americas*, Max J. Castro, ed. (Miami: North/South Center Press, 1999), 203; Human Rights Watch/Americas, "Cuba: Stifling Dissent in the Midst of Crisis," *Human Rights Watch/ Americas* 6 (1994): 8. Some accounts report that two policemen were killed in the incident in Havana after the rioting. See, for example, "Protesters Battle Police in Havana, Castro Warns U.S.," *New York Times*, August 6, 1994, http://www.nytimes.com/1994/08/06/world/protesters-battle-police-in-havana-castro-warns-us.html, accessed May 21, 2012.

18. "Protesters Battle Police in Havana, Castro Warns U.S."

19. Pérez, *The End of Exile*, 202–203; United States Coast Guard, Alien Migrant Interdiction Overview, http://www.uscg.mil/hq/cg5/cg531/AMIO/amio.asp#; Human Rights Watch/Americas, "Cuba: Stifling Dissent in the Midst of Crisis," 8.

20. A vulgarity that loosely translates as "dicks."

Chapter 3

1. Johnson Hansen, *Guantánamo: An American History* (New York: Hill and Wang, 2011), 181–182.

2. Hansen, *Guantánamo*, 214–215.

3. Lynn-Darrell Bender, "Guantánamo, Its Political, Military and Legal Status," *Caribbean Quarterly* 19, no. 1 (March 1973): 82; Marion E. Murphy, *The History of Guantánamo Bay 1494–1964* (Guantánamo Bay, Cuba: US Navy, 1953); Jana Lipman, *Guantánamo: A Working Class History between Empire and Revolution* (Berkeley: University of California Press, 2009), 32; Nicholas Reynolds, *A Skillful Show of Strength: U.S. Marines in the Caribbean, 1991–1996* (Washington, DC: US Government Printing Office, 2003), http://www.mcu.usmc.mil/historydivision/Pages/Publications/Publication%20PDFs/A%20Skillful%20Show%20of%20Strength%20U.S.%20Marines%20in%20the%20Caribbean%201991-1996.pdf.

4. Hansen, *Guantánamo*, 266–271.

5. Hansen, *Guantánamo*, 266–272.

6. Hansen, *Guantánamo*, 266–277, quote on 272.

7. Hansen, *Guantánamo*, 276–277.

8. For an extremely thorough examination of the legal precedents set during the internment of Haitians on the base, see Brant Goldstein, *Storming the Court: How a Band of Law Students Sued the President and Won* (New York: Scribner, 2005); Paul Farmer, *The Uses of Haiti* (Monroe, ME: Common Courage Press, 2003), 37; Hansen, *Guantánamo*, 276–278.

9. Reynolds, *A Skillful Show of Strength*, 58–64; Kathleen Newland, "The Impact of US Refugee Policies on US Foreign Policy: A Case of the Tail Wagging the Dog?" in *Threatened Peoples, Threatened Borders: World Migration and US Policy*, Michael Teitelbaum and Myron Weiner, eds. (New York: W. W. Norton, 2004); Howard French, "Haiti Pays Dearly for Military Coup," *New York Times*, December 25, 1991, http://www.nytimes.com/1991/12/25/world/haiti-pays-dearly-for-military-coup. html?pagewanted=all &src=pm; for the military's version of this, see Reynolds, *A Skillful Show of Strength*, 283.

10. Hansen, *Guantánamo*, 283–284.

11. Hansen, *Guantánamo*, 287.

12. Amy Kaplan, "Where Is Guantanamo?" *American Quarterly* 57, no. 3 (September 2005): 838–839.

13. Clinton continued a long-standing US policy to label 99.9 percent of Haitians fleeing unrest on the island as economic migrants, contrary to UN principles. See Goldstein, *Storming the Court*, 181; Farmer, *The Uses of Haiti*, 37.

14. Reynolds, *A Skillful Show of Strength*, 22–23.

15. Felix Raul Masud-Piloto, *From Welcomed Exiles to Illegal Immigrants: Cuban Migration to the U.S., 1959–1995* (Lanham, MD: Rowman and Littlefield, 1996), 141; for a good explanation of what makes the base anomalous, see Gerald Neuman, "Surveying Laws and Borders: Anomalous Zones," *Stanford Law Review* 48 (1996): 1197–1234.

16. J. J. Pelton, J. L. Beuhrer, and D. L. Cull, "Surgical Support of Operation Sea Signal: Adaptability of the 59th Air Transportable Hospital in Cuba," *Military Medicine* 168, no. 12 (December 2003): 957–960.

17. I happened to be working at FEMA during this time and was aware of the decisions being made.

18. Joseph B. Treaster, "Guantánamo Refugee Camps Fill with Fury," *New York Times*, August 30, 1994, A1.

19. Reynolds, *A Skillful Show of Strength*, 58–64.

20. A *jutia*, or banana rat in English, is a large opossum-like rodent that lives in abundance in the trees on the base. Certain subspecies are endangered on the rest of the island.

21. David Martin and Audrey Solis, "Cuba. U.S. Response to the 1994 Cuban Migration Crisis," *Congressional Research Service* (Washington, DC: United States General Accounting Office, 1995), 4.

22. The INS repeatedly displayed incompetence in its operations on the base; when the Haitian Refugee Center sued the government in 1991 for sending the Haitians back to Haiti without due process, much of the evidence that Senior Judge C. Clyde Atkins, District Court for the Southern District in Florida, heard during a court procedure on December 2, 1991, was stories of INS incompetence. This was when the government began to argue that there is no jurisdiction on migrants being processed outside the territorial limits of the United States. See *Memorandum, Sitrep*

9—*Haitian Refugee Center, Inc. v Baker* (Southern District of Florida, Case number 91-2563), Document 16217, December 30, 1991.

23. For a good description of the medical challenges and an account of the types and numbers of surgeries carried out at the 69th ATH during the operation, see Pelton, Beuhrer, and Cull, "Surgical Support of Operation Sea Signal."

24. See Reynolds, *A Skillful Show of Strength*, 85–87.

25. In fact, military history touts the success of the Marines in "subduing" residents of Camp Two, where these incidents occurred. For a complete description from the military's point of view, see Reynolds, *A Skillful Show of Strength*, 75–85.

26. For example, see Ben Dolorfino, *Small War Manual's Strategic and Psychological Principles in Philippine Counterinsurgency (COIN) Operations* (Washington, DC: US Marine Corps, 1940) and the manual itself, US Marine Corps, *Small Wars Manual* (Washington, DC: US Marine Corps, 1940), www.marines.mil/Portals/59/Publications/FMFRP%2012-15%20%20Small%20Wars%20Manual.pdf.

27. *El Yuma* is a slang term for the United States. It reflects the popularity of 1950s-era Westerns set in the Yuma area of Arizona, which were still televised during the Revolution.

Chapter 4

1. Richard F. Mollica, *Healing Invisible Wounds* (Nashville, TN: Vanderbilt University Press, 2006).

2. Noel Walsh, "Life in Death," in *Trauma and Self*, C. B. Strozier and M. Flynn, eds. (Lanham MD: Rowman and Littlefield, 1996), 252.

3. Viktor Frankl, *Man's Search for Meaning: An Introduction to Logotherapy*, 3rd ed. (New York: Simon and Schuster, 1984), 147.

4. Richard G. Tedeschi and Lawrence G. Calhoun, *Trauma and Transformation: Growing in the Aftermath of Suffering* (Thousand Oaks, CA: Sage, 2000), 40–41.

5. Tedeschi and Calhoun, *Trauma and Transformation*, 20–25; Walsh, "Life in Death," 252.

6. Tedeschi and Calhoun, *Trauma and Transformation*, 40–43, 78; Ronnie Janoff-Bulman and Andrea R. Berger, "The Other Side of Trauma: Towards a Psychology of Appreciation," in *Loss and Trauma: General and Close Relationship Perspectives*, J. H. Harvey and E. D. Miller, eds. (Philadelphia: Brunner-Routledge, 2000), 29–44; Aiko Sawada, Julia Chaitin, and Dan Bar-On, "Surviving Hiroshima and Nagasaki: Experiences and Psychosocial Meanings," *Psychiatry* 67, no. 1 (2004): 43–60.

7. Tedeschi and Calhoun. *Trauma and Transformation*, 20–25.

8. Alexander McFarlane and Bessel A. van der Kolk, "Trauma and Its Challenge to Society," in *Traumatic Stress: The Effects of Overwhelming Experience on Mind, Body, and Society*, Alexander McFarlane, Bessel A. van der Kolk, and Lars Weisaeth, eds. (New York: Guilford Press, 1996), 24.

9. Kai Erikson, *A New Species of Trouble: The Human Experience of Modern Disasters* (New York: W. W. Norton, 1994), 230–231.

10. People also made their own "wine" from the mixed fruit that came in some of the MREs.

Chapter 5

1. See the following studies by folklorists and anthropologists: Guy Brett, *Through Our Own Eyes: Popular Art and Modern History* (Philadelphia: New Society Publishers, 1986); Marsha MacDowell, "Textiles of Refugee Women: New Ways with Old Traditions," in *New Threads in the Fabric of American Culture*, A. Skillman,

ed. (St. Louis: International Institute of Metropolitan St. Louis, 1989); James Phillips, "The Politics of Refugee Identity in Central America," in *Selected Papers on Refugee Issues: IV*, Anne Rynearson and James Phillips, eds. (Arlington, VA: American University Press, 1996); Varick Chittenden, *A Vietnam Remembered: The Folk Art of Marine Combat Veteran Michael D. Cousino Sr.* (Jackson: University Press of Mississippi, 1995); Linda Pershing, *The Ribbon around the Pentagon: Peace by Piecemakers* (Knoxville: University of Tennessee Press, 1996); Dwight Conquergood, "Fabricating Culture and Identity: The Textile Art of Hmong Refugee Women," in *Performance, Culture and Identity*, E. C. Fine and J. H. Spencer, eds. (Westport, CT: Praeger, 1992), 207–248; Margarie Agosín, *Scraps of Life: Chilean Arpilleras* (Trenton, NJ: Red Sea Press, 1987).

2. Judith Weiss, "The Emergence of Popular Culture," in *Cuba: Twenty-Five Years of Revolution, 1959–1984*, S. Helebsky and J. M. Kirk, eds. (New York: Praeger, 1985), 117–130.

3. Weiss, "The Emergence of Popular Culture," 117–130.

4. Here, "strike" refers to the incident in early September 1994 in which several thousand balseros breached the razor wire around their camps and roved around the base for a couple of days after learning that US-Cuba migration talks had not produced an agreement to admit them into the United States.

5. The collection of the camp newsletters is housed in the Richter Library at the University of Miami.

Chapter 6

1. Unfortunately, there has never been a study of PTSD among the adults who were held at the base.

2. Eugenio M. Rothe et al., "Posttraumatic Stress Disorder among Cuban Children and Adolescents after Release from a Refugee Camp," *Psychiatric Services* 53, no. 8 (2002): 970–976.

3. Alberto Sarrain, "Algunos Aspectos Relevantes del Proceso Adaptación-Aculturación de los Cubanos Procedentes de los Campos de Refugiados de la Base Naval de Guantánamo, 1995," unpublished conference paper, 1995, in possession of the paper's author.

4. Holly Ackerman interviewed the balseros as they came into Miami and collected more evidence suggesting that initially they experienced discrimination from their fellow Cubans in Miami. She found that some in the community considered them to be deceivers who concealed their identities or fakers who were not genuine in their political disaffection. Others considered the balseros "damaged goods," since they had grown up under the Revolution. She concluded that Clinton's redefinition of the balseros as illegal immigrants in the midst of the exodus was responsible for this. See Holly Ackerman, "The 'Balsero' Phenomenon, 1991–1994," in *Cuban Studies/Estudios Cubanos*, vol. 26, J. Domínguez, ed. (Pittsburgh, PA: University of Pittsburgh Press, 1996).

5. Ruth Wasem, "Cuban Migration to the United States" (Washington, DC: Congressional Research Service, 2009), 4–5, accessed January 5, 2014; Max J. Castro, *The Cubans Are (Still) Coming: U.S. Immigration and Foreign Policy on Cuba* (Washington, DC: Center for Latin American Studies, Georgetown University, 2001), 7.

6. USCG (U.S. Coast Guard) website. "Alien Migrant Interdiction" (http://www.uscg.mil/hq/g-o/g-opl/mle/AMIO.htm), 2004 http://www.uscg.mil/hq/cg5/cg531/AMIO/amio.asp; Ted Henken, "Balseros, Boteros and El Bombo: Post-1994 Cuban Immigration to the United States and the Persistence of Special Treatment," *Journal of Latino Studies* 3 (2005): 393–416.

Epilogue

1 Government Accountability Office. *Economic Sanction: Agencies Face Competing Priorities in Enforcing the Embargo on Cuba*. Washington DC: GAO. Report GAO-08-80, November 2007, p. 70.

2 Government Accountability Office. *Economic Sanction: Agencies Face Competing Priorities in Enforcing the Embargo on Cuba*. Washington DC: GAO. Report GAO-08-80, November 2007, p. 70

3 Anne Louise Bardach: *Cuba Confidential: Love and Vengeance in Miami and Cuba*. New York: Random House, 2002

4 Julie Hirschfeld Davis and Michael R. Gordon, *Obama Intends to Lift Several Restrictions Against Cuba on His Own*. New York Times, December 18, 2014; Julie Hirschfeld Davis. Announcing Cuba Embassy Deal, Obama Declares 'New Chapter.' New York Times, July 1, 2015.

5 U.S. Coast Guard, Alien Migrant Interdiction. U.S.Coast Guard website. http://www.uscg.mil/hq/cg5/cg531/AMIO/amio.asp

6 Azadeh Dastari. United States Migrant Interdiction and the Detention of Refugees in Guantánamo Bay. New York: Cambridge University Press, 2015, 55-56.

7 Agence France Press, *Guantánamo Base to be US Immigration Welcome Center*. Final Edition, May 8, 2007 http://rawstory.com/news/afp/Guantanamo_base_to_be_US_immigratio_0508.html.

8 Jane Franklin. *How Did Guantánamo Become a Prison?* History News Network. April 11, 2005. http://hnn.us/articles/11000.html.

9 Linda Greenhouse, *Justices, 5-3, Broadly Reject Bush Plan to Try Detainees*. The New York Times. June 30, 2006.

10 William Glaberson, *Detention Camp Remains, But Not its Rationale*. The New York Times, June 13, 2008.

Appendix

1 Holly Ackerman, "The 'Balsero' Phenomenon, 1991–1994," in *Cuban Studies/ Estudios Cubanos*, vol. 26, J. Domínguez, ed. (Pittsburgh, PA: University of Pittsburgh Press, 1996), 179–180.

2 Susan Eva Ekstein, *The Immigrant Divide: How Cuban Americans Changed the US and Their Homeland* (New York: Routledge, 2009), 45–46.

3 Elián González was the five-year-old boy at the center of an international custody battle and diplomatic dispute in 2000. He was found alone on a raft off the coast of Miami on Thanksgiving Day in 1999 after his mother and stepfather drowned while attempting to cross the Florida Straits on a raft with him. The Immigration and Naturalization Service placed him in the temporary custody of his relatives in Miami without consulting his biological father, Juan Miguel, who had remained in Cuba. When Juan Miguel stated that he wanted the child to return to the island, his Miami relatives refused to relinquish custody. The Cuban exile community in Miami rallied around the relatives' house with dramatic displays of defiance while the Cubans on the island participated in weekly marches demanding Elián's return. In the end, the Justice Department returned the child to his father and the Cuban exile community had to cope with a self-imposed public relations disaster. For an account of this episode, see Ann Louise Bardach, *Cuba Confidential: Love and Vengeance in Miami and Havana* (New York: Random House, 2002).

Bibliography

Ackerman, Holly. "The 'Balsero' Phenomenon, 1991–1994." In *Cuban Studies/Estudios Cubanos*, vol. 26. In J. Domínguez, ed. Pittsburgh, PA: University of Pittsburgh Press, 1996, pp. 169–200.

Agence France Presse. "Guantánamo Base to Be U.S. Immigration Welcome Centre." *DailyTimes*, May 10, 2007. http://archives.dailytimes.com.pk/foreign/10-May-2007/guantanamo-base-to-be-us-immigration-welcome-centre.

Agosín, Margarie. *Scraps of Life: Chilean Arpilleras*. Trenton, NJ: Red Sea Press, 1987.

Anderson, Benedict. *Imagined Communities*. New York: Verso, 1991.

Balmseda, Liz. "Now-Grown 'Pedro Pan' Seeks to Unravel CIA Mystery." *Miami Herald*, May 19, 1998.

Bardach, Ann Louise. *Cuba Confidential: Love and Vengeance in Miami and Havana*. New York: Random House, 2002.

BBC. "Guantánamo Refugee Plan Scrapped." BBC World Service, Final Edition, April 19, 1999. http://news.bbc.co.uk/2/hi/americas/315391.stm.

Behar, Ruth. *The Vulnerable Observer: An Anthropology That Breaks Your Heart*. Boston: Beacon Press, 1996.

Bender, Lynne-Darryl. "Guantánamo: Its Political, Military, and Legal Status." *Caribbean Quarterly* 19, no. 1 (March 1973): 80–86.

Bentley, David. "Operation Sea Signal: U.S. Military Support for Caribbean Migration Emergencies, May 1994 to February 1996." *National Defense University Strategic Forum* 73 (May 1996): 1–5.

Boone, Margaret S., Linda Camino, and Ruth Krulfeld. "Thirty-Year Retrospective on the Adjustment of Cuban Refugee Women." In *Reconstructing Lives, Recapturing Meaning: Refugee Identity, Gender, and Culture Change*. Linda Camino and Ruth Krulfeld, eds. Amsterdam: Gordon and Breach, 1994, pp. 154–173.

Brett, Guy. *Through Our Own Eyes: Popular Art and Modern History*. Philadelphia: New Society Publishers, 1986.

Campisi, Elizabeth. "Guantánamo: Safe Haven or Traumatic Interlude?" *Latino Studies* 3, no. 3 (November 2005): 375–392.

Caruth, Cathy, ed. *Trauma: Explorations in Memory*. Baltimore, MD: Johns Hopkins University Press, 1995.

Castro, Max J. *The Cubans Are (Still) Coming: U.S. Immigration and Foreign Policy on Cuba*. Washington, DC: Center for Latin American Studies, Georgetown University, 2001.

Castro, Max J. "Cuba, the Continuing Crisis." *North-South Agenda Papers*. Coral Gables, FL: North South Center of the University of Miami, 1995.

Centers for Disease Control. "Health Status of Haitian Migrants—U.S. Naval Base, Guantánamo Bay, Cuba, November 1991—April 1993." *MMWR Weekly* 42 (1993): 138–140.

Chávez, Karma R. "Act UP, Haitian Migrants, and Alternate Memories of HIV/AIDS." *Quarterly Journal of Speech* 98, no. 1 (2012): 63–68.

Chittenden, Varick A. *Vietnam Remembered: The Folk Art of Marine Combat Veteran Michael D. Cousino Sr.* Jackson: University Press of Mississippi, 1995.

Cobb, Kim. "The Haiti Crisis: Island Conditions Called Too Risky for Refugees to Return from Guantánamo." *Houston Chronicle*, September 20, 1994.

Conquergood, Dwight. "Fabricating Culture and Identity: The Textile Art of Hmong Refugee Women." In *Performance, Culture and Identity*. E. C. Fine and J. H. Spencer, eds. Westport, CT: Praeger, 1992, pp. 207–248.

De Young, Karen. "Obama Moves to Normalize Relations with Cuba as American Is Released by Havana." *Washington Post*, December 17, 2014. https://www.washingtonpost.com/world/national-security/report-cuba-frees-american-alan-gross-after-5-years-detention-on-spy-charges/2014/12/17/a2840518–85f5–11e4-a702-fa31ff4ae98e_story.html.

Didion, Joan. *Miami*. New York: Random House, 1987.

Doherty, Carroll J. "Influx of Cubans Forces Clinton to Halt Automatic Asylum." *Congressional Quarterly Weekly Report* 52, no. 33 (August 20, 1994): 2464–2465.

Doherty, Carroll J. "Presidential News Conference: Clinton Changes Policy on Cuba, Describes View of Crime Bill." *Congressional Quarterly Weekly Report* 52, no. 33 (August 20, 1994): 2472–2473.

Dolorfino, Ben. *Small War Manual's Strategic and Psychological Principles in Philippine Counterinsurgency (COIN) Operations*. Washington, DC: U.S. Marine Corps, 1940. www.marines.mil/Portals/59/Publications/FMFRP%2012–15%20%20Small%20Wars%20Manual.pdf.

Dominguez, Jorge. "Immigration as Foreign Policy in U.S.-Latin American Relations." In *Immigration and U.S. Foreign Policy*. R. W. Tucker, C. B. Keely, and L. Wrigley, eds. Boulder, CO: Westview Press, 1990, pp. 150–166.

Duany, Jorge. *Blurred Borders: Transnational Migration between the Hispanic Caribbean and the United States*. Chapel Hill: University of North Carolina Press, 2011.

Eckstein, Susan Eva. *Back from the Future: Cuba under Castro*. Princeton, NJ: Princeton University Press, 1994.

Eckstein, Susan Eva. *The Immigrant Divide: How Cuban Americans Changed the US and Their Homeland*. New York: Routledge, 2009.

Erikson, Kai T. *A New Species of Trouble: The Human Experience of Modern Disasters*. New York: W. W. Norton, 1994.

Fagen, Richard R. *The Transformation of Political Culture in Cuba*. Stanford, CA: Stanford University Press, 1969.

Farber, Samuel. *The Origins of the Cuban Revolution Reconsidered*. Chapel Hill: University of North Carolina Press, 2006.

Farber, Sonia R. "Forgotten at Guantánamo: The *Boumediene* Decision and Its Implications for Refugees at the Base under the Obama Administration." *California Law Review* 9 (2010): 989–1022.

Farmer, Paul. *Pathologies of Power*. Berkeley: University of California Press, 2004.

Farmer, Paul. *The Uses of Haiti*. 3rd ed. Boston: Common Courage Press, 2005.

Fernández, Alfredo A. *Adrift: The Cuban Raft People*. Houston: Arte Público, 2000.

Fernández, Damián. *Cuba and the Politics of Passion*. Austin: University of Texas Press, 2000.

Franklin, Jane. "How Did Guantánamo Become a Prison?" History News Network, April 11, 2005. http://hnn.us/articles/11000.html.

Frankl, Viktor. E. *Man's Search for Meaning: An Introduction to Logotherapy*. 3rd ed. New York: Simon and Schuster, 1984.

Freedland, Jonathan. "U.S. Soldiers 'Abuse Haiti Children.'" *Guardian*, January 26, 1995.

French, Howard. "Haiti Pays Dearly for Military Coup." *New York Times*, December 25, 1991. www.nytimes.com/1991/12/25/world/haiti-pays-dearly-for-military-coup.html?pagewanted=all &src=pm.

Fullerton, Carol S. "Shared Meaning Following Trauma: Bridging Generations and Cultures." *Psychiatry* 67, no. 1 (2004): 61–62.

García, Maria Cristina. *Havana USA: Cuban Exiles and Cuban Americans in South Florida, 1959–1994*. Berkeley: University of California Press, 1996.

Glaberson, William. "Detention Camp Remains, but Not Its Rationale." *New York Times*, June 13, 2008. http://www.nytimes.com/2008/06/13/washington/13gitmo.html.

Gluck, Suzanne. "Intercepting Refugees at Sea: An Analysis of the United States' Legal and Moral Obligations." *Fordham Law Review* 61, no. 4 (1993): 865–893.

Goldstein, Brandt. *Storming the Court: How a Band of Yale Law Students Sued the President—and Won*. New York: Scribners, 2005.

González-Pando, Miguel. *The Cuban Americans*. Westport, CT: Greenwood, 1998.

Greenhill, Kelly. *Weapons of Mass Migration: Forced Displacement, Coercion and Foreign Policy*. Ithaca, NY: Cornell University Press, 2010.

Greenhouse, Linda. "Justices, 5–3, Broadly Reject Bush Plan to Try Detainees." *New York Times*, June 30, 2006. http://www.nytimes.com/2006/06/30/washington/30hamdan/html.

Greenhouse, Steven. "The Flight from Cuba: Clinton Will Open Talks with Cuba on Refugee Crisis." *New York Times*, August 28, 1994.

Greenhouse, Steven. "The Flight from Cuba: The Policy; Cuba Strategy: Reactive or Planned?" *New York Times*, August 23, 1994.

Grenier, Guillermo J., and Lisandro Pérez. *The Legacy of Exile: Cubans in the United States*. Boston: Allyn and Bacon, 2003.

Haitian Refugee Center, Inc. v. Baker, 953 F.2D 1498 (11th Cir. 1992).

Hansen, Jonathan M. *Guantánamo: An American History*. New York: Hill and Wang, 2011.

Hatchwell, Emily, and Simon Calder. *Cuba: A Guide to the People, Politics and Culture*. London: Latin America Bureau, 1995.

Henken, Ted. "Balseros, Boteros, and El Bombo: Post-1994 Cuban Immigration to the United States and the Persistence of Special Treatment." *Latino Studies* 3 (2004): 393–416.

Herman, Judith Lewis. *Trauma and Recovery: The Aftermath of Violence—from Domestic Abuse to Political Terror*. New York: Basic Books, 1997.

Hermanos al Rescate/Brothers to the Rescue. http://www.hermanos.org.

Hobsbawm, Eric, and Terence Ranger. "Introduction: Inventing Traditions." In *The Invention of Tradition*. Eric Hobsbawm and Terence Ranger, eds. New York: Cambridge University Press, 1983, pp. 1–14.

Hoffman, Alice, and Howard Hoffman. *Archives of Memory*. Lexington: University Press of Kentucky, 1990.

Holland, Dorothy. *Identity and Agency in Cultural Worlds*. Cambridge, MA: Harvard University Press, 1997.

Holland, Dorothy, and Jean Lave, eds. *History in Person: Enduring Struggles, Contentious Practice, Intimate Identities*. Santa Fe, NM: School of American Research Press, 2001.

Human Rights Watch. "Cuba: Repression, the Exodus of August 1994, and the US Response." *Human Rights Watch/Americas* 6, no. 12 (1994).

Human Rights Watch. "Cuba: Stifling Dissent in the Midst of Crisis." *Human Rights Watch/Americas* 6, no. 2 (1994b).

Janoff-Bulman, Ronnie, and Andrea R. Berger. "The Other Side of Trauma: Towards a Psychology of Appreciation." In *Loss and Trauma: General and Close Relationship Perspectives*. J. H. Harvey and E. D. Miller, eds. Philadelphia: Brunner-Routledge, 2000, pp. 29–44.

Jatar-Hausmann, Ana Julia. *The Cuban Way: Capitalism, Communism and Confrontation*. West Hartford, CT: Kumarian Press, 1999.

Kapcia, Antoni. *Cuba: Island of Dreams*. New York: Berg, 2000.

Kaplan, Amy. "Where Is Guantanamo?" *American Quarterly* 57, no. 7 (September 2005): 831–858.

Keane, Terence M., Danny G. Kaloupek, and Frank W. Weather. "Ethnocultural Considerations in the Assessment of PTSD." In *Ethnocultural Aspects of Posttraumatic Stress Disorder: Issues, Research, and Clinical Applications*. A. J. Marsella, M. J. Friedman, E. T. Gerrity, and R. M. Scurfield, eds. Washington, DC: American Psychological Association, 2001, pp. 183–208.

Keely, Charles B. "The United States of America: Retaining a Fair Immigration Policy." In *The Politics of Migration Policies: Settlement and Integration, the First World in the 1990s*. D. Dubat, ed. New York: Center for Migration Studies, 1993.

Kifner, John. "Refugees' Perilous Voyage Starts and Finishes in Cuba." *New York Times*, August 23, 1994.

Kleinman, Arthur, Veena Das, and Margaret Lock, eds. *Social Suffering.* Berkeley: University of California Press, 1997.

Krulfeld, Ruth M. "When the 'Powerless' Take Control: Self-Empowerment through Organization-Building among Lao Refugee Women." In *Beyond Boundaries: Selected Papers on Refugees and Immigrants*, vol. 5. D. Baxter and R. Krulfeld, eds. Arlington, VA: American Anthropological Association, 1997.

Kuramitsu, Kristine C. "Internment and Identity in Japanese American Art." *American Quarterly* 47, no. 4 (December 1995): 619–658.

Langer, Lawrence L. *Holocaust Testimonies: The Ruins of Memory.* New Haven, CT: Yale University Press, 1991.

Lifton, Robert Jay. *The Protean Self: Human Resilience in an Age of Fragmentation.* Chicago: University of Chicago Press, 1993.

Lindsay, Arturo, ed. *Santeria Aesthetics in Contemporary Latin American Art.* Washington, DC: Smithsonian Institution Press, 1996.

Lipman, Jana. *Guantánamo: A Working Class History between Empire and Revolution.* Berkeley: University of California Press, 2009.

Loescher, Gil, and John A. Scanlan. *Calculated Kindness: Refugees and America's Half-Open Door, 1945 to Present.* New York: Free Press, 1986.

Long, Lynellyn. *Ban Vinai: The Refugee Camp.* New York: Columbia University Press, 1993.

Luis, William. "Reading the Master Codes of Cuban Culture in Cristina García's 'Dreaming in Cuban.'" *Cuban Studies/Estudios Cubanos* 26 (1996): 201–223.

MacDowell, Marsha. "Textiles of Refugee Women: New Ways with Old Traditions." In *Needlework of New American Women: New Threads in the Fabric of American Culture.* A. Skillman, ed. St. Louis: International Institute of Metropolitan St. Louis, 1989, pp. 25–28.

Malkki, Liisa. "National Geographic: The Rooting of Peoples and the Territorialization of National Identity among Scholars and Refugees." In *Culture, Power, Place: Explorations in Critical Anthropology.* A. Gupta and J. Ferguson, eds. Durham, NC: Duke University Press, 1997, pp. 52–74.

Martin, David R., and Audrey Solis. *Cuba. U.S. Response to the 1994 Cuban Migration Crisis.* Congressional Research Service. Washington, DC: United States General Accounting Office, 1995.

Martinez, Juan A. *Cuban Art and National Identity: The Vanguardia Painters 1927–1950.* Gainesville: University Press of Florida, 1994.

Masud-Piloto, Felix Raul. *From Welcomed Exiles to Illegal Immigrants: Cuban Migration to the U.S., 1959–1995.* Lanham, MD: Rowman and Littlefield, 1996.

McFarlane, Alexander C., Bessel A. van der Kolk, and Lars Weisaeth, eds. *Traumatic Stress: The Effects of Overwhelming Experience on Mind, Body, and Society.* New York: Guilford Press, 1996.

Mesa-Lago, Carmel. "Cuba and the Downfall of Soviet and Eastern European Socialism." In *Cuba after the Cold War.* Carmelo Mesa-Lago, ed. Pittsburgh, PA: University of Pittsburgh Press, 1993, pp. 133–196.

Mesa-Lago, Carmelo. "Cuba's Raft Exodus of 1994: Causes, Settlement, Effects, and Future." *North-South Agenda Papers* no. 12, April 1995. Coral Gables, FL: North-South Center of the University of Miami, 1995.

Mollica, Richard. *Healing Invisible Wounds: Paths to Hope and Recovery in a Violent World.* Nashville: Vanderbilt University Press, 2006.

Murphy, Marion E. *The History of Guantánamo Bay, 1494–1964.* Guantánamo Bay, Cuba: United States Naval Station, 1953. http://archive.is/UdHH.

Nackerud, Larry, Alison Springer, Christopher Larrison, and Alicia Isaac. "The End of the Cuban Contradiction in U.S. Refugee Policy." *International Migration Review* 33 (1999): 176–192.

Navarro, Mireya. "Florida Nearing Emergency as Cuban Exodus Increases." *New York Times,* August 18, 1994.

Neimeyer, Robert A., and Heidi M. Levitt. "What's Narrative Got to Do with It? Construction and Coherence in Accounts of Loss." In *Loss and Trauma: General and Close Relationship Perspectives.* J. H. Harvey and E. D. Miller, eds. Philadelphia: Brunner-Routledge, 2000, pp. 401–412.

Neuman, Gerald L. "Surveying Laws and Borders: Anomalous Zones." *Stanford Law Review* 48 (May 1996): 1197–1234.

Newland, Kathleen. "The Impact of US Refugee Policies on US Foreign Policy: A Case of the Tail Wagging the Dog?" In *Threatened Peoples, Threatened Borders: World Migration and U.S. Policy.* Michael Teitelbaum and Myron Weiner, eds. New York: W. W. Norton, 1995, pp. 190–214.

Ojito, Mirta. "Castro Foe's Legacy: Success, Not Victory." *New York Times,* November 30, 1997.

Oppenheimer, Andrés. *Castro's Final Hour.* New York: Touchstone, 1993.

Pedraza, Sylvia. "Cuba's Refugees: Manifold Migrations." In *Origins and Destinies: Immigration, Race, and Ethnicity in America.* Sylvia Pedraza and Rubén Rumbaut, eds. Belmont, CA: Wadsworth, 1996, pp. 1–20.

Pedraza, Sylvia. *Political Disaffection in Cuba's Revolution and Exodus.* New York: Cambridge University Press, 2007.

Pelton, Jeffrey J., Jeffrey Beuhrer, and David Cull. "Surgical Support of Operation Sea Signal: Adaptability of the 59th Air Transportable Hospital in Cuba." *Military Medicine* 168, no. 12 (2003): 957–960.

Pérez, Lisandro. "The End of Exile? A New Era in U.S. Immigration Policy toward Cuba." In *Free Markets, Open Societies, Closed Borders? Trends in International Migration and Immigration Policy in the Americas.* Max J. Castro, ed. Miami: North/South Center Press, 1999, pp. 197–212.

Pérez, Louis A. Jr. *Cuba and the United States: Ties of Singular Intimacy.* Athens: University of Georgia Press, 1997.

Pérez, Louis A. Jr. *Cuba: Between Reform and Revolution.* New York: Oxford University Press, 2006.

Pérez, Louis A. Jr. *On Becoming Cuban: Identity, Nationality and Culture.* Chapel Hill: University of North Carolina Press, 1999.

Pérez-Stable, Marifeli. *The Cuban Revolution: Origins, Course, Legacy.* New York: Oxford University Press, 1993.

Pershing, Linda. *The Ribbon around the Pentagon: Peace by Piecemakers.* Knoxville: University of Tennessee Press, 1996.

Phillips, James. "The Politics of Refugee Identity in Central America." In *Selected Papers on Refugee Issues: IV.* A. M. Rynearson and J. Phillips, eds. Arlington, VA: American Anthropological Association, 1996.

Portelli, Alessandro. *The Death of Luigi Portelli and Other Stories: Form and Meaning in Oral History.* Albany: State University of New York Press, 1990.

Poyo, Gerald. "The Cuban Experience in the United States, 1865–1940: Migration, Community and Identity." *Cuban Studies/Estudios Cubanos* 21 (1991): 19–36.

"Protesters Battle Police in Havana, Castro Warns U.S." *New York Times,* August 6, 1994. http://www.nytimes.com/1994/08/06/world/protesters-battle-police-in-havana-castro-warns-us.html.

Public Law 104–114, March 12, 1996.

Reynolds, Colonel Nicholas. *A Skillful Show of Strength: U.S. Marines in the Caribbean, 1991–1996.* Washington, DC: US Government Printing Office, 2003.

Rhem, Kathleen. "Guantánamo Bay Base Has Storied Past." American Forces Press Service. Final Edition, August 25, 2004. http://www.news.navy.mil/search/display.asp?story_id=14902.

Ricardo, Roger. *Guantánamo: Bay of Discord.* Melbourne, Australia: Ocean Press, 1994.

Rieff, David. "From Exiles to Immigrants." *Foreign Affairs* 74, no. 4 (1995): 76–89.

Robben Antionius, C. G. M., and Marcelo M. Suárez-Orozco, eds. *Cultures under Siege: Collective Violence and Trauma.* New York: Cambridge University Press, 2000.

Robbins, Carla Anne. "Dateline Washington: Cuban American Clout." *Foreign Policy* 88 (Fall 1992): 162–183.

Rohter, Larry. "Many Cubans Don't Share Havana's Pride in Pact with US." *New York Times,* May 7, 1997.

Rohter, Larry. "U.S. Starts the Return of Haitians from Guantánamo." *New York Times,* January 7, 1995.

Rose, Gillian. *Visual Methodologies: An Introduction to the Interpretation of Visual Materials.* 2nd ed. Thousand Oaks, CA: Sage, 2007.

Rosenberg, Carol. "Guantánamo Base Free of Land Mines but U.S. Officials Fear a Wave of Defectors." *Miami Herald,* June 29, 1999.

Rosendahl, Mona. *Inside the Revolution: Everyday Life in Socialist Cuba.* Ithaca, NY: Cornell University Press, 1997.

Rothe, Eugenio M., et al. "Posttraumatic Stress Disorder among Cuban Children and Adolescents after Release from a Refugee Camp." *Psychiatric Services* 53, no. 8 (2002): 970–976.

Rutter, Terri. "Cuban Refugees Injured Themselves to Get into the United States." *British Medical Journal* 336 (1997): 1297. http://bmj.bmjjournals.com/cgi/content/full/314/7090/1297?mastoshow=&HITS=10&hitsbmj.com.

Rynearson, Ann M. "Living within the Looking Glass: Refugee Artists and the Creation of Group Identity." In *Selected Papers on Refugee Issues: IV.* A. M. Rynearson and J. Phillips, eds. Arlington, VA: American Anthropological Association, 1996, pp. 20–44.

Sarrain, Alberto. "Algunos Aspectos Relevantes del Proceso Adaptación-Aculturación de los Cubanos Procedentes de los Campos de Refugiados de la Base Naval de Guantánamo," 1995. Unpublished manuscript, in the possession of the paper's author, Miami, Florida.

Saul, Jack. *Collective Trauma, Collective Healing.* New York: Routledge, 2013.

Sawada, Aiko, Julia Chaitin, and Dan Bar-On. "Surviving Hiroshima and Nagasaki: Experiences and Psychosocial Meanings." *Psychiatry* 67, no. 1 (2004): 43–60.

Scanlan, Gil, and John A. Loescher. *Calculated Kindness: Refugees and America's Half-Open Door, 1945 to Present.* New York: Free Press, 1986.

Schacter, Daniel L. *The Seven Sins of Memory: How the Mind Forgets and Remembers.* New York: Houghton Mifflin, 2001.

Schaefer, Jeanne A., and Rudolf H. Moos. "The Context for Posttraumatic Growth: Life Crisis, Individual and Social Resources, and Coping." In *Posttraumatic Growth: Positive Change in the Aftermath of Crisis.* R. G. Tedeschi, C. L. Park, and L. Calhoun, eds. Mahway, NJ: Lawrence Erlbaum, 1998, pp. 99–125.

Schmitt, Eric. "Cuban Refugees Riot in Panama." *New York Times*, December 7, 1994.

Silverman, Jon. "Guantánamo's Legal Limbo Ends." BBC News, Final Edition, June 28, 2004. http://news.bbc.co.uk/2/hi/americas/3848279.stm.

Simon, Jonathan. "Refugees in a Carceral Age: The Rebirth of Immigration Prisons in the United States." *Public Culture* 10, no. 3 (1998): 577–607.

Skidmore, Thomas, and Peter Smith. *Modern Latin America.* New York: Oxford University Press, 1989.

Smelser, Neil J., et al. "Psychological Trauma and Cultural Trauma." In *Cultural Trauma and Collective Identity.* C. Alexander, R. Eyerman, B. Giesen, and N. J. Smelser, eds. Berkeley: University of California Press, 2004, pp. 31–59.

"A Stunning Decision for the Rule of Law. Supreme Court Ruling Decisively Repudiates Bush." *Minneapolis Star Tribune*, June 30, 2006. http://nl.newsbank.com/date:B, E&P_text_date-0=2006&p_field_advanced.

Suárez-Orozco, Marcelo M., and Antonius C. G. M. Robben. "Interdisciplinary Perspectives on Violence and Trauma." In *Cultures under Siege: Collective Violence and Trauma.* M. M. Suárez-Orozco and A. C. G. M. Robben, eds. New York: Cambridge University Press, 2000, pp. 1–41.

Suro, Ro. "U.N. Refugee Agency Says U.S. Violates Standards in Repatriating Haitians." *Washington Post*, January 11, 1995.

Tedeschi, Richard G., and Lawrence G. Calhoun. *Trauma and Transformation: Growing in the Aftermath of Suffering.* Thousand Oaks, CA: Sage, 2000.

Tedeschi, Richard G., et al. "Posttraumatic Growth: Conceptual Issues." In *Posttraumatic Growth: Positive Change in the Aftermath of Crisis*. R. G. Tedeschi, C. L. Park, and L.G. Calhoun, eds. Mahwah, NJ: Lawrence Erlbaum, 1998, pp. 1–22.

Tedlock, Dennis. *Envelopes of Sound: The Art of Oral History*. New York: Praeger, 1991.

Thomas, Hugh. *Cuba, or the Pursuit of Freedom*. New York: Da Capo Press, 1998.

Torres, Maria de los Angeles. "Elian and the Tale of Pedro Pan." *Nation* 270, no. 12 (March 27, 2000): 21–24.

Torres, Maria de los Angeles. *In the Land of Mirrors: Cuban Exile Politics in the United States*. Ann Arbor: University of Michigan Press, 1997.

Treaster, Joseph B. "Flight from Cuba. The Refugees: Guantanamo: Refugee Camps Camps Fill with Fury." *New York Times*, August 30, 1994.

Trippany, Robyn L., Victoria E. White Kress, and S. Allen Wilcoxon. "Preventing Vicarious Trauma: What Counselors Should Know When Working with Trauma Survivors." *Journal of Counseling and Development* 82 (Winter 2004): 31–37.

Turner, Victor. *From Ritual to Theatre: The Human Seriousness of Play*. New York: PAJ Publications, 1982.

United States Coast Guard. Alien Migrant Interdiction 2004, Overview. http://www.uscg.mil/hq/g-o/g-opl/AMIO/AMIO.htm.

United States Coast Guard. Alien Migrant Interdiction. U.S. Department of Homeland Security, U.S. Coast Guard. www.uscg.mil/hq/cg5/cg531/AMIO/amio.asp.

United States Coast Guard. 2004. Operation Able Vigil. http://www.uscgmil/hq/g-o/g-opl/AMIO/AbV.htm.

United States Coast Guard. "Operation Able Vigil: Service Participates in Its Largest Peacetime Efforts Ever, Keeping Cuban Rafters Alive." *Commandant's Bulletin*. November 1994, pp. 4–5. http://www.uscg.mil/history/ops/1994_AbleVigil/docs/AbleVigil1994.pdf.

United States Department of State, United States Interests Section. http://havana.usint.gov/cuban_family_reunification_parole_program2.html.

United States Department of State. U.S.-Cuba Joint Communiqué on Migration. *U.S. Department of State Dispatch* 5, no. 37 (September 12, 1994): 603.

United States Navy. Fact File: Naval Station Guantanamo Bay, Cuba. Updated 2011. http://www.jtfgtmo.southcom.mil/xWEBSITE/fact_sheets/NavstaGTMO_08NOV11.pdf.

Uriarte, Miriam. *Cuba: Social Policy at the Crossroads: Maintaining Priorities, Transforming Practice*. Boston: Oxfam America, 2002.

Ursano, Robert J., Brian G. McCaughey, and Carol S. Fullerton, eds. *Individual and Community Responses to Trauma and Disaster: The Structure of Human Chaos*. New York: Cambridge University Press, 1994.

Valdés, Nelson. "Cuban Political Culture: Between Betrayal and Death." In *Cuba in Transition: Crisis and Transformation.* S. Halebsky and J. M. Kirk., eds. Boulder, CO: Westview, 1992, pp. 207–228.

Van der Kolk, Bessel A., ed. *Traumatic Stress: The Effects of Overwhelming Experience on Mind, Body, and Society.* New York: Guilford Press, 1996.

Walsh, Noel. "Life in Death." In *Trauma and Self.* C. B. Strozier and M. Flynn, eds. Lanham, MD: Rowman and Littlefield, 1996, pp. 245–254.

Wasem, Ruth Ellen. "Cuban Migration to the United States: Policy and Trends." Washington, DC: Congressional Research Service, June 2, 2009.

Weiss, Judith. "The Emergence of Popular Culture." In *Cuba: Twenty-Five Years of Revolution, 1959–1984.* S. Helebsky and J. M. Kirk, eds. New York: Praeger, 1985, pp. 117–133.

Yanez, Luisa. "Pedro Pan Was Born of Fear, Human Instinct to Protect Children." *Miami Herald,* May 16, 2009. http://www.miamiherald.com/2009/05/14/1050851/pedro-pan-was-born-of-fear-human.html.

Young, Allan. *The Harmony of Illusions: Inventing Post-Traumatic Stress Disorder.* Princeton, NJ: Princeton University Press, 1995.

Zucker, Norman, and Naomi Flink Zucker. *Desperate Crossings: Seeking Refuge in America.* Armonk, NY: M. E. Sharpe, 1996.

Index

THE OXFORD ORAL HISTORY SERIES

J. Todd Moye (University of North Texas)
Kathryn Nasstrom (University of San Francisco)
Robert Perks (The British Library)
Series Editors

Donald A. Ritchie
Senior Advisor